PSYCHE
at work

PSYCHE
at work

edited by

Murray Stein & John Hollwitz

Chiron Publications ■ Wilmette, Illinois

Library of Congress Catalog Card Number: 92–12176

Printed in the United States of America.
Copyediting and design by Siobhan Drummond.
Cover design by Michael Barron.
Cover photography by Kurt Hasselquist.

Library of Congress Cataloging-in-Publication Data:

Psyche at work : workplace applications of Jungian
    analytical psychology / Murray Stein and John Hollwitz, editors.
        p.   cm.
    Includes bibliographical references.

    1. Psychology, Industrial. 2. Organizational behavior. 3.
    Work—Psychological aspects. 4. Jung, C. G. (Carl Gustav),
    1875–1961.
    I. Stein, Murray. II. Hollwitz, John.
    HF5548.8.P748 1992
    158.7—dc20   92–12176
                                                     CIP

ISBN   978-0-933029-61-3

CONTENTS

PREFACE

Jungian psychology has traditionally concerned itself with the individual, since the practitioners of its methods and theories have been engaged mainly in the personal analysis and psychotherapy of individuals. Only in recent years have occasional attempts been made to carry the insights derived from Jung's theoretical formulations into the public arena. Applications to group dynamics and processes, to world politics, and to the arts have been carried out to varying degrees of success. Now the authors in this volume turn their attention to organizations and to the issues of organizational development.

As several of our authors note, Jung regarded organizations with suspicion and tended to see them as inimical to the process of individuation. Individuation was conceived by Jung and by most traditional Jungians as an introverted endeavor in which persons faced their own souls in the privacy of analysis, using fantasies and dreams to explore the unconscious dimensions of personal life. These essays take the question of individuation in another direction, asking how individuals may develop and grow psychologically within the context of organizational life and how organizations themselves may reflect individuation themes in their structures and structural changes. It should also be noted that Jung himself engaged in cultural analysis and culture therapy in his last period (cf. Murray Stein, *Jung's Treatment of Christianity*).

From the other side of the aisle, industrial and organizational psychology has begun to ask questions that sound familiar to analytical psychologists. How does the corporate world, heavily invested as it is in patriarchal values, confront these changing times in which other (e.g., feminine) values are coming forward and challenging long-held assumptions about power and structure? How can organizations acknowledge their unconscious and do something about it? Where are their creative sources? What are the possibilities for transformation in the structures of traditional organizations, and how will such changes affect labor and management?

The essays in this volume suggest that the theories and insights elaborated originally within the context of Jungian analysis and practice can address these kinds of questions in fruitful and potentially creative ways. Some of them focus on selection, development, and evaluation of employees; others use case study and application to probe the dynamics of organizational life. Some consider the tensions between individual and organizational needs. Despite this variety of perspective and concern, several common themes emerge: organizational life holds great potential for individuation, traditional norms for organizational development are changing, and organizational interventions are similar to personal analyses.

Above all, these essays demonstrate that industrial and organizational psychology and analytical psychology share common interests and offer one another fruitful opportunities for further exchange.

The Editors

Organizational Life as Spiritual Practice

Murray Stein

Organizations can be murder. Is there anyone who has not been badly mauled by one?

We begin dealing with organizations in our families of origin. In fact, our earliest infant experience with mother is organizational life, a dyad. And families, we know, can be murder.

Multiplying that, one thinks of all the other organizations that have to be dealt with: schools, army, corporations, government. If these don't get you, the IRS will. Then there are the still-larger groups: tribes, ethnic and racial groups, nations, the international network of national and business organizations.

So pervasive and psychologically deep-reaching are the effects and influences of these organizations on our inner lives that one may well ask if there is such a thing as "the individual." If one removes all the layers of identification, introjection, and projective identification, is there anything left?

What is left is the center of the ego, the self, the core of potential individuality and the essence of personhood. Here is one's signature, the unique fingerprint, the still, small voice of a personal, nonrational conscience. But to get to this essence and to stay with it is demanding. It requires a great effort of consciousness. And it is precisely this kernel of irreducible individuality that organizations often seek to murder. It threatens their dominance and authority. Perhaps it is unfortunate that we need the collective, relationships, involvement with the organizational world—"work and love"—in order to come into consciousness. For it is precisely this need that makes organizations so dangerous and so alluring to the individual. Precisely because we need them in order to become ourselves and to become whole, human organizations are fraught with danger and have the power to overwhelm and destroy us.

My premise is that in dealing with organizations the individual is also dealing with the unconscious, personal and collective,

and the more intense this relationship becomes, the more potentially fruitful that engagement can be for individuation. But it can
also destroy. How to turn the corner from experiencing the organization as destroyer to finding in this relationship an opportunity
for contacting the self and making this a more-conscious relationship is the problem I am setting out to explore.

A fairy tale that Jung used to open his masterful paper, "The
Spirit Mercurius" (1948), sets the stage.

> Once upon a time there was a poor woodcutter. He had an only
> son, whom he wished to send to a high school. However, since
> he could give him only a little money to take with him, it was
> used up long before the time for the examinations. So the son
> went home and helped his father with the work in the forest.
> Once, during the midday rest, he roamed the woods and came
> to an immense old oak. There he heard a voice calling from the
> ground, "Let me out, let me out!" He dug down among the
> roots of the tree and found a well-sealed glass bottle from
> which, clearly, the voice had come. He opened it and instantly
> a spirit rushed out and soon became half as high as the tree.
> The spirit cried in an awful voice: "I have had my punishment
> and I will be revenged! I am the great and mighty spirit Mercu-
> rius, and now you shall have your reward. Whoso releases me,
> him I must strangle." This made the boy uneasy and, quickly
> thinking up a trick, he said, "First, I must be sure that you are
> the same spirit that was shut up in that little bottle." To prove
> this, the spirit crept back into the bottle. Then the boy made
> haste to seal it and the spirit was caught again. But now the
> spirit promised to reward him richly if the boy would let him
> out. So he let him out and received as a reward a small piece of
> rag. Quoth the spirit: "If you spread one end of this over a
> wound it will heal, and if you rub steel or iron with the other
> end it will turn into silver." Thereupon the boy rubbed his
> damaged axe with the rag, and the axe turned to silver and he
> was able to sell it for four hundred thaler. Thus father and son
> were freed from all worries. The young man could return to his
> studies, and later, thanks to his rag, he became a famous doc-
> tor. (Jung 1948, par. 239)

Like the spirit sprung loose from long captivity in the bottle,
the unconscious side of organizations can be overwhelming. Jung
(1936) felt that the fierce Germanic god of thunder and martial
fury, Wotan, had been released in Nazi Germany, for example. On
a lesser level, a similar spirit of destructiveness was released in

Ruth's relationship with her corporation. "It" had her by the throat.

Ruth was an attractive woman in her late thirties, single, well-placed at the executive level of a large corporation. When she had been offered the job a couple of years earlier, it had seemed like a dream come true. She would get to work at the top levels of a large company, report to the president, and make a lot of money. But the best part was that this company was about to embark on a major transformation of its culture. It was committed to a program for excellence and had hired a topflight consultant to come in and shake things up. There would be change. Creativity and new ideas were highly prized by the president. This was an old, established company that badly needed to change its outmoded ways, to introduce new technology, and to reeducate all the middle-level managers. All of this was intensely exciting for Ruth and promised a high level of job satisfaction. But what had actually happened as she got into the position was that the demands of the job and the rapidity of the changes initiated by the consultant, and the consequent pileup of responsibilities, were overwhelming. She worked through weekends, she stayed late into the wee hours during the week, and her personal life was reduced to nil. She had not dated for a year, she felt no sexual desire, she suffered from sleeplessness and anxiety states, while the demonic consultant felt free to call her at any time of the day or night with more suggestions. When I first saw her, she was near collapse physically and emotionally. Truly the spirit was out of the bottle and had her by the throat, and it presented itself in the form of the creative, dynamic agent of change, the consultant.

How to trick the spirit back into the bottle and contain it? Cleverness and ingenuity are needed. When the unconscious is released, it often sweeps us up in a gust of enthusiasm. We may become inspired with creative ideas, so many of them that it would take an army to accomplish them. We are pumped up with energy, "beside ourselves" with emotional intensity, fervor, and belief. Jung called this ego inflation (1966, pp. 143ff). The ego gets inflated when the plug is pulled on the bottled-up unconscious, and it is then overwhelmed with the flood of ideas, fantasies, wishes, and projects that come pouring out. When the ego identifies with them and claims them as its own, it creates a problem. If the ego could let them go, observe them, consider and sift and discern which are the better ones, the problem of inflation would not arise. But to the ego it seems that each idea and fantasy is a jewel, and so the responsibilities become enormous. Ruth felt an urgent need to be a part of this corporate change, to be at the center of the team that was transforming this company; this was why they had brought her in, after all, and she couldn't let them down. She was identified with the spirit of transformation, and it was killing her.

In Ruth's own personal history, her mother had been excessively controlling and intrusive. It had been all she could do to get away from home, so strong was the glue. It almost killed her mother when she moved away, and she had to move far in order to get away at all. Now she could not get away from the job, and the only solution seemed to be to quit and to move away again. Like the mother, the job had taken over everything, had intruded into every aspect of life, and had destroyed any chance for a personal life outside of its embrace. The job had become the devouring mother, and the organization was allowing this to happen.

One of the essential functions of a *good* organization is to contain the spirit of the organization's unconscious and to keep it from devouring its members. The Great Mother archetype, which is projected upon all large organizations that claim to take care of their members—paying them, giving them benefits like medical insurance and pension plans and the perks that make life comfortable—has a double aspect. Erich Neumann's classic work on this subject, *The Great Mother* (1955), reveals how images of the Great Mother show her to hold, nourish, and contain on the one hand and to smother, devour, and destroy on the other. A well-run, consciously managed organization—if there can be such a thing—would attempt to ameliorate the negative side of this archetype by setting limits on involvement, which would protect its members from becoming overinvested and devoured. Because members of these organizations project the Great Mother upon them and then become so dependent and look to them for the very basis of material life and comfort and sustenance, the power held is enormous. This is especially true in a materialistic, non- or anti-spiritual culture such as ours is. Beyond rational considerations, it is felt that the organization controls life and death. To be banished from one of them is to starve and collapse into an abandonment depression. The base of support for the ego's existence in the world is threatened. So tied into organizational life can the individual become that the self seems at stake, the core of the personality at risk. Promotion comes to mean self-esteem and life; demotion, abandonment and death.

When individual and organization come together, one can observe the intermeshing of the spirit of the organization's unconscious and the unconscious of the individual. In Ruth's case, this was not necessarily a bad thing to have happen. As in the fairy tale, the release of the spirit Mercurius in the first place is bad, but only temporarily. It would have been worse had it not ever been released at all. In that case, there would be no chance to have an encounter with the unconscious, which is essential for personal growth and individuation.

Are there people for whom the genie never springs from the bottle and threatens to destroy? Some years ago I wrote *In Midlife* (1983), where I describe the transformation that typically occurs at this stage of the life cycle. Often it begins with a feeling of failure or loss, then deepens into crisis and a deathlike experience, followed by a period of "floating" that I call liminality. In this period of extended crisis, reevaluation, inner struggle for renewal and for identity at a deeper level, there often occur major dreams and visions that lead the way ahead. The release of the spirit of the unconscious, which must then be contained and harnessed, is typical of the midlife period. In the end, a person emerges from this transformational experience with a broader and more complex sense of self, a deeper feeling of who one is, a clarified personal voice, a more individualized signature. Often this period of life is full of *Sturm und Drang*, with divorces, vocational changes, transformations of life-style, and other inner upheavals.

I once presented this material to a church group. Many heads nodded knowingly as I spoke. People smiled with recognition; questions and responses were lively and affirming. But afterwards, as I was about to pack up and leave, a well-dressed gentleman of about seventy and his wife came up to me. He told me he was a retired banker, and, hard as he tried, he couldn't remember anything in his life that was even remotely like what I was talking about! To myself I thought: William James writes about the once-born and the twice-born, and this is one of those healthy-minded, once-born souls. Perhaps these are the lucky ones. Yet it seems clear that they miss out on something essential, at least from individuation's point of view.

Jung himself went through a most horrendous midlife crisis, with bloody dreams, horrifying images, fears of psychosis, inner upheavals so severe he thought he was losing his sanity and had to practice yoga to calm himself. This struggle with Mercurius went on for about five years. Day after day he recorded his dreams, worked with his inner images, drew pictures of his visions, struggled to understand this material, and was finally able to contain it and make it yield up its treasures for life. It transformed him, and at the end of it all, in old age, he wrote about this period of "creative illness" (Ellenberger 1970) as follows:

> The years when I was pursuing my inner images were the most important in my life—in them everything essential was decided. It all began then; the later details are only supplements and clarifications of the material that burst forth from the unconscious, and at first swamped me. It was the *prima materia* for a lifetime's work. (Jung 1961, p. 199)

Prima materia is a phrase from alchemy, and I would like to turn to some alchemical notions now to discuss the problem of containing the unconscious and relating to it, in an organizational structure or generally in life, in such a way as to promote individuation.

I think of individuation in the second half of life and spiritual growth as being synonymous. Spiritual practices all have the common goal of increasing awareness of the divine, of the god or goddess that is, or should be, at the center of one's conscious being. Jung's spiritual practice, as outlined in his works and autobiography, involved dealing with the unconscious in such a way that the self becomes more and more clearly articulated. The self is, for Jung, the "God within." The methods for pursuing this goal may be broadly useful, while the content is always unique and different in each case. It is about some of the methods that I wish to comment.

Jung found in alchemy a useful model for discussing the individuation process, one that corresponded in many ways to his own practices of active imagination, dream interpretation, and working with the unconscious in any and every form in which it appears, including projections. What the alchemists did was to project the unconscious and its processes onto their work. By studying their reports, Jung felt he could find parallels to how the unconscious is revealed and can be worked with in the modern psyche, of himself and his patients. In the course of studying the works of the alchemists, Jung learned some methods for working with the unconscious.

We face the situation that the unconscious is powerfully projected onto organizational life, and that what we meet there is also the spirit of the organization's unconscious. Both are often uncontained and therefore potentially exceedingly dangerous for the individual's emotional stability (witness Ruth). But this fact, that organizational life constellates the spirit of the unconscious and releases the genie from the bottle, also offers the opportunity for greater consciousness and for transformation of both individual and organization. Through an intense engagement with organizational life, one may find the opportunity to become twice-born, and the organization may also grow and change. The reward for this is what the alchemists called "philosophical gold," which Jung speaks of as the self. It is the *medicina catholica*, the magical transformer of lead into gold, the access to creative life. But how is one to capture this prize of spirit? First the genie must be tricked back into the bottle, and only then can one enter into a more-conscious dialogue with it. This is the first step of the process, after the initial release has taken place.

When the spirit is released, we have found the *prima materia*, but this is an extremely volatile spirit and needs containment. When Mercurius is freed in a real-life situation—a relationship, a workplace, a family, or elsewhere—we are confronted with a lot of affect, with intense pressures to discharge an impulse, and our self-protective defenses naturally come into play. This is when we resist, and these defenses—such as denial, repression, splitting, projection—are an instinctive attempt at containment. If these defenses work, the situation will cool off and calm down, but unfortunately the potential benefit will be lost, too. The unruly spirit may be driven back into hiding, only to reappear again later and perhaps more destructively; or, worse yet, to stay away, in which case the fizz goes out and the system becomes lifeless and flat. On the other hand, if these defenses do not work, something else must be done to contain the unconscious. It was Jung's genius to discover a way to contain the spirit of the unconscious without losing track of it or repressing it.

The alchemists called their container the *vas bene clausam* ("the well-sealed vessel"). Into it they placed the *prima materia*, a highly ambiguous substance often made up of disgusting ingredients. Yet the *prima materia* had to be a precise material, not just any old rotten thing. It had to contain the potential for development and hold within it the untransformed essence of the gold to come. Jung would speak of this as the shadow. The shadow is the first appearance of the unconscious, and it contains the germ of future developments.

In the context of organizational life, shadow projections can be caught, for instance, in envy reactions and rivalries. One envies someone who has some sort of perceived access to the self, perhaps in the form of a creative spirit or a privileged position vis-à-vis the power throttle in the organization. You may pity someone whom you genuinely perceive to be inferior to yourself, but you will not envy such a person. Envy tells you that you have hit upon some of the nasty pay dirt, the *prima materia.*

Systemically, too, if your organization envies another, it is projecting the collective, or organizational, self onto the other organization. Somehow they've got "it"—i.e., special access to markets, more creative people, stronger charismatic leadership—and that is what you hate them for and why you want to destroy them.

Envy reactions, though, are often covered up and disguised as contempt. You can fool yourself into thinking the envied one is actually inferior and yet find yourself continuing to compete, within your own mind or outwardly, just the same. Once you actually see the other as lesser and inferior, however, the threat is removed and competitive strivings disappear. You don't have to overcome, better, or destroy an inferior other.

Analysis is a *vas bene clausam* where such reactions can be contained and considered. This is the great value of the analytic vessel. Every sort of psychic substance can be poured into it with the assurance of safety and confidentiality. (At least, in theory this is the case.) The analytic vessel is a free and sheltered space where the shadow can be acknowledged, the *prima materia* collected and contained. Within organizational life this is more problematic. How safe is it to reveal shadow reactions within an organization? Power issues and complex interpersonal relationships may make it extremely dangerous to be too open about one's thinking and feelings. Better to keep these private. And yet, by doing so, one stands in the way of potential transformation in the organization. When the unconscious becomes repressed and blocked, creativity falls. If members of an organization do not feel free to share themselves openly and spontaneously, the spirit of the unconscious gets bottled up in a way that yields no benefits. You end up with an uptight, stagnant organization.

If an organization is well put together, it will have the capacity to contain the shadow and to work with this unsavory material as it arises. By containing the shadow, I am not suggesting utilizing mechanisms of defense like splitting, projecting, and repressing. I am thinking of conscious containers where personal confrontation and working through of conflict is given a safe place to happen. This requires consciousness and safeguards. Perhaps it means including experts in managing such matters on the staff, and a third party is sometimes indispensable for hearing, reflecting, and balancing such emotionally intense and potentially explosive exchanges. Doing this organizationally is more than good human relations management; it facilitates releasing and utilizing the creative fizz that sparks an organization and keeps it vital and alive. Competition and rivalry, even envy, are deadly and corrosive only if they are rampant and unmanaged; contained, they promise to yield enormous benefits. For this is the form in which the unconscious makes its initial appearance.

In alchemy, this was called the *nigredo* state, the stage of fertile blackness, and the alchemists rejoiced when they arrived at it. It means the transformational process is under way and is working. The *prima materia* is in the vessel, and it is cooking. There is a spark of life, which inevitably creates imbalance and conflict and draws the psyche into the work. Wherever people are involved in their work, their psyches are powerfully engaged, and with this comes the energy for the organization to become creative and to grow and differentiate as a collective.

For the individual, however, containment may well mean backing away from the organization for a time, in order to make conscious what had been projected onto the institution or onto some of its members. When we enter an organization and our unconscious becomes activated by our relationship to its other members and structures, we typically enter into a state of unconscious identity with some part of it, with a role, a function, or a position. This identification is most likely based on an archetype that the group psyche needs to have represented and enacted, and the individual's unconscious is ready to identify with the needed archetype and to participate in it. Jung called this state of unconscious identification *participation mystique* (1948, par. 253). This refers to a state of nondifferentiation between subject and object, in this case between oneself and an aspect of the organization. As psyches mingle and merge, the person begins enacting an archetypal role offered, or even demanded, by the group unconscious. This may be the role of savior/hero, for instance, the one who comes in to save a company, to transform it through charismatic leadership. It may be the role of the Great Mother, the head of the personnel department, for instance, who takes up the job of looking out for the interests of all the employees and making sure that no one gets hurt or neglected, that all are nurtured and cared for. It may be the shadowy role of the scapegoat, not explicitly hired for this purpose, but ending up acting as the receptacle into which the group shadow is poured, then attacked and driven away in order to relieve the shadow burden for the whole group.

In all these cases—and many more that one could mention,

like the trickster, the lover, the king, the *femme fatale*, the *soror mystica*, the wise old man or woman—the hallmark is *participation mystique*. The organization uses its individual members to act out roles as they become activated in the group's collective unconscious. The constellation and enactment of these archetypal roles forms the psychological underpinning for what is called an organization's "culture." A group culture is made up of many such archetypally determined roles and enactments, most of them unconsciously motivated and shaped. Only the rare individual or organization has any insight at all into how this works or what the most crucial archetypes active in its midst are.

Generally, individuals and groups are not motivated to become conscious of what is going on with such unconscious identifications and archetypal enactments until the shoe starts pinching. Without pain, there is little desire or demand for consciousness. When the pain becomes intense, as it did for Ruth, then the demand for consciousness reaches the pitch of life and death.

The alchemists spoke of a death that took place in the early phases of their work. In a set of operations outlined by Gerard Dorn and elucidated by Jung in his late *magnum opus* on alchemy, *Mysterium Coniunctionis* (1955–1956), there is a stage in which the soul separates from the body and joins the spirit. This is a second union, the first being the original union between soul and body. This second union Dorn called *unio mentalis*. Physically what has happened is that the moisture (the "soul") has been driven out of the *prima materia* by the heat applied to the flask and has risen to the top of the vessel in the form of steam, where it has condensed and formed droplets. The alchemist's notion was that the soul (water) had been united with the spirit (air) to form a new combination, leaving the body (earth) dead and inert in the bottom of the vessel. This was compared to the death of Christ, whose soul departed from his body for three days. Jung interprets this psychologically to mean the dissolution of *participation mystique* and the dawning awareness of that with which one had been unconsciously identified and how the identification had come about. The soul (or psyche) has been unconsciously fused with an object (another person, an organization, a role) without awareness of this. Now, in the stage of *unio mentalis*, there is insight into what has been going on.

This also means death, since the identification is destroyed and the object that was identified with is now much less animated. When a projection drops away from a person or organization, they become much less important, fascinating, repugnant, or emotionally stimulating. The emotional situation is neutralized, and one realizes, "Aha, so that is what was going on!" The projection can now be contained mentally, in conscious understanding.

Psychological theories and constructs can be extremely useful for the purpose of containing unconscious, projected contents and holding them in consciousness while they are examined and analyzed. For this reason, a psychological education is recommended for everyone. Good psychological concepts increase the possibility of containment.

Organizations and individuals resist this movement toward consciousness, however, for a good reason, since it results in a symbolic death. Consciousness is threatening. Becoming conscious of projection sounds appealing in the abstract, but when one actually gets down to particulars, it is extremely upsetting and disturbing. Why is this? To break off *participation mystique* is to risk loss of meaning and depression. One's unconscious identifications give one a sense of place, of purpose, of attachment, and as long as they do not seem to threaten life itself, one is loath to give them up. Even painful identifications are held on to. It is well known among psychotherapists that unproductive and harmful attitudes and thoughts are clung to with great tenacity, because they are so familiar and therefore comforting. They stand in for the lost mother, and to risk giving them up provokes abandonment anxieties. It is not at all unusual that a person will repeat, in a work situation or organization, the role played in childhood within the family. The work group becomes the family, and the archetypal roles adopted by the individual reflect childhood roles. As the original family meant having a mother and the security of a parental presence, so the work organization provides the same. If the father was an alcoholic and the mother was hysterical and intrusive, a crazy company is ideal: goalless and uncontained, it feels just like home! There is a sense of security in this.

But the greater Self presses for something else. It wants conscious wholeness.

Individuation is driven by the Self, by a necessity other than the repetition compulsion. The Self presses for consciousness even against the resistances of one's neurotic attachments. Development, in Jung's understanding, moves like a spiral, coming back over the same ground again and again, but at increasingly higher levels of consciousness. Such is the purpose in repeating. The unconscious will choose an organization where one can repeat, so that in repeating one can also spiral upwards toward consciousness. A Jungian view of the unconscious must include this teleo-

logical tendency on the part of the Self. The spirit of the unconscious, while it can and does overwhelm the ego sometimes, also
wants to be released for a purpose. So the drive toward consciousness, towards greater and more precise articulation of the Self
within the realm of ego consciousness, is fueled by this teleological
pressure forward and upward. The human being demands to
know, to understand, to become aware of what is going on. This
curiosity is inspired by the Self.

A first result is the "death" of the "body," the loss of a psychological identification, through *participation mystique*, with an
object. When this occurs, the individual's quality of participation
in the organization changes, too. There is less of the knee-jerk
response. There is less routine predictability, less power for the
organization to coerce a person psychologically without some conscious reflection and independent judgment. Now the secretary
does not smile automatically when the boss comes huffing and
puffing by her desk; the CEO takes a day off to be with his wife or
child; the chief accountant takes an interest in organizing the
office picnic. People step out of defined roles a bit more. They come
across as more-whole persons. A sense of their greater complexity
is communicated. The individual feels less compulsively involved
in the organization. There is some freedom, some room for personality, some privacy and personal space in the aura. For a time,
there may also be flatness, depression, emotional absence, a dead
period. There is a corpse at the bottom of the vessel. Something
has disappeared from the organization, and there is less energy
coming into its unconscious system. It is a time of stepping back
and evaluating: Is this what you really want to do with your life? Is
this role, this position, this activity how you want to spend your
life energy? Do you really need the organization as desperately as
you thought, now that you know it is not the Great Mother? At this
time, people may lose interest and drop out of the organization.
The *unio mentalis* offers one a position of strength, a standpoint,
over against that with which one has identified in *participation
mystique*. Here marriages break up, families dissolve, business
partnerships change, and individuals make important life
decisions.

In Dorn's description of the alchemical *opus*, the stage of *unio
mentalis* is followed by a reunion between the soul-spirit substance and the body. The body becomes reanimated. This is compared to the resurrection of Christ, and the new body to his glo-
ried, symbolic body. Jung speaks of this as the birth of the
symbolic attitude, the second birth if you will, in which the con-

crete tasks of life are taken up again but now in a more-conscious way. One may play the same role again, but now with consciousness, not identified with it or driven by an archetypal imperative, but by conscious choice and with insight. This is the spiritual attitude par excellence, in which spirit and matter are united, so that concrete activities are undertaken with the kind of conscious seriousness ordinarily reserved for sacramental acts.

Without an archetypal connection, work is sheer labor. The archetypal connection transforms labor into meaningful work. One's role in organizational life similarly must be infused with archetypal energy in order to carry personal value and meaning. This relation of activity to archetype can be entirely unconscious and acted out in a state of *participation mystique*. When one returns to the task after achieving *unio mentalis*, however, there is an awareness of the symbolic dimension of doing it right. The archetype gives the activity meaning, but consciousness is required if that activity is to become symbolic for the performer of it.

The Protestant reformation affirmed the possibility of a vocation for all persons no matter what particular activity or work they engaged in. Vocation was not reserved only for the religious. What this said, psychologically, is that archetypes are connected to many human activities besides the officially sacramental ones. Pluralism of vocation, rather than exclusivity and elitism, was at the center of the Protestant theological perception. This means that all human activities and roles are potentially meaningful if there is an archetypal connection, and all can be rendered symbolic for the performer of them if consciousness is brought to bear. In the ancient world, this was commonplace; the gods and goddesses were plural and each presided over a particular set of activities and over specific areas of life. Homemaking (Hestia), lovemaking (Aphrodite), warring (Ares), blacksmithing (Hephaestus), and other activities were divinely ordained and guided. In the East, too, this notion is familiar, and the most humble service tasks and roles in organizations take on significant symbolic meaning:

> From ancient times, in communities practicing the Buddha's Way, there have been six offices established to oversee the affairs of the community. The monks holding each office were all disciples of the Buddha and all carry out the activities of a buddha through their respective offices. Among these officers is the *tenzo*, who carries the responsibility of preparing the community's meals. . . .
>
> This work has always been carried out by teachers set-

tled in the Way and by others who have aroused the bodhi-sattva spirit within themselves. Such a practice requires exerting all your energies. If a man entrusted with this work lacks such a spirit, then he will only endure unnecessary hardships and suffering that will have no value in his pursuit of the Way. . . .

Down through the ages, many great teachers and patriarchs, such as Guishan Lingyou and Dongshan Shouchu, have served as *tenzo*. Although the work is just that of preparing meals, it is in spirit different from the work of an ordinary cook or kitchen helper. . . .

Renyong of Baoneug said, "Use the property and possessions of the community as carefully as if they were your own eyes." (Dogen and Uchiyama 1983, pp. 3–4)

In treating organizational life as spiritual practice, one holds a conscious attitude toward the nature and symbolic significance of the role one is playing in the organization. In the case of the *tenzo*, it is the role of nurturer, food preparer, a positive Great Mother archetypal function performed for the community. The same would be done with other roles as well, be they Father, Guide . . . or Scapegoat.

The scapegoat in a group is usually regarded, from a detached distance, as an unfortunate and innocent victim of group process. This viewpoint is accurate precisely because the role has not been consciously adopted and symbolically understood. We do not yet fully understand the role of the scapegoat in organizational life, but it does seem to be the case that the scapegoat makes it possible for the rest of the group to feel freed from shadow contamination. The scapegoat carries shadow projections and, if successful in containing them, manages to dispose of them, temporarily at least. The scapegoat performs a cleansing function. To take on this role consciously and to do it well is perhaps the hardest part anyone can play in organizational life. It is a therapist function. It should be reserved for the wisest and most spiritually developed, though of course it often is not. If carried out successfully, the entire organization will grow in consciousness, because the scapegoat becomes the issue around which central conflict swirls, and through this conflict and the clash of opposites the light of new consciousness and resolution of the tension of opposites can take place. The scapegoat functions as a sort of lightning rod, and this person must be extremely tough, spiritually, to take the hits.

In our collective cultural history, the scapegoat archetype was played out consciously and with full symbolic understanding by Jesus Christ. The symbol of the cross is the lightning rod that takes the full charge of the clash between the opposites good and evil. This symbol became the moral center of Western consciousness for two thousand years.

As told by scriptural texts, Jesus consciously accepted the role of suffering servant and scapegoat, carrying the sins of the world as projected upon him willingly as a mission from the Father. He assumed this role for the collective of which he was part. The Apocalypse of Peter, a Gnostic text (Robinson 1977), speaks of the laughing Savior, indicating his spiritual attitude of being in the role but not identified with it. Out of this drama came the birth of a new consciousness.

The return to archetypal role, after due conscious consideration and acceptance, is the second stage of our alchemical *opus*.

In the third and final stage, Dorn says, there is another union. The integrated substance, made up of spirit, soul, and body, unites with the *anima mundi* (world soul). Jung interprets this to mean a still-wider conscious connection with the world and a broadening of interest and meaning beyond the individual. In our terms, it would mean extending the horizon beyond a particular organization or time period to a more-universal perspective. Few individuals, much less organizations, reach this stage of development.

Religious aspire to this, joining the unique particularity of their originating figures and specific beliefs and practices to the universal, to the Godhead. The continuous awareness of this connection is maintained through rite and ritual, where the temporal and the eternal meet in a sacred space and time, which recapitulates what happened *in illo tempore*, as Eliade (1959) terms it. Our secular organizations stop short of this stage, perhaps for modesty's sake, and limit their concerns to self-interest. Indeed, it would be hard to say with conviction that the interests of General Motors or Exxon Corporation coincide with those of humankind throughout all of human history. This, however, is precisely what religions do say: the Law is eternally valid and divinely given; Christ is for all the ages; Muhammad is the one true Prophet of the one true God; Buddha and Buddha consciousness are timeless. As repeated and reinforced through rite and ritual, this kind of consciousness is carried through the generations of the religious organization's life. It is the role of the sacramental specialists, the priests and priestesses, to remind the members of a religious tradition of this connection of the individual and the universal. This priestly role is quite different from that of the CEO-type Protestant minister, who sets goals and leads the organization forward; it is also different from the scapegoat who provokes new consciousness. The priest is the ritual master who, through symbolic actions and gestures, points the organization beyond itself to the source of its being, to the spiritual light from which all of history descends and to which it returns. The function of this role is to remind organizations and individuals of their finitude, of temporality, and of the eternal backdrop against which all of human life is played out. The priest, by gesture and symbolic action, by dress and symbol, rather than by intellect or creative thinking, grounds time in eternity.

Most of the organizations to which we belong and in which we play roles, consciously and unconsciously, do not (and cannot) provide a context for this third level of consciousness. It would be false to their identities to try. Yet perhaps some lesser degree of this level could be attempted. To have someone in a company who considers wider and longer range ramifications than the quarterly bottom line; who considers the impact of an organization's activities upon the environment not only for this generation but for the coming ones; who reflects upon and brings consciousness of the impact of certain products and sales practices upon the quality of life of the wider population—such a person in an organization would move it in the direction of the third level of consciousness.

Individuals can, to some extent, bring this level of consciousness into their organizations, if they have reached it themselves. If they do, they may begin to play the role of scapegoat, the bringer of new consciousness, through the conflict they provoke in the group. They may also find themselves playing the archetypal role of the wise old man or woman, who can see further than one generation and can look intuitively into the ageless depths. To maintain this kind of consciousness in the midst of the dynamic forces of organizational life, which place tremendous pressure on the ego to cope and manage, it is helpful to practice some private daily rituals and to keep at hand some symbolic objects. Keeping a journal of dreams, reading a Scripture, praying, meditating, practicing active imagination are essential and generally available practices. Beyond that, individually meaningful rites and rituals, consciously practiced and symbolically understood, can be of immense value, and this value will carry over into the life of the organization as well.

I have deliberately used the words *organization* and *organizational life* rather than *community*, which is a much warmer and emotionally appealing word. *Organization* has a sort of harsh, impersonal edge to it. I did this deliberately, because to speak of community, it seems to me, is often deceitful, since community most likely does not exist in the organizations to which we belong. It is a highly seductive word, because we want community so much, precisely because it is so infrequently experienced. But even more important, the notion of community sets up a polarity, community being the positive side of a tension that reaches across the divine into the opposite sort of murderous organizational experience that many people witness and feel personally. I hope, in these reflections, to indicate some possibilities for positive development, individual and collective, without constellating the opposite devolutionary process. While the best wine often comes from the harshest and most unpromising soil, and the greatest individuation often appears in the toughest and least tolerant organizations, nevertheless I feel it is worthwhile to try improving organizational life and to assist its development toward greater consciousness. Ultimately I imagine this will assist in the evolution of human consciousness generally.

References

Dogen, and Koshu Uchiyama. 1083. *Refining Your Life*. New York: Weatherhill.

Eliade, M. 1959. *Cosmos and History: The Myth of the Eternal Return*. New York: Harper Torchbooks.

Ellenberger, H. 1970. *The Discovery of the Unconscious*. New York: Basic Books.

Jung, C. G. 1936. Wotan. In *CW* 10:179–193. New York: Pantheon Books.

_____. 1948. The spirit Mercurius. In *CW* 13:193–250. Princeton, N.J.: Princeton University Press, 1967.

_____. 1955–1959. *Mysterium Coniunctionis*. *CW*, vol. 14. Princeton, N.J.: Princeton University Press, 1970.

_____. 1961. *Memories, Dreams, Reflections*. New York: Random House.

_____. 1966. *Two Essays in Analytical Psychology*, 2nd ed. New York: Pantheon Books.

Neumann, E. 1955. *The Great Mother*. Princeton, N.J.: Princeton University Press.

Robinson, J., ed. 1977. The Apocalypse of Peter. In *The Nag Hammadi Library*. New York: Harper and Row, pp. 339–345.

Stein, M. 1983. *In Midlife*. Dallas: Spring Publications.

Murray Stein, Ph.D., is a Jungian analyst in private practice in Wilmette, Illinois, and author of numerous papers and two books, In Midlife *and* Jung's Treatment of Christianity.

Individuation at Work

Considerations for Prediction
and Evaluation

John Hollwitz

Introduction

Applied psychology addresses the nature of work from multiple perspectives, few of which take a Jungian approach. In part, this oversight represents the legacy of positivism and the preference in American academic psychology for behavioral models. As several papers in this volume indicate, it may also represent Jung's preference for conceptualizing individuation in individual terms.

Yet the times are changing. The paradigm of positivism is yielding to other conceptualizations. Industrial/organizational (I/O) psychology, like the other disciplines, has expanded to accommodate a slow revolution in psychological research. The organizational literature seldom uses Jungian analytical constructs to describe this revolution. As we shall see, though, workplace psychologists are now exploring such issues as individuation, shadow, archetypal images, and the constellation of the Self in organizational life. My purpose here is to review some of these developments. This paper will concentrate on ways that I/O psychologists conceptualize the psychological climate of work. The paper will argue that the field is beginning to articulate an archetypal model of organizational life. My purpose here is to review some of these developments. This paper will concentrate on ways that I/O psychologists conceptualize the psychological climate of work. The paper will argue that the field is beginning to articulate an archetypal model of organizational life. Finally, I will describe a methodology that offers promise as a way to explore archetypal variables in organizational life and development.

Traditional Models of Organizational Motivation

A central concern of I/O psychology is employee motivation, which is believed to influence virtually all areas of worker behavior. In their review of historical approaches to motivation, Steers and Porter (1987) trace the influence of three dominant models of motivation management.

The first, associated with the "scientific management" approach of F. W. Taylor early in the twentieth century, represents labor from a classical economic perspective that dates from *The Wealth of Nations* (Smith 1776). Adam Smith argued that the utility of production is a function of specialization. Taylor (1911) extended this principle to the industrial setting. He described a psychology of management that emphasized repetitive tasks, "scientifically" designed and sufficiently well-compensated to overcome workers' inherent distaste for them. This distaste represents an important assumption in Taylor's theory, which imagines work as inescapably alienating and unfulfilling, opposed to individuation—a perspective that finds an echo in Jung's distaste for organizational life.

Later motivational approaches moved closer to describing work as a path to individuation. The human relations model of motivation attempted to address insufficiencies in the scientific management fantasy. Human relations theory focuses on needs for affiliation and accomplishment; management's role is to help employees satisfy these needs in the workplace and thereby to increase productivity. An implicit assumption in human relations theory is that career provides a container for individuation. The workplace can both satisfy developmental needs and improve the bottom line.

The human resources model, a third approach to worker motivation, represents an important psychological development. Human resources theory assumes that people are differentially motivated by various workplace factors. In general, the model assumes that people *want* to produce: that their individuation needs can be met through accomplishment if the workplace is able to identify those needs and allow their play. An important distinction between human relations theory and the human resources model is a focus on internally generated motivators. While human relations emphasizes the extraverted world of the interpersonal, human resources acknowledges the inner world.

Developments in personality theory offered a further advance in motivational management. Herzberg (1966) and his associates distinguished internal motivators from external job factors. Various need hierarchies emphasized levels of motivation that included individuation-related drives for growth or self-actualization (Maslow 1954, Alderfer 1969). Although the empirical evidence may not fully support the type of invariant hierarchy that needs theorists suggest, factor analysis indicates the existence at least of a general higher-order motivator, a factor that we might reasonably label a drive for individuation.

The Psychological Climate of Work

More recently, organizational theorists have devoted considerable attention to the psychological climate of work and to the psychological cultures of work organizations. These developments begin to employ analytical constructs in their predictive and explanatory models. Early attempts to examine these variables attempted to combine the methodologies of organizational research with some of the constructs of depth psychology. Faucheux, Amado, and Laurent (1982) reviewed organizational development research, focusing on approaches that examined the "unlearned assumptions" of organizational life. They pointed out that the depth psychological model, based on psychoanalytic constructs, has found a place in Europe, where researchers are comfortable discussing "the unconscious reality of an organization" (p. 359). On the other hand, the United States has typically looked to humanistic and behavioral psychologies for its dominant models. As a result, the unconscious remains unexamined. At times, American organizational theory accepts some elements of psychodynamic theory. It does so most often with respect to the Tavistock and interpersonal models, stressing adaptation to the external world of the workplace. In any event, American approaches have stressed bottom-line utility analyses which attempt to subject psyche to cost-accounting procedures.

In recent years, American organizational analysis has approached psychodynamic theory from the perspectives of psychological culture and climate analyses. Work in this area, as in others of applied psychology, often has a mechanistic feel. Much of it stresses ego adaptation. But a new tradition is developing in climate and culture research, going beyond ego and including the analytical perspective as part of mainstream approaches to organizational psychology.

Research on climate and culture includes a wide number of perspectives, methods, and assumptions. In general, "climate" examines interactions. As Glick (1985) points out, there is frequent inconsistency in how researchers conceptualize the appropriate unit of climate analysis. Some have aggregated individuals' scores to compute an overall measure; others focus upon the organization as a whole as the unit of analysis. Still, some generalizations emerge. First, it's clear that organizations have something like unique climates. Chatman (1989) stresses the importance of accounting for the "fit" between a job candidate and on organization: a valid assessment of fit would help predict not only an individual's success within an organization, but also the ways in which an overall climate might change over time as a result of hiring decisions—an index, in other words, of organizational individuation. Rynes and Gerhart (1990) found that personnel interviewers are able to assess job candidates' "fit" with their organizations, and that ratings of candidate fit differ from ratings of "general employability." Such findings suggest future research to determine the characteristics of organizational climate or culture that produce differential expectations for employee selection (a topic, as we shall see, that occupies other researchers as well).

In a review of the climate research, Rousseau (1988) points out that climate stems from Lewinian social psychology, which conceptualizes behavior largely as a function of environment. The way to examine an employer's organizational climate is therefore to compute individual workers' *perceptions* of the organization. The assumption is that an aggregate of these perceptions represents an attribute of the organization (Rousseau 1988, p. 147).

There are two implications to this view of climate. The first is that climate research is consistent with traditional behavioral and social learning theories of person-situation interactions. Climate and culture are typically described as "learned" through some process of workplace socialization. The second implication is that mainstream organizational theorists (especially in America) have pursued inquiries quite different from their European counterparts. The American models are ego-based, even when culture or climate researchers admit to the existence of something like a depth factor (the term *unconscious* is seldom used) in organizational life. In a recent essay on organizational culture, Schein (1990) claims that climate is "only a surface manifestation of culture," that culture involves "deeper" realities (p. 109). But he proceeds to argue that culture is transmitted more or less consciously within organizations through the transmission of norms and the experience of exemplars, leaders who serve as social models. The result is a heavily rational and ultimately contradictory approach to organizational analysis: the organization has this "deeper" essence, but the essence loses its depth by being reified into cookbook-style management concepts. Similarly, organizational theorists claim that organizations express themselves through the rites and symbols of workplace life, through what are in effect archetypal dominants. These dominants are examined through perspectives as diverse as folklore studies (Jones 1990, Scheiberg 1990), organizational mythology (Bowles 1989), and psychohistory (Dervin 1984). But the same theorists avow rational causal models which make such symbols ultimately uninterpretable to them (Schein 1990; James, Joyce, and Slocum 1988).

Unfortunately, mainstream psychology has made causal analysis its ultimate ideal, and the products of the organizational psyche may be as far beyond (or beneath) the causal as are the products of the individual psyche. In fact, a relatively new approach to culture and climate offers an alignment between I/O theory and depth psychology. This approach accepts the idea that organizations have inner psychological lives, apparent in collective symbols, ritual behaviors, and cultural narrative.

Most researchers in this area speak of "organizational culture" instead of "climate." The distinction between the two can be fuzzy, but culture owes less to Lewinian theory than to symbolic interactionism. Culture also tends to be more dynamic, more concerned with organizational change over time. The primary difference, though, is the data accepted for analysis. Some examples of these data demonstrate the psychodynamic orientation implicit in culture research. Killman (1985) uses the image of the descent to the underworld to describe culture: he talks about an "invisible quality" to organizations, an "underground world of corporate cultures" (p. 62). In an early text on corporate culture, Turner (1971) speaks of the "myths and mysteries" (p. 7) of organizational life; he invokes Victor Turner and van Gennep to illuminate rituals of organizational behavior, suggesting for example that career progressions represent the enactment of an archetypal pattern. From this perspective, the workplace is not just a goal-oriented environment driven by the bottom line. It is instead a container for individuation.

If organizational culture accepts a wider variety of data than does traditional climate research, it also appears willing to employ alternative schemes of data analysis. Pettigrew (1979) defines organizational culture as an "amalgam of beliefs, ideology, language, ritual, and myth" (p. 572); it includes "the organization's vocabulary, the design of [its] buildings, the beliefs about the use and distribution of power and privilege, the rituals and myths which legitimate those distributions" (pp. 574–575). He, too, advocates an ethnographic research method based on Victor Turner for studying culture, and he concludes with a statement that would be shocking to conventional behavioral research: the collected symbology of an organization represents a mythology, "a narrative of events often with a sacred quality which explores in dramatic form issues of origin and transformation" (p. 576).

This approach may represent the beginnings of an archetypal perspective on organizational behavior. As yet, the movement refers to itself as the study of organizational symbolism, a distinct subdiscipline of culture analysis. In its most conservative form, the organizational symbolism movement studies the ways individuals attach meanings to their working environments. These meanings then help predict or explain workforce performance (Joyce, Slocum, and von Gilnow 1982). The symbolism expresses common realities (Louis 1983) or distinguishes an organization's expressive contents (which satisfy members' emotional needs) from its instrumental content (its conscious goal-orientation) (Daft 1983).

But organizational symbolism is seldom so conservative. Bowles (1989) argues that the workplace has assumed religious importance, supplanting the preindustrial church. "Motivation" and "management" are surrogates for meaning. From this perspective, transpersonal mythologies are better models of organizational life than theories X, Y, or Z. Others take an explicitly analytic approach. One group of researchers argues that the symbols serve the Self and awaken consciousness (Dandridge 1983) or embody "an underlying archetype which embodies a predisposition to organize" (Morgan, Frost, and Pondy 1983). The organizational symbolism movement takes as its concern the amplification of the archetypal pattern that guides workforce behavior.

Psyche in Climate and Culture Research

From the perspective of academic psychology, a construct is only as useful as the validity of attempts to measure it. In the particular case of I/O psychology, measurement strategies serve several purposes. They can be descriptive, attempting to articulate organizational dynamics or worker-situation interactions. They can be predictive, used to estimate (or evaluate) individual performance. As a corollary to prediction, they can be used with various statistical formulas to assess the economic utility (the bottom line) of new measures or interventions.

Finally, they can be causal. From the perspective of mainstream applied psychology, causal analysis is the ultimate god, representing a fantasy of enlightenment, clarity, and aesthetic elegance. The causal model lives in the imagination of Apollo. It requires clarity of concept; control over subjects, variables, environments; and a considerable amount of abstraction that inevitably removes it from the real world. The real world of organizational life does not offer that much unfiltered sunshine. Rather, it seems uncontrolled, messier, loose. It has more to do with Dionysus than with Apollo.

Together with the organizational symbolism movement, among the most interesting changes in organizational psychology has been the sense that maybe it would be okay to loosen up. Although few behavioral researchers would use just these terms, maybe measurement can accommodate some of the Dionysian by turning to quasi-experimental (nonrandomized or partially controlled) designs (Cook and Campbell 1979, especially the article by Macias and Santos). Maybe, too, the Apollonian ideal has caused us to misspecify our models of climate and culture research; maybe the depths contain something that conventional behavioral analysis has missed from looking too hard at the sun.

Consider two arguments that have been advanced recently in the research literature. First, James and James (1989) claim that efforts to measure the perceptions of work environments derive from a pair of assumptions: first, that we respond in organizational environments as a result of our perceptions; second, that the most important part of our perceptions is our attribution of meaning to events. They point out that the psychological climate research has failed so far to specify what they believe is a single latent component, a g-factor, that composes a high-order psychological structure by which we evaluate our "fit" with an organization's environment or our sense of "meaning" in our organizational settings. Factor analysis and linear structured relations models provide some support for such a factor, which James and James (1989) describe as a kind of internal mechanism, a predisposition to find meaning in particular kinds of organizational environments. Although they use the constructs of social psychology, their formulation resembles the archetypal predisposition posited by Morgan *et al.* (1983). In the old days, organizational theory might have tried to specify this predisposition according to the mechanistic models of classical or operant conditioning. Today it is possible to suggest that this factor represents the activity of the Self.

Second, Schneider (1987) and Schneider and Reichers (1983) question whether conventional research strategies are even applicable outside the artifice of the laboratory. They undermine both an assumption of behaviorism and the Apollonian fantasy upon which much organizational research has been based. Schneider (1987) challenges Lewinian theory (which argues that situations determine behavior) and claims instead that individuals determine environment. He then argues that social behaviorism (including Lewinian social psychology) is based on laboratory-oriented research and statistical tests which typically require assumptions (like randomization) and a fantasy of control, according to which researchers appear to manipulate conditions for the sake of clarity. Again, the model represents the imagination of Apollo. Schneider (1987) argues that randomization does not occur in the real world or organizational life. The restriction of range introduced by personnel selection and normal attrition means that the workplace is homogeneous, and measures of these organizations will necessarily demonstrate decreased variability, restriction of range, and limited or even misleading results.

These arguments suggest that psychological life at work is not very much under the control of the organization. Quite the contrary, the organization functions at the whim of the people within it, sometimes in ways counter to conscious goals. Schneider and Reichers (1983) use the example of an organization that consciously implements an organizational development program intended to decentralize decision making (increasing autonomy, which is predicted to affect job satisfaction). Such a conscious decision does not account for the depth psychology of the people who constitute the organization's life. In their terms:

> This approach, in the extreme, seems to suggest that individuals in an organization would perceive themselves to have little personal autonomy with respect to decision making, *regardless* of the organization's stance on centralized decision-making authority. Some internal, psychological trait, such as low internal locus of control, perhaps, would have to be hypothesized to account for low perceived autonomy. (Schneider and Reichers 1983, p. 28)

Once again, the research implicates an archetypal construct, a predisposition to organize. The search for this "internal, psychological trait" could degenerate into a heroic quest involving just the inadequate research methods and assumptions that Schneider and Reichers intend to criticize.

One other line of research deserves attention in this regard. In the past two decades, scientists in groups as disparate as topology, climatology, fluid dynamics, astronomy, and information systems have begun to describe a mathematics of "chaos" (Gleick 1987). Among other things, chaos theory treats the evolution of organized systems toward apparent disorganization. Prediction breaks down relatively quickly as these systems enter disorder. Yet upon examination, this disorder may show coherence, although the coherence is nonlinear. It is as though random processes were meaningful, but without cause (or at least without *linear* cause). This aspect of chaos theory sounds like synchronicity. Other parts of the theory suggest Jung as well. "Strange attractors," for example, emerge as innate (archetypal?) predispositions to order.

Conventional psychology traditionally shuns any suggestion of chaos. Noise in the system is bad. Instead it adheres to the linear model, to exactly the kind of predictive formulation that will fall apart in the prospect of chaos. In personnel selection, for example, prediction is straightforward according to the relationships among independent variables and criteria. Anything that falls outside the linear relationship is "error variance," and the whole point is to minimize the error as much as possible. But if chaos exists, it is both inevitable and *non*linear. In that case, what we are discarding as error is not, strictly speaking, erroneous. Attempts to minimize error in order to improve prediction are probably both short-sighted and futile. The chaos perspective reaches some of the same conclusions as Schneider and Reichers (1983). Real systems don't function according to controlled models.

This is not to suggest that chaos theory is yet very useful in applied psychology. Although it is receiving speculative attention, the methodologies of chaos can be stunningly complex and hard to relate to the immediate task of classifying employees, diagnosing schizophrenia, or mapping perception. However, it provides another justification for the Schneider and Reichers (1983) argument. We need to seek the determinants of systems and climates elsewhere than in the reductive linear method. We need to include the unconscious in the search and to take seriously the archetypal structures through which psyche is expressed. It may not be as useful in organizational settings as widely supposed. Instability in its scores could affect selection and classification (Druckman and Bjork 1991).

Assessing Archetypal Dominants in the Workplace

Few measures have been developed to assess analytical psychological constructs in the workplace. Both Jungian theory and the research reviewed above suggest some standards that such a measure would have to meet. At a minimum, it would have to achieve accepted standards of reliability and validity to be accepted by the conventional psychological community. At the same time, it would have to capture potentially wide individual differences in unconscious content and, at the same time, detect consistencies which would make it possible to profile the archetypal dominants active in an organizational setting.

Such measures as have been advanced are probably insufficient for these purposes. The Jungian Type Survey (Wheelwright, Wheelwright, and Buehler 1942), the Myers-Briggs Type Indicator (MBTI) (Myers 1962), and the Singer-Loomis Inventory of Personality (SLIP) (Singer and Loomis 1984a) are typology measures. Despite its enormous popularity in clinical and organizational settings, the MBTI will provide little assistance in articulating an archetypal climate of work. Like the Jungian Type Survey, the MBTI is a forced-choice instrument whose structure can be criticized on several grounds (Singer and Loomis 1980, 1984b). It may not be as useful in organizational settings as widely supposed. Instability in its scores could affect selection and classification (Druckman and Bjork 1991). SLIP, now in a third experimental edition, has a different format. Stuart (1989) points out that no information is available on the stability of its scores, its external validity needs further work, and its construct validity is unresolved. Houston (1989) raises some questions in particular about its introversion scale (see also Houston 1988). But the SLIP may prove useful in helping to classify employees. Singer and Loomis (1984b) report differences in cognitive modes between artists and psychotherapists based on SLIP scores. They use multiple t-tests, reporting strong significance, but the instrument really requires a multivariate analysis (and the sample size to support it) before it can be usefully applied to selection or classification.

A number of organizational specialists use Jungian typology measures for management development. Given Singer's and Loomis's (1980, 1985b) critique of the traditional measures, this use is problematic, at best. Schneider (1987) argues that personality and interest measures should not be used at all in organizational settings that require fine-grade distinctions. However, he suggests that such measures may have a different utility: maybe organizations have something like "personality" (an early notion of climate research), and maybe personality, interest, or typology measures can provide a useful picture of them.

In any event, the typology measures do not describe archetypal dominants. If an organization has a kind of "collective personality," as Schneider (1987) believes, then it likely has an archetypal structure that can be revealed in its imagination—its symbols, narratives, and rituals. Assessing this structure and articulating its dominants is a field that has been almost entirely ignored in the organizational literature.

The main question is how to do it. Given the resistance of depth processes (or the James and James (1989) g-factor) to conventional empirical methods, some alternative method for discovering archetypal dominants in the workplace must be found. The practice of analytical and archetypal psychology suggests a clinical method based on amplification. Some behavioral researchers regard clinical methods with suspicion. In a classic paper on clinical judgment, for instance, Goldberg (1968) points out that statistical models do at least as good a job of clinical classification as do practitioners. But simply to adopt the conventional models is again to engage an ego-based fantasy of organizational research. Furthermore, the actuarial model typically ignores the importance of transference and of the analytical vessel in the elucidation of the Self. More precisely, and much worse, the conventions would regard transference as a source of rater unreliability or error variance. The whole point of these statistical models is to reduce such variance because it has the effect of diluting statistical significance, perhaps ensuring that (statistically) a Jungian or arche-typal clinical model will produce null results even in the presence of real effects.

The literature suggests that it is possible to derive measures based on personal biography that can assist in a number of work-place decisions. One of the primary considerations of biographical measures is the extent to which they are criterion-related—that is, the amount of validity they have in predicting something like per-formance or "fit." The culture has established norms which would make such prediction problematic. Employment law, as we shall see, prohibits decision making on irrelevant criteria, or on criteria which systematically discriminate against protected groups, and a simple reliance on personal history or psychological experience can risk adverse impact. Yet biographical methods (biodata) hold promise. Asher (1972) points out that a single question ("Did you ever build a model airplane that flew?") was almost as good a predictor of flight training success in World War II as was the whole Air Force Battery. Although single items will seldom have that much power, biodata approaches to personnel decisions may provide a way to yield conclusions that simply cannot be reached according to traditional methods (Howe 1982).

Perhaps the best contribution of Jungian analytical psychol-ogy to personnel selection and evaluation would be the develop-ment of a measure that could assess the archetypal climate of an organization and, perhaps, help predict the degree of fit between employees and the climate. In addition to meeting the usual psy-chometric standards, such an instrument would probably have two characteristics. First, it would probably derive from some qualitative approach to organizational culture. Although content analyses are not often used in conventional personnel research, they clearly have a place. The critical incident technique (Flana-gan 1965) is a well-established method for job analysis; Boland and Greenberg (1988) describe a content-analytic method for look-ing at dominant metaphors within organizations. Schein (1987a), among the most prominent specialists in organizational culture and development, argues for clinical and descriptive approaches to institutional analysis. Such approaches could be applied to archetypal structures as well as to operational metaphors. As Macias and Santos demonstrate, this kind of methodology closely resembles the process of individual analysis (Cook and Campbell 1979).

Second, it would have to be legally justifiable. There are per-haps three areas of legal concern regarding potential uses of archetypal analysis (or of any manifestation of the unconscious) as part of the personnel function. The first is the question of discrimination, or adverse impact against legally designated protected groups. The Civil Rights Act of 1974 prohibits personnel measures which discriminate by race, color, religion, sex, or national origin. The law does not address the unconscious contents of individuals, much less organizations, and the burden of proof would likely rest on the organization to demonstrate that an analytically based measure does *not* have adverse impact.

The courts examine statistical records as part of the evidence for (or against) adverse impact, but Jungian analytical constructs raise another question. Although the courts typically address ego, one area of employment law pertains directly to any possible use of depth psychological constructs in workplace decisions. If archetypal images are culturally specific, then selection or evaluation instruments based on them would be inaccurate and could expose users to legal liability. There are clearly intercultural differences that affect variability between organizations (Schein 1990). What passes for acceptable practice in one culture becomes shadow in another. In other words, the assumption that a Greek pantheon (or anything like it) is a universally applicable taxonomy fails to represent cultural subgroups and also ignores the possibility that the organizational psyche might evolve over time as a result of a workforce that operates from archetypally different cultures. In any event, a sensitive measure of archetypal dominants would provide a way to measure those dynamics over time.

A second legal issue relates to the right to privacy. Would any attempt to assess individuals' psychological constellations, even for the sake of deriving an organizational profile, constitute a violation of this right? Privacy law generally focuses on the procedures by which data are gathered and issues related to record keeping or access to information. As a rule, the courts have allowed the use of psychiatric information in selection procedures. Perhaps because of their devotion to the world of ego, the courts are much less comfortable with personal material that could be regarded as protected by confidentiality. The bottom line is that the material used in personnel decisions must be clearly job-related. Fortunately, job-relatedness is an area in which the conventional Apollonian model works quite well. (For a recent review of the legal issues, see Jones, Ash, and Soto 1990.)

The final legal question has to do with the standards of reliability and validity that personnel procedures must meet in order to be job-related. Conventional methodologists are often suspicious about alternatives to the customary statistical procedures (such as regression, ANOVA, and the parametric multivariate techniques). Content analysis seems a bit unreliable; nonparametric procedures seem somehow weaker. But content analysis can be very strong (Krippendorff 1980), and the nonparametrics are very useful. They are indeed weaker than their parametric counterparts. But they are now known to be not *much* weaker. Given the tendency of many mainstream research methods to play fast and loose with statistical assumptions—a tendency, as Schneider (1987) says, which has sent us down the wrong paths for years already—we should welcome the chance to trade a little power for a lot of security (Lehmann 1975).

A measure of archetypal structures is feasible, and some precedent appears in the work of McAdams (1988). Part of his research involves life narratives among undergraduate college students and midlife adults, who were administered a semi-structured interview. Among other things, McAdams was interested in analyzing the "imagoes" that emerged from the interviews. He defined the imagoes in terms that are heavily ego-related. But he also established an archetypal coding scheme based on the Greek pantheon. He defined interview features which he associated with Zeus, Hera, Hermes, Ares, Apollo, Athena, Prometheus, Demeter, Aphrodite, Hestia, Hephaestus, and Dionysus. These figures constituted a content analysis dictionary. He further grouped the archetypal images into categories of power, communion (or intimacy), or joint power and communion, and then used the Thematic Apperception Test to demonstrate that the resulting imago scores, based on the coded archetypal dominants, discriminated power motivation (McAdams 1988, pp. 187ff).

There are some problems with McAdams's approach. Perhaps the most important, from an Apollonian perspective, is the absence of reported reliability data on the coding dictionary, which is based on observer ratings. Further, it is unclear that the categories meet the criterion of independence that would be required by the strictest statistical analyses. The mythologies portray these figures as closely related by blood, marriage, or both; too rigorous an attempt to isolate them might violate their psychological grounds. But there are advanced significance tests which might handle this problem.

Some of the criteria for scoring a subject on particular archetypal dominants are also questionable. For instance, the criteria for determining a constellation of Hera included narrative themes suggesting the roles of spouse, helpmate, friend, confidante, servant, and subordinate. As Kerenyi (1975) demonstrates, Hera is much more complicated. Some important figures (like Persephone) are omitted from the dictionary. Dionysus seems peculiarly mild. McAdams (1988) characterizes him almost as an Edwardian gentleman: Dionysus is a "man of leisure," an "epicure who tries many different things but commits himself to nothing. He is the carefree dilettante who dabbles in photography, visits museums, and regularly attends the theatre" (p. 206). A bacchanalia is much less restrained. In addition, this kind of research might be more suitable to between-subjects analysis: that is, by categorizing subjects on the basis of "archetypal image scores," it inevitably ignores intraindividual variability and inevitably becomes somewhat reductive in driving for an overall assessment.

However, the research is formative, and too much emphasis on its initial shortcomings overlooks its enormous potential for a Jungian analytical approach to organizational research. Although the McAdams model assumes the primacy of ego, the method in fact probes beneath conscious expressions in an attempt to sort the tacit themes from the archetypal perspective. With some further refinement, the system offers a way to assess dominant archetypal structures in organizations. It seems eminently suitable to a paper-and-pencil measure which would see whether the gods' defining characteristics might emerge as empirically derived factors. If so, we would have at least initial evidence for a reliable and construct-valid assessment of collective archetypal content. A preliminary version of such a measure now exists (Hollwitz 1991). If such a measure passes the full psychometric tests, it could potentially be used to characterize workgroup climates, to examine characteristics of subgroups, or to look at the natural history of organizational development—the individuation of the workplace.

It is possible, too, that a biodata scheme based on archetypal codings could assist personnel placement and development. Hunter and Schmidt (1983) and a number of their colleagues describe ways to compute the expected utility of assessment measures or organizational development interventions. In brief, the methods use the normal distribution and expert rating scales to distinguish highly effective performers. In theory at least, it is possible to use a valid archetypal measure to assess the salience (or degree of consciousness) of an archetypal dominant within an organization and (again in theory) to determine whether this consciousness predicts long-term employee fit or deviation from the organization's climate. Given a sound measurement device to begin with, the computation of expected utilities is straightforward. Dollars are the way to keep score. They could have enormous persuasive value regarding analytical constructs in mainstream personnel work.

Conclusion

In fact, the greatest use of a measure sensitive to the archetypal components of organizational climate would be to help articulate the process of individuation in the workplace. A recursive model of psychological effects is almost certainly too narrow to capture the Self at work or in any other area of development: simply to use the assessment to predict job success largely ignores the influence of the organization on the employee's soul. This is the heart of the Schneider (1987) model, rephrased in analytical terms: if the worker individuates, so must his or her organization.

In sum: if psyche is a part of climate, and the organizational symbolism movement suggests that it must be so, then industrial and organizational psychology has done a poor job so far of describing psyche's organizational movements. The traditional models, sophisticated as they seem to be, have severe limits. They cannot detect archetypal movement over time, either in organizations as aggregates or in the souls of employees. The subtler process of individuation is at work. Its exploration may represent a significant advance for I/O research.

References

Alderfer, C. 1969. An empirical test of a new theory of human needs. *Organizational Behavior and Human Performance* 4:142–175.

Asher, J. 1972. The biographical item: Can it be improved? *Personnel Psychology* 25:251–269.

Boland, R., and Greenberg, R. H. 1988. Metaphorical structuring of organizational ambiguity. In *Managing Ambiguity and Change*, L. Pondy, R. Boland, and H. Thomas, eds. New York: Wiley, pp. 17–36.

Bowles, M. L. 1989. Myth, meaning, and work organization. *Organization Studies* 10:405–421.

Chatman, J. A. 1989. Improving interactional organizational research: A model of person-organization fit. *Academy of Management Review* 14:333–349.

Cook, T., and Campbell, D. 1979. *Quasi-Experimentation*. Boston: Houghton Mifflin.

Daft, R. 1983. Symbols in organizations: A dual content framework for analysis. In *Organizational Symbolism*, L. Pondy, P. Frost, G. Morgan, and T. Dandridge, eds. Greenwich: JAI Press, pp. 199–206.

Dandridge, T. 1983. Symbols' function and use. In *Organizational Symbolism*, L. Pondy, P. Frost, G. Morgan, and T. Dandridge, eds. Greenwich: JAI Press, pp. 69–79.

Dervin, D. 1984. Group fantasy models and the imposter. *Journal of Psychohistory* 12:240–250.

Druckman, D., and Bjork, R. A., eds. 1991. *In the Mind's Eye: Enhancing Human Performance*. Washington, D.C.: National Academy Press.

Faucheux, C., Amado, G., and Laurent, A. 1982. Organizational development and change. *Annual Review of Psychology* 33:343–370.

Flanagan, J. 1954. The critical incident technique. *Psychological Bulletin* 51:327–358.

Gleick, J. 1987. *Chaos: Making a New Science*. New York: Viking.

Glick, W. 1985. Conceptualizing and measuring organizational and psychological climate: Pitfalls in multilevel research. *Academy of Management Review* 10:601–616.

Goldberg, L. R. 1968. Simple models or simple processes? Some research on clinical judgments. *American Psychologist* 23:483–496.

Herzberg, F. 1966. *Work and the Nature of Man*. Cleveland: World.

Hollwitz, J. 1991. *Survey of Archetypal Dominants*. Unpublished manuscript, Creighton University, Department of Communication Studies.

Howe, M. J. A. 1982. Biographical evidence and the development of outstanding individuals. *American Psychologist* 37:1071–1081.

Houston, H. 1988. Construct validity of the Singer-Loomis Inventory of Personality: measuring moral maturing based on Jungian typology. Ph.D. diss., Loyola University of Chicago.

_____. 1989. Personal correspondence.

Hunter, J. E., and Schmid, F. L. 1983. Quantifying the effects of psychological interventions on employee job performance and work-force productivity. *American Psychologist* 39:473–478.

James, L. A., and James, L. R. 1989. Integrating work environment perceptions: explorations into the measurement of meaning. *Journal of Applied Psychology* 74:739–751.

James, L., Joyce, W., and Slocum, J. 1988. Organizations do not cognize. *Academy of Management Review* 13: 129–132.

Jones, J., Ash, P., and Soto, C. 1990. Employment privacy rights and pre-employment honesty tests. *Employee Relations* 15: 561–575.

Jones, M. O. 1990. A folklore approach to emotions in work. *American Behavioral Scientist* 33:278–286.

Joyce, W., Slocum, J. W., and von Glinow, M. 1982. Person-situation interaction: Competing models of fit. *Journal of Occupational Behavior* 3:265–280.

Killman, R. H. 1985. Corporate culture. *Psychology Today* (April), pp. 62–68.

Kerenyi, K. 1975. *Zeus and Hera: Archetypal Image of Father, Husband, Wife*, C. Holme, trans. Princeton, N.J.: Princeton University Press.

Lehmann, E. L. 1975. *Nonparametrics: Statistical Methods Based on Ranks*. New York: McGraw-Hill.

Louis, M. R. 1983. Organizations as culture-bearing milieus. In *Organizational Symbolism*, L. Pondy, P. Frost, G. Morgan, and T. Dandridge, eds. Greenwich: JAI Press, pp. 39–54.

Krippendorff, K. 1980. *Content Analysis*. Beverly Hills, Calif.: Sage.

Maslow, A. 1954. *Motivation and Personality*. New York: Harper.

McAdams, D. 1988. *Power, Intimacy, and the Life Story*. New York: Guilford Press.

Morgan, G., Frost, P., and Pondy, L. 1983. Organizational symbolism. In *Organizational Symbolism*, L. Pondy, P. Frost, G. Morgan, and T. Dandridge, eds. Greenwich: JAI Press, pp. 3–35.

Myers, I. 1962. *The Myers-Briggs Type Indicator*. Palo Alto, Calif.: Consulting Psychologists Press.

Pettigrew, A. 1979. On studying organizational cultures. *Administrative Science Quarterly* 24:570–581.

Rousseau, D. 1988. The construction of climate in organizational research. In *International Review of Industrial and Organizational Psychology*, C. Cooper and I. Robertson, eds. New York: John Wiley, pp. 139–158.

Rynes, S., and Gerhart, B. 1990. Interviewer assessments of applicant "fit": An exploratory investigation. *Personnel Psychology* 43:13–35.

Scheiberg, S. L. 1990. Emotions on display: The personal decoration of work space. *American Behavioral Scientist* 33:330–338.

Schein, E. 1987a. *The Clinical Perspective in Fieldwork*. Beverly Hills, Calif.: Sage.

———. (1987b). Culture as an environmental context for careers. In R. Steers and L. Porter (Eds.), *Motivation and work behavior* (pp. 348–359). New York: McGraw-Hill. (Reprinted from *Journal of Occupational Behavior*, 1984, 5, 71–81.)

———. 1990. Organizational culture. *American Psychologist* 45:109–119.

Schneider, B. 1987. The people make the place. *Personnel Psychology* 40:437–453.

Schneider, B., and Reichers, A. 1983. On the etiology of climates. *Personnel Psychology* 36:19–39.

Singer, J., and Loomis, M. 1980. Presenting the Singer-Loomis Inventory of Personality. In *Depth Dimensions of Physical Existence*, J. Beebe, ed. Fellbach: Bonz, pp. 386–397.

_____. 1984a. *The Singer-Loomis Inventory of Personality*, experimental ed. Palo Alto, Calif.: Consulting Psychologists Press.

_____. 1984b. *Manual for the Singer-Loomis Inventory of Personality*. Palo Alto, Calif.: Consulting Psychologists Press.

Smith. A. 1776. *The Wealth of Nations*. Chicago: University of Chicago Press, 1976.

Steers, R., and Porter, L., eds. 1987. *Motivation and Work Behavior*. New York: McGraw-Hill.

Stuart, R. 1989. The Singer-Loomis Inventory of Personality. In *The Tenth Mental Measurements Yearbook*, J. Connoley and J. Kramer, eds. Lincoln: University of Nebraska Press, pp. 748–749.

Taylor, F. 1911. *The Principles of Scientific Management*. New York: Norton, 1967.

Turner, B. 1971. *Exploring the Industrial Subculture*. London: Macmillan.

Wheelright, J. B., Wheelwright, J. H., and Buehler, J. 1942. *Jungian Type Survey*. San Francisco. Society of Jungian Analysts of Northern California.

John Hollwitz, Ph.D., is chairperson of the Department of Communication Studies at Creighton University. In addition to his research and consulting in organizational development, he has written extensively on Jungian and archetypal approaches to literature and film.

Analytical Psychology and Organizational Development at Work

Richard Auger and Pauline Arneberg

The changes that have been occurring in the workplace and workforce have given the meaning to the word *work* that Jung attributed to it more than forty years ago—that it is Psyche's invitation to personal transformation and individuation. Although Jung was wary of organizations, within which most work takes place, much of current organizational development theory supports Jung's concerns and goals. Organizational development seeks to transform the fundamental processes of the organization for the good of both it and the individuals within it. Analytical psychology's philosophy, principles, and processes for change are being used by organizational development practitioners within organizations. In this essay, we consider the philosophy of analytical psychology and of organizational development to see where they are complementary, similar, and opposed.

Work: Psyche's Invitation

People expect more from work today than just "making a living." For decades counseling psychologists wrote that work provides meaning and fulfillment to one's life. Yet when they surveyed workers about the definition of work, they found about 80% said it was simply a means of making a living. As the educational level of workers improved, and the hours of work necessary to meet subsistence needs declined, work became for many that which counseling psychologists had proclaimed it to be.

Employment has always been a special part of a man's life. Women traditionally placed their primary emphasis on their relationships, while men did so on their positions. To have positive self-esteem, men have needed to feel good about themselves in their work. Women were taught that their lives would be fulfilled through their careers as homemakers and mothers. During the 1960s, women read Betty Friedan's book, *The Feminine Mystique* (Friedan 1963), and from her and other feminists they heard they were guilty of living nonfulfilling lives if they were satisfied to stay at home. Many began to enter the workforce by choice. During the 1970s, as home prices escalated, more married women entered the workforce to enable their families to maintain their life-styles. Pioneering women developed new role models. The energy of many goddesses, arising initially in women, transformed not only women's self-image but attitudes men had toward work. We are all aware of many changes that have taken place in the last decade regarding men entering the daddy track, the growth of child care centers, and changing family roles and patterns. Employers found new definitions of work and new relationships to their employees. Phrases like human resource development (HRD) and organizational development have become common. As employment philosophies have changed, work has come to have the meaning Jung assigned to it more than forty years ago.

In Jung's *Collected Works*, the word *work*, by implication, is used in three ways. One work is that which one does to make a living (which we will call a *job*) (Jung 1917, par. 428). In another, work refers to activity or employment pursued after the necessities of food, shelter, and clothing are provided for (which we will call a *career*) (Jung 1948, pars. 80–82). The third, the way Jung most often uses it, is the work of individuation, of alchemy (the *opus*) (Jung 1946, par. 486). We will consider the second meaning in this essay—that which we call a career to distinguish it from the other two meanings it has in Jung's writings.

Work in the sense of a career is Psyche's invitation to transform, to find fulfillment, to individuate. It can promote one's life's work, the opus. Psyche's call, which leads one to spiritual depths, is often frightening to people. Thus we may understand why so often we fill our lives with credit requirements and unnecessary financial obligations to escalate our "basic needs" and reduce our employment to a job, thereby avoiding Psyche's call.

Through the process called "work," Psyche invites one to undertake a process of transformation. This transformation can be similar to alchemy where adepts manipulated and processed matter subsequently to find that the sought-for gold was contained in their souls. Within the workplace, individual experience with others much of what they encounter in their own psyches: conflict, projections, difficulties with their ruling principles, etc. The dis-ease in our souls is lived in the workplace, and the problems in the workplace infect our psyches.

Our estrangement from work's historic connection to nature and survival has increased our vulnerability to such infections. Since the Industrial Revolution, work increasingly has become a fragmented, meaningless activity. The need to find a cure for such dis-ease was one catalyst for the birth of Freud's depth psychol-ogy. Work today separates people from their families and, for too many, their souls. Until recently employers assumed that the per-sonal problems of their employees were not their concern. The accompanying dilemmas in the employer's organization, such as frequent turnover, role-bound communication, and ineffective leadership, demanded that solutions be sought. Social scientists began to explore the problems of organizations as they had been doing with individuals. They found that when the development of organizations considered the development of their members, the age-old problems were lessened. Thus organization development became a field of study in its own right.

Work takes place in an environment, and the quality of that environment affects the work. There is an interplay: an employee who feels fulfilled offers more to the work environment; the fulfill-ing workplace offers the individual more. Whereas analytical psy-chology has focused on the concerns of the individual, organiza-tional development emphasizes the concerns of organizations. We contend the two are intertwined and have many similarities. Many organizational development practitioners have found the values and processes for change employed in analytical psychology are directly or indirectly relevant to their discipline. Organizational development is a process which parallels the personal in the collec-tive and seeks to help the transformation of a particular collective, the organization. Its enlightened use also may facilitate the devel-opment of the individual.

Jung and Organizations

C. G. Jung, the founder of analytical psychology, was known for his antipathy to groups and organizations. Regarding the founding of the Jung Institute in Zurich, he reportedly said, "If there is to be an institute, let it be as disorganized as possible." He was against organizations that superseded the individuals within them. The antonym of organization is chaos, and Jung would have seemed to prefer the latter.

> Large political and social organizations must not be ends in themselves, but merely temporary expedients. Just as it was felt necessary in America to break up the great Trusts, so the destruction of huge organizations will eventually prove to be a necessity because, like a cancerous growth, they eat away man's nature as soon as they become ends in themselves and attain autonomy. From that moment they grow beyond man and escape his control. He becomes their victim and is sacrificed to the madness of an idea that knows no master. All great organizations in which the individual no longer counts are exposed to this danger. There seems to be only one way of countering this threat to our lives, and that is the "revaluation" of the individual. (Jung 1958, par. 719)

Jung implies a distinction between organizations that stifle individuals' autonomy by usurping it, and those that allow for, and support, the growth of the individual. The latter is a primary consideration of organizational development. Jung's point of view is not troubling to organizational development practitioners but may be to bureaucrats. (The events in Eastern Europe in 1989, where the freedom of the individual replaced the "state first" principle, retrospectively seem to have been predicted by Jung.)

Comparison of AP and OD

Jung's analytical psychology is a theory and method that values individuals and seeks to help them become conscious and whole. It is a psychological treatment practiced by an analyst who participates in interviews with an analysand, usually on a one-to-one basis. The treatment often continues once or twice a week over many years. Analytical psychologists, called Jungian analysts, work for the development of individuals.

Organizational development is a process that works for the development of an organization through long-range planned change. It focuses on the organizational culture, processes, values, and attitudes of its members, as well as the organization's structure, technology, services, products, and how the organization relates to its external environment. Organizational development's activities are carried out by one or more consultants, called organizational development (OD) practitioners. They conduct data-collection activities, individual interviews, and group meetings and design surveys to understand the current and desired states of the organization. OD consultants initially work intensively with an organization to define a long-range change plan and then spend less time within the system as its members learn the skills, values, and attitudes to implement the plan themselves. The goal of both the analytical psychologists and OD practitioners is to foster self-reliance.

Structures of Individuals and Organizations

Jungian analysts understand the individual's personality as consisting of an ego (the conscious will of a person) and various complexes and subpersonalities, e.g., the inner child or each individual's contrasexual side (the anima or animus). The totality of the personality, with the archetypal images of the collective unconscious, is the Self. Ultimately the pilgrim who undertakes the individuation journey, a process of Self discovery and growth, seeks to be guided by and serve the Self, which psychologically is indistinguishable from God. The board of directors, CEO, or manager can be compared to an individual's ego in that they are responsible for the long-range survival of the organization, for managing turbulent environments, and for constantly posing quality issues. An organization's hierarchy may be analogous to subpersonalities, and sometimes, complexes of an individual.

These comparisons, and those that follow, are not complete or exhaustive. They are not always direct correspondences but suggest similar ideas or functions inherent in both approaches. They are intended to be examples of how analytical psychologists and OD practitioners manage comparable issues and processes.

It is not uncommon for workers to project the Self onto the organization or its leader. When the Self is projected onto someone or something, one's growth is impeded even if the organization appears to benefit. This can be seen in the lives of people who seemingly "marry" the organization, or who become workaholics. Often the Self is projected onto the organization early in one's career, and that may be helpful to one's development. By placing the company's needs first, one rises in esteem, responsibility, and income. In maturity the projections are taken back. One must

Figure 1. *Partial Comparison of Analytical Psychology and Organization Development*

	AP	OD

Structure	INDIVIDUAL
	Self
	Ego
	Complexes, subper-
	   sonalities
	Hero
	Psychological typol-
	   ogy
		ORGANIZATION
		(Projections of Self)
		CEO, manager
		
		Staff, hierarchy
		Leadership
		
		(Myers-Briggs Type Indicator)

Values	Individual Soul Transformation Spirituality Wholeness	Organization (Collective self) Transformation, change Philosophy of the organization Meeting goals

Problems	Lack of meaning
	Symptoms: physical,
	   mental, emotional
	
	Poor relationship(s)
	Power, ego-self
	
	Shadow
	Defense mechanisms
		Not meeting goals
		
		High turnover, lack of profit-
		   ability, customer dissatisfaction
		Conflicts
		Power sharing, centralization/
		   decentralization
		Sabotage
		Goal displacement

Processes	Self-report
	History
	Dreams, images
	
	Active imagination
	Feedback
	Mirroring
	Transference
	Analysis, diagnosis
		Self-reports, observation
		History/organizational culture
		Brainstorming, organizational
		   vision
		Group building
		Feedback/process consultation
		Organizational mirroring
		Transference (expert role)
		Data collection, needs assess-
		   ment, data analysis, action
		   planning

reclaim them before one can make substantial contributions to an organization. Sometimes this results in a sense of disillusionment with that which carried the projection. Unless individuals can work this through, they will experience alienation from the organization and its members and goals and, in a worst-case scenario, are likely to seek employment elsewhere.

An archetypal image that is particularly important in organizational development work is that of the hero, which may correspond to the leader. Leadership is crucial in any organization. The leader's role often is to exercise power to keep the organization's subsystems (technology, processes, resources, etc.) in balance. The leader may be seen as a "good" or "bad" father or mother, and for some the original family constellation will affect how they relate to the organization and to authority figures. In general, one must work through one's family issues before one is able to be a contributing member of an organization without the family constellation being paramount in relating to it.

Explicit and Implied Values of Analytical Psychology and Organizational Development

When comparing the inherent or implied values of analytical psychology and organizational development, one encounters Jung's crucial concern that organizations are destructive to individuals. The primacy of the individual is almost holy writ to Jungians.

There may be some truth to the idea that organizations are antithetical to the individual. The degree of potential harm depends on the philosophy of the particular organization and where the individuals are in their development. Some social systems exploit their members. Yet, the more dependent persons are on the organization, the more their individuality is threatened. It is possible to evolve to the position where one is not psychologically or emotionally dependent, that is, one may not need an organization but can choose membership in one. Some organizations do allow that. OD practitioners assist organizations in examining how to create processes for greater power sharing, openness, and trust in dealing with both internal and external environments. The organization then can become a tool to foster the individual's transformation. This doesn't happen for everyone and perhaps people are not ready for this before mid-life. Careers tend to plateau, and it is on that plateau that people begin to grapple with who they are and what they want to serve for the rest of their lives. Depending on how that conflict is resolved, if they choose to stay in the organization, there can be a certain transcendence that wasn't there before. People at this level have worked through their authority issues and have discovered their inner authority, their inner work, and know their own issues apart from those of the organization.

Organizational development was born in a more-conservative era than we are in now. People were less likely genuinely to engage each other around work issues, and our whole culture was much more role-bound. We have experienced a shift. The revolutions of the 1960s and 1970s have helped free us as people to say what we think. We now recognize that what we perceive as individuals is important.

Transformation and change are the raison d'être of both organizational development and analytical psychology. Analytical psychology often seeks to strengthen the ego; organizational development seeks to enhance the decision-making processes of a group by encouraging wider involvement by those who do the work and who often have different perspectives on problems and opportunities. Pushing decision making down into the organization where the work is done, as well as where the concomitant responsibility and authority is, are basic organizational development values. Analytical psychology encourages individuals to look within; organizational development seeks to revitalize an organization from within. Organizational development encourages building on the strengths of existing resources to cope with new problems.

The goal of the analytical psychologist is to help analysands move toward wholeness: to become the full and unique individuals they are. The OD consultant seeks to help the organization meet its goals and to enhance the quality of working life while meeting them. Commonly, the goals in either case are not immediately, directly, or consciously perceived, and, in each discipline, ideally it is not the practitioner who selects the goals. They are selected by dialogues with the clients, and ultimately it is the latter who make the choices. Sometimes compelling inner or outer events supersede the ego's or manager's primary objectives. The analysand may be forced to surrender to the demands of the Self; the organization may have to alter its course in light of changing market, political, social, or financial circumstances. Problems encountered in assisting the desired changes, and the interventions used to achieve them, are also similar for analytical psychology and organizational development.

We contend that there is nothing in the values of organizational development and analytical psychology that are necessarily at odds. While concepts like soul and spirituality, which are highly valued by analytical psychology, have no direct counterparts in organizational development, OD consultants may incorporate them in their individual approaches to their tasks.

Problems Addressed

When people enter analysis, they are usually suffering from assorted physical, emotional, or mental symptoms. Their life may lack meaning, or they may have problems in their primary relationships with a spouse, child, or employer. To deal with these and other issues, it is necessary to confront one's shadow: that part of one's personality of which one is unaware. Ultimately, if the work (opus) goes deeply enough, the ego must learn to share power with other parts of the psyche and surrender to the Self.

Correspondingly, OD practitioners are asked to help organizations solve comparable problems. The organization may not be meeting its goals: there may be low productivity, low profitability, customer dissatisfaction, or seemingly unresolvable conflicts. Some employees, consciously or unconsciously, may be sabotaging the objectives of the organization. Power may be too centralized, or misused.

Organizations as well as individuals have shadows. A new manager, after attending a lecture on team building, asked an OD practitioner for assistance in determining why teamwork in his organization was nonexistent. He was new to his role but had successfully managed a similar agency in another state. He perceived himself to be consistently supportive of the ideas of his people, to delegate well, and to have a good deal of skill in dealing with a complex external environment. He believed his staff trusted him, and yet he was beginning to consider moving to another position because he felt he faced a "battlefield" daily. He saw his staff as competent, energetic, and "a little bit green." The OD practitioner conducted extensive interviews with the manager and his staff. The staff experienced him to be creative, capable of dealing with a complex external environment, and consistently trying to build his image in this outer environment. They perceived him to be subtly controlling and did not trust what he said. The manager's perception that he behaved collaboratively was not shared by the staff. They found the manager's need to be liked cloying and could not understand how he set priorities. The manager gave his directives through an assistant, who had spent many years in the role, was well respected by the external environment, and, for a variety of reasons, had begun to feel uninterested in the agency's mission and was making plans to leave. This is a common scenario faced by OD practitioners. The manager was given extensive feedback both by the consultant and the group; the assistant's contribution to an environment of constant chaos surfaced; his views of the agency and the manager were aired; eventually, the group members were ready to define their desired state and ready to engage in problem-solving/action-planning activities that would help them achieve this state. In time it became clear that the assistant was carrying much of the leader's shadow.

Power redistribution is a central consideration in organizational development activities. The OD practitioner works to help individuals and groups understand how they use influence. If necessary, training can be offered in developing new influence styles. Power and influence patterns are deeply tied into the political processes and structures of an organization. Normative reeducative approaches to change (organizational development is one of these) help people examine their current practices and to choose other, more satisfying and productive approaches. OD practitioners work to clarify and build upon differences, not to avoid them. Organizations need not be pictured as negative mothers that eat people up. There are also nourishing mothers and benevolent fathers who help people grow and who support their freedom and creativity. Mentoring programs are increasingly becoming a part of organizational development efforts. A pioneer of organizational development in California, Neely Gardner, said, "You'll never find the perfect employee; you have to grow 'em" (Gardner 1982).

Recently, economic realities have forced many organizations to reduce the number of employees. OD practitioners have been asked to help with the out-placement effort, to help in work reallocation, and to restructure the organization, as well as to help people deal with their feelings of anger, grief, or loss. Interestingly, streamlined units often become more responsive to the public they serve; and, frequently, a certain amount of decentralization of power occurs.

Processes Employed

The analytical psychologist and OD practitioner rely on self-reports, history taking, mirroring, giving and receiving feedback, and analyzing and diagnosing presenting problems. In organizational development circles, the latter is commonly called the diagnostic or "needs assessment" phase. Unconscious processes are projected onto OD practitioners in their roles as outside experts just as the analyst experiences them in the process called transference. Each also brings their countertransference to the relationship with the clients.

One advantage organizational development has over analytical psychology is a greater opportunity to observe and measure the client population. Although the analyst observes behavior during the analytical sessions, inferences must be made about behavior outside the consulting room. On the other hand, while the organizational development person may more fully observe how the people in the organization work and relate, they seldom are privy to the inner processes of the clients in the deeper way affordable to the AP practitioner.

Both analytical psychology and organizational development ask the clients to take responsibility for change. Both Jungian analysts and OD consultants mirror to the clients what they are saying but cannot hear. Both mirror the image of what's desired. This is done by bringing the client's data to greater consciousness and focus. It is always their data, and rarely does expert knowledge need to intrude.

Clinically, many analysands spend hours talking about their jobs or careers. They may be venting frustrations about personal and collective values, or interpersonal conflicts. They also may be experiencing a parallel process in which their outer concerns are reflections of inner dynamics. If an analyst listens to them in this way, it is possible to mirror to them their inner processes. This is especially true if the analysand is more extraverted than introverted.

Analytical psychology encourages clients to talk with their inner, subpersonalities via a process called active imagination. Organizational development works for the empowerment of those who have felt powerless, or without influence, by supporting problem-solving dialogues across levels of the organization. This helps to reduce the projections members of the organization have upon each other. Analytical psychology stresses integration of the dark, shadow parts of the personality; organizational development encourages the development of a climate of trust where the negative, dark feelings can be shared nondefensively and the creative energy in them can be released. Intimacy, comradeship, and collegiality are part of the value base of organizational development.

There are many ways of being an OD consultant or a Jungian analyst. No two people or circumstances are the same. An OD consultant often helps an organization in collecting data about itself; the consultant and a representative group from the organization analyze the data, and results are fed back to the organization as a whole. Ideally, a broad sample, or all members of the organization, participate in the data-generation stage. The consultant's role is to help initiate a process, provide some expert guidance on that process (e.g., survey design), and serve as a facilitator to the process. In later stages, where action is planned, the consultant may serve as a conscience, reminding the group of its plans and new objectives.

The analysis of dreams is a central process in many Jungian analyses. Most Jungian analysts would not encourage people to reveal dreams outside the protective *temenos* (sacred structure) of the analytical relationship. To do so is to invite contamination and infection into one's psyche. Such disclosures only may be done in an understanding, protective environment. To some OD consultants, the organization may function as a tribe and perform the same identity functions tribes did long ago. This allows for the possibility of "tribal dreams and visions" serving to clarify problems or to suggest the direction of desired changes.

Reflections

At last the disciplines of analytical psychology and organizational development are beginning to talk to each other. This is always a difficult process. We see a profession devoted to the inner world of the psyche learning to dialogue with an applied in-the-world profession. Thus far, organizational development has learned more from analytical psychology than has analytical psychology from organizational development: Jungian thinking has stimulated many OD consultants. The philosophy of analytical psychology revitalizes many ideas of organizational development. For some, organizational development can be an outreach of analytical psychology by taking its soulful and spiritual contributions to the workplace. But for too long, analytical psychology's contributions to organizational development have been a one-way street.

An early, substantial contribution to organizational development was Jung's ideas about psychological types. Instruments such as the *Myers-Briggs Type Indicator* (Myers 1962) and the *Singer-Loomis Inventory of Personality* (Singer and Loomis 1984) have been administered by OD consultants to help groups understand differences, for conflict-resolution training, and for team building. Many people have been introduced to Jungian thought through such instruments.

The Jungian analyst helps individuals to live in the embrace of their souls. Joseph Campbell called this "following one's bliss." OD consultants do something similar, but in some ways the Jungian approach goes deeper than organizational development does. The transcendent function, that process in which one contains the opposites, is related to finding God and allowing that to alter one's life. For some people, it is possible to find the transcendent function in what they do and let that define the next step in their career. It is difficult to find or to live the transcendent function without integrating one's career.

Most organizations have not evolved to the point where seeking soulful communication is highly prized. Organization development practice is in some ways limited by instrumental values. The shadow of the organization is not likely to be dealt with, although there is movement in this direction. A branch of organizational development, organization transformation, has evolved. This approach seems to seek to transform directly, rather than change incrementally, the processes and values of the organization.

Earlier we claimed that so far organizational development has learned more from analytical psychology than has analytical psychology from organizational development. In large part, this has resulted from the Jungian bias that only individuals and not organizations are important, and that organizations can be neutral or benign for individuals at best, and harmful at worst. This also stems from the fact that 85 percent of Jungian analysts are introverts who find it difficult or unrewarding to relate to the world of organizations (Bradway and Wheelwright 1978). Thus analytical psychology sometimes dismisses organizational development as unnecessary or superficial. Their argument is that if one concentrates on the organization, it is because the Self is projected onto it. To the Jungian this must be avoided at all costs, of course. But one need only observe how organizations of Jungian analysts are operated to realize how greatly organizational development could make positive contributions to them. If the present beginning dialogue between the two disciplines flourishes, we anticipate a beneficial advancement in both. Jung's early views about organizations are a reminder to OD consultants about the need for organizational change, and point to a way the change may evolve. As organizations and organizational development attempt to improve, analytical psychology also may move beyond Jung's earlier views.

One of the fathers of organizational development, Herb Shepard, was fond of saying, "What's important is that what you are doing is nourishing to you and to others" (Shepard 1985). Both parts of the equation are important. If one side dominates, there is reason for considering change.

Analytical psychologists benefit from seeing the individual as a personal collective; OD practitioners can gain insight by seeing the collectives with whom they work as spiritual entities.

We began with the proposal that work was Psyche's invitation for transformation. The transformation of the workplace as women and minorities have gained more influence, and the concomitant changes in social values, have caused many organizations to be more caring places. When work is a career, rather than a job, it is an endeavor where people can be engaged in their individual journeys toward wholeness. An enlightened organizational development, building on the spiritual contributions of analytical psychology, can help the workplace become an environment in which an individual's soul may take root and find nourishment.

Job, career, opus: many people in organizations experience all three levels daily. Hopefully one can spend the main part of the day doing the work that one wants to do from a professional point of view. When that occurs, the individuals are also working on themselves as well. We are working to remember ourselves.

References

Bradway, K., and Wheelwright, J. 1978. The psychological type of the analyst and its relation to analytical practice. *Journal of Analytical Psychology* 23:134–146.

Friedan, B. 1963. *The Feminine Mystique*. New York: W. W. Norton.

Gardner, N. 1982. Personal communication.

Jung, C. G. 1917. New paths in psychology. In *CW* 7:407–441. Princeton, N.J.: Princeton University Press, 1966.

_____. C. G. 1946. The psychology of the transference. In *CW* 16:353–539. Princeton, N.J.: Princeton University Press, 1966.

_____. C. G. 1948. On psychic energy. In *CW* 8:1–130. Princeton, N.J.: Princeton University Press, 1969.

_____. C. G. 1958. Flying saucers: a modern myth of things seen in the skies. In *CW* 10:589–824. Princeton, N.J.: Princeton University Press, 1970.

Myers, I. 1962. *Manual: The Myers-Briggs Type Indicator*. Palo Alto, Calif.: Consulting Psychologists Press.

Shepard, H. 1985. Personal communication.

Singer, J., and Loomis, M. 1984. *The Singer-Loomis Inventory of Personality, Experimental Edition*. Palo Alto, Calif.: Consulting Psychologists Press.

Richard Auger, Ph.D., is a clinical psychologist, trained as a Jungian analyst at the C. G. Jung Institute of Los Angeles, where he served five years as director of training. He conducts a private practice in Los Angeles and is involved in organizational training and development as a guest lecturer at the University of Southern California's School of Public Administration and as organization development consultant for the Asia Foundation and the Republic of Singapore. He is the author of "Being a Man in a Woman's World" and "The Jungian Community in the 1980s."

Pauline Arneberg, Ph.D., is currently director of the Center for International Training and Development, School of Public Administration, University of Southern California. She has taught applied behavioral sciences for the past fifteen years and has carried out organization development projects for more than 100 organizations in the U.S. and abroad. She is the author of A Team Building Guide: Facilitation Skills *and, with Dr. David Hartl, "So Near, Yet So Far: An Experiment in Cross Cultural Consulting."*

The Role of Evaluator as Program Analyst

Parallels Between Evaluation and Jungian Analysis

Cathaleene J. Macias and Gregory J. Santos

There is an ongoing debate within evaluation research on the relative merits of experimental versus interpretative methods of inquiry. These two different approaches to evaluation have been variously referred to as traditional versus naturalistic (Madaus and McDonagh 1982), causal versus noncausal (Cook and Shadish 1986), and utilitarian versus intuitionist/pluralist (House 1980). Briefly stated, while some evaluation theorists stress the importance of rigor in determining effectiveness, their opponents emphasize the importance of creativity and intuition in collecting descriptive data. This ideological debate parallels a similar duality within the field of psychology in general, a duality that pits such adjectives as *experimental, positivist, deterministic, Lockean, behaviorist,* and *quantitative* against the supposedly oppositional terms *interpretative, phenomenological, teleological, Kantian, dialectical,* and *qualitative.* The proponents of the first set of adjectives criticize their proponents for being metaphysical and nonscientific, while proponents of the latter set of adjectives accuse so-called positivists of being reductionist and Machiavellian.

It is our intention in this chapter to demonstrate the fallacy of the experimental-interpretative dichotomy for describing evaluative research. We will first compare evaluation to mainstream experimental research in psychology to see how well evaluation fits into this category of research. Then we will compare evaluation to a more interpretative field of psychology, Jungian analysis. Through these two sets of comparisons, we hope to illustrate the unique aspects of evaluation research that make it both a rigorous and a highly subjective method of inquiry.

Evaluation as Applied Experimental Research

Evaluation research occupies an ambiguous position in regard to mainstream psychological research. On the one hand, it is the application of rigorous quantitative research methodologies to a real-world setting, while on the other hand, it is essentially an intuitive, adaptive, and collaborative process that can only approximate laboratory experimental designs. The conduct of organizational evaluation has been likened to the interpretative pursuits of law (Guba 1981), literary criticism (Della-Piana 1981), art criticism (Eisner 1979), folk song collecting (Madaus and McDonagh 1982), storytelling (Wachtman 1982), and watercolor painting (Gephart 1981). In these comparisons of evaluation to the arts and humanities, experienced evaluators point out the necessity for recognizing that evaluative research entails not only inquiry into how an organization functions, but also inquiry into the worth of what is discovered and the implications of the evaluation findings for organizational change (Smith 1981). These last two interpretative aspects of evaluation, i.e., to decide the value and the implications of evaluative findings, are considered critical tasks in the arts and the applied humanities, such as law and journalism, as well as in applied psychological research, such as psychotherapy. On the other hand, they are relatively undervalued by experimental psychological research in general, which has as a primary concern the verification of cause-effect relationships between specific variables. For this reason, evaluators who favor an experimental or quasi-experimental approach to evaluation may view the interpretative approach as lacking in validity and empirical rigor.

The experienced evaluator is well aware that laboratory methods for experimental research are usually too restrictive for field application, but most evaluation methodology texts suggest that the field researcher should try to approximate laboratory research designs. The implicit message in such an approach is that field research, and evaluation research in particular, is second-rate research, only approximating the rigor of laboratory research. Rossi and Wright (1977) describe this "second-rate" status succinctly:

> If there is a Bible for evaluation, the Scriptures have been written by Campbell and Stanley (1966), along with a revised version by Cook and Campbell (1976). The "gospel" of these popular texts is that all research designs can be compared more or less unfavorably to randomized controlled experiments, departures from which are subject to varying combinations of threats to internal and external validity. (p. 13)

However, the rigor of a research design is not only in the process of demonstrating a cause-effect finding, e.g., program effectiveness, but also in validating that the finding is meaningful in specific, theoretically relevant ways. That is, a good evaluation will attempt to explain *why* a program has been effective. It is in this latter task of meaningful explanation, i.e., conceptual validation, that evaluation research has the capacity to surpass laboratory research in rigor by validating its measurements and testing procedures in relation to a specific population at a specific time, by gathering supportive evidence that a certain interpretation of the findings is correct, and/or by investigating the parameters of effectiveness to determine who benefitted the least or most from the program and what were the essential components of the program.

Evaluation practice is grounded in practical meaning. A good evaluation requires the validation of measurement instruments and emphasizes the importance of relating theoretical inferences to real-world observations. By comparison, measurement validation has usually received a cursory nod from mainstream research psychologists: empirical measures are considered valid if they have commonsense, face validity; if they were constructed by the researcher in a way that ensures high content validity; or if the researcher elects to limit his concept generalizability to the specific measurement itself (Wicklund 1990). When criterion or construct validity is demonstrated, it is usually via the correlation of a measure with a similar measure (e.g., one test of self-esteem with another). Such a single demonstration of criterion validity has long been considered inadequate for establishing measurement validity in evaluation research (Cronbach 1989, Messick 1989). However, even these minimal validity efforts are usually absent from reported experiments if the measurement is behavioral rather than instrumental, i.e., a spontaneous human response rather than a test. It is rare that the validity of behavioral measures is assessed in any way, including even the most accepted procedure for variable clarification, conceptual replication. The replication of demonstrated causality has remained imperative, but only in the sense that it instills faith in the reliability of a finding rather than in its conceptual meaning. A majority of psychological studies are simply demonstrations, providing interesting, albeit theoretically ambiguous, evidence that if "X," then "Y." The theoretical relationship of "X" to "Y," the conceptual meaning of the empirical measures, is of less importance to many contemporary researchers than the simple predictive ability they have gained (Wicklund 1990).

The neglect of conceptual validation goes against the teachings of distinguished evaluation theorists, such as Anne Anastasi (1988), Donald Campbell (1966), Robert Linn (1979), Jane Loevinger (1957), Samuel Messick (1989), and Lee Cronbach (1989), who have pointed out for decades that the meaningfulness of any demonstrated effect rests upon a careful delineation of what has taken place and what has been measured. If evaluative research is to attain the rigor necessary to provide pragmatic consultation for organizational administrators, it is essential that evaluators reject the criticism that program evaluation is a poor imitation of mainstream psychological research and come to see themselves as experts in a separate field that demands greater rigor in conceptual validity than laboratory experimental research.

Evaluation as Interpretative Analysis

The importance of conceptual validation to evaluative research, and to psychological research in general, can be seen more clearly through a comparison of evaluation with the practice of Jungian analytical psychology. The relevance of Jungian analysis to program evaluation is immediately apparent in the shared concern of both practices for worker, consumer, or client welfare and the common goal of improving individual as well as organizational functioning. However, the correspondence between the two practices runs much deeper. A more basic correspondence between evaluation and Jungian psychology concerns the rigor with which each practice approaches the empirical verification of conceptual theories.

Table 1. *Correspondence Between Tasks in Evaluation and Jungian Analysis*

	Hypothesis Generation	Hypothesis Confirmation	Conceptual Clarification
Organizational Evaluation	Documentation	Demonstration	Validation
Jungian Analysis	Elicitation	Exploration	Elaboration

Table 1 provides a comparison of the essential procedures in organizational evaluation and Jungian analysis in terms of a general model of intellectual inquiry. These procedures are divided into three categories which reflect the empirical, theory-testing nature of both practices: (1) hypothesis generation, (2) hypothesis confirmation, and (3) conceptual clarification. The distinction between these last two categories, hypothesis confirmation and conceptual clarification, will be the focus of our following discussion of the parallels between organizational evaluation and Jungian analysis.

Evaluation Tasks

Because of the diversity of methodological orientations in contemporary evaluation research theory, it is impossible to speak confidently of a single evaluative procedure. In practice, however, evaluators generally follow a process of hypothesis-testing akin to the model we have proposed. In the early years of evaluation, organizational objectives served as a basis for formulating hypotheses addressing organizational effectiveness; currently, hypotheses are more likely to be derived from evaluator observation and consultation, from descriptive data on organizational functioning, or from stakeholder concerns and information needs (Cook and Shadish 1986). For evaluation, the essential tasks described by most handbooks and research texts are (1) to *document* organizational functioning, (2) to *demonstrate* that an organization is functioning in a particular way, and (3) to *validate* the meaning of the demonstration in terms that are relevant to organizational effectiveness (see Table 1).

Analytic Tasks

For purposes of our comparison to evaluation research, we will focus on the methodological practice of Jungian analysis. That is, we will consider the interpretative methods which an analyst follows in helping the analysand "to gain insight into the specific unconscious structures and dynamics that emerge during analysis" (Stein 1984, p. 29). Our focus will be on the analyst's method of identifying, interpreting, and verifying the specific "unconscious structures and dynamics" that reflect the analysand's psychological functioning. While Jung's writings on his analytic treatment focused primarily on the education and transformation of the analysand, rather than on methods for eliciting and interpreting case material (McCurdy 1984), he nevertheless provided sufficient examples of his own methods of interpretative verification to allow us to posit a general hypothesis-testing model.

Interpretation in Jungian analysis follows a hypothesis-testing procedure similar to that of organizational evaluation. Jung himself formulated the verification goal of analytical psychology when he wrote: "Every interpretation is a hypothesis, an attempt to read an unknown text" (Jung 1934, par. 322). While Jungian interpretation verification is usually more subjective and/or introspective than hypothesis-testing in the typical research study (Jung 1963) and less likely to be causal, the same intellectual rigor is required for analysis as for evaluation. For Jungian analysis, the essential interpretative tasks are (1) to *elicit* personal associations from the analysand, (2) to *explore* interpretations of this information with the analysand, and (3) to *elaborate* on interpretations of the case material through amplification (see Table 1).

Like the evaluator, the Jungian analyst follows a flexible, often circular and repetitive, investigative procedure, looping back to gather previously overlooked data and reformulating interpretations (i.e., hypotheses) as the work progresses. Both practices adhere to an assumption of multiplicity, i.e., that more than one inference or interpretation can be appropriate for the same data. Both practices also presuppose theoretical stances, but rely upon empirical observation and personal experience to judge the relevance of these preliminary stances to the individual case.

In the remaining section of this paper, we will discuss these essential tasks of evaluation and Jungian analysis in order to point out the correspondence between the two practices and the value of reconceptualizing each practice in terms of the other.

Task I: Hypothesis Generation

The hypothesis generation task is referred to as the discovery phase of research by philosophers of science. Although mainstream experimental psychology publications rarely report a corresponding preliminary observation period, naturalistic research often relies only on discovery. For this reason, a verification-discovery dichotomy has become a common way of describing the distinction between experimental and interpretative ideologies. However, discovery can also be considered an integral step in verification. Even Cronbach (1982), a stanch experimentalist, acknowledged the value of initial observation and organizational interaction to the design of evaluation, and he has even suggested that such preparatory question-gathering is essential to the process of conceptual validation (Cronbach 1989). In organizational evaluation, a preliminary period of observation and documentation allows a researcher to design an appropriate research plan and to formulate pertinent and situationally relevant hypotheses.

The elicitation of personal information, associations, and dream material from an analysand corresponds to the task of documentation in evaluation. From personal case material presented by the analysand, the analyst moves toward the formation of hypotheses about the analysand's psychological functioning just as an evaluator would move toward the construction of hypotheses about organizational effectiveness after having observed organizational functioning and interacting informally with administrators and personnel. However, while Jungian psychology is most certainly an interpretative practice, it should not be conceptualized as simply a discovery endeavor. Like evaluation, Jungian analysis utilizes careful observation and interaction with the client to facilitate the formulation of hypotheses which will then be subjected to verification. The elicitation of dreams, associations, fantasies, confessions, and reflections from the analysand is but one critical step in a sophisticated verification process.

Task II: Hypothesis Confirmation

The essential difference between the hypothesis-testing of experimental research and the hypothesis-testing of analytical psychology is simply the degree to which the investigator or analyst can substantiate his findings. Social science generally places more confidence in experimental or quasi-experimental demon-

strations of causality than in introspective client reports or corroborative personal disclosures. When hypothesis-confirmation is the
end product of a research endeavor, such differences in confidence
become critical, leading critics of psychoanalysis to claim that
there is insufficient evidence that psychoanalytic interpretations
are accurate (e.g., Scharnberg 1984) or that findings from evaluation designs that only approximate experimental rigor are incon-
clusive (Cook and Campbell 1979). However, when the demonstration of causality or interpretative appropriateness (Task II:
Hypothesis Confirmation) is considered to be a separate task from
measurement or interpretation (Task III: Conceptual Clarification),
then it becomes evident that the demonstrated effect or interpretation must be explicated in order for it to have meaning (i.e., validity) for a particular organization or analysand.

The theoretical, conceptual validity of an empirical finding
(or an analytical interpretation) must be established independently of its demonstration in order for the meaning inherent in
the finding (or the interpretation) to be clear and unequivocal. This
distinction between hypothesis confirmation and conceptual clarification is identical to the distinction made by Campbell and Stanley (1966) between internal and external validity when they posited that internal validity is the *sine qua non* of social science
research. However, like Chen and Rossi (1987), we are suggesting
that both internal validity (i.e., evidence of an effect) and external
validity (i.e., meaningfulness of the effect) are essential in social
research, and that each type of validity elucidates and supports
the other. For instance, demonstrating that an employee training
program has significantly increased employee knowledge via a
knowledge-acquisition test provides an employer with evidence
that training can make a difference. Exactly what that difference is
and how it relates to employee on-the-job efficiency must be
spelled out separately through a detailed analysis of the test and
its relationship to employee characteristics and job performance.
Strong confidence in the demonstrated effectiveness of training is
meaningless without a clear conceptual understanding of what
that effectiveness means. On the other hand, lack of confidence in
a demonstrated finding, e.g., when the finding is based on herme-
neutic, interpretative inquiry rather than on experimental results,
becomes less relevant when the finding is carefully explored and
substantiated through corroborative evidence. For instance, ethnographic observation or organizational functioning may lead an
evaluator to conclude that an organization is effective in certain
regards. Corroborating this observational evidence with employee

interview data, production schedules, and consumer reports could provide support for the ethnographic finding that would substantiate its validity, clarify its meaning, and make irrelevant the issue of how much confidence should be placed in this particular ethnographer's observation.

Likewise, in the analytical process, there is a clear distinction between hypothesis-testing through exploration and conceptual clarification through interpretative elaboration. After the analyst has formulated interpretative hypotheses in reaction to the analysand's dreams, confessions, and reflections, she or he then obtains confirmation or refutation of those hypotheses by exploring relevant topics with the analysand and carefully probing for supportive or discrediting information. This hypothesis-testing task in analysis obviously requires skill and sensitivity and is certainly influenced by the theoretical and personal leanings of the analyst, and yet it is as critical to the analytic endeavor as demonstrated effectiveness is to evaluative research. However, the process of exploring and probing for hypothesis confirmation is strictly an empirical attempt to find a tenable interpretation of an analysand's dream, association, or experience. The task of validating these interpretations lies in the realm of symbolic elaboration and amplification. If an analyst were to confuse demonstration with validation, then that analyst would mistakenly believe he has validated his interpretative diagnosis of an analysand if he receives confirmation of his hypotheses in response to his probes, either directly from the analysand or on the basis of observed criteria. Certainly, more than a few therapists proceed in this manner, resting their diagnoses on simple confirmatory evidence supporting specific symbolic interpretations, and this has been a significant criticism of the psychoanalytic process in general (Scharnberg 1984). However, a trained Jungian analyst will not rely solely on hypothesis confirmation, but will pursue a conceptual validation through the process of symbol amplification.

Task III: Conceptual Clarification

Jungian analysis offers evaluation research a very explicit model for conceptual clarification. In the Jungian tradition, conceptual clarification is achieved by elaborating and amplifying the conclusions and inferences drawn from the collaborative exploration of case material. Amplification in Jungian theory can be defined as the "elaboration and clarification of a dream-image by means of directed association and of parallels from the humane science" (Storr 1983). Inferences and interpretations are judged valid or invalid on the weight of associative memories or fantasies, corroborative dreams, artistic expressions of the analysand, and/or previous case material. Moreover, the extensive training of the Jungian analyst in mythology, theology, folklore, and ethnology allows an analyst to present relevant cultural motifs from history, literature, and art to the analysand for his or her consideration, and the responses of the analysand to these motifs and archetypes then become important criteria for judging the validity of analytical insights. Dream and fantasy symbols are not considered fixed in meaning, for it is "only through comparative studies in mythology, folklore, religion and philology that we can evaluate their nature scientifically" (Jung 1934, par. 351). The validity of an interpretation, therefore, is judged not by its intuitive or theoretical appropriateness for describing the analysand's psychological functioning, nor simply by the analysand's confirmation of its explanatory relevance, but by its meaningful correspondence from both the analyst's and the analysand's perspectives with multiple instances of the same symbolic imagery. In essence, Jung validated his analytical interpretations by seeking parallel meanings from other "texts" which would elucidate the contextual meaning of a particular psychological symbol and clarify the relevance of the symbol for a particular person (Jung 1935, par. 173).

This dialectical approach to conceptual clarification provides the Jungian analyst with knowledge about what universal archetypes are evident in an analysand's associations, as well as what is distinctly different from the archetypes in an analysand's personal archetypal images. For instance, for the analyst, the archetype of Mother can mean many things, but the individual meaning of the archetypal figure for an analysand can be refined through a comparison to multiple dream images, responses to expressions of the archetype in myth and fairy tales, or an active imagination dialogue with the archetypal figure itself. The individual symbolism of Mother for the analysand may be revealed as similar to cultural manifestations of the archetype in some respects, but very different in other respects which may have significance for the analysand's well-being. Relating particular, personally meaningful aspects of the archetypal figure to particular events in the analysand's life can then help the analysand toward self-insight and a better understanding of his or her life circumstances.

Dialectical validation through amplification in Jungian anal-

ysis corresponds directly to convergent and discriminant validation (Campbell and Fiske 1959) in organizational evaluation. With
convergent and discriminant validity, the meaning of a specific
measure is ascertained by its high or low correlation with several
independent criteria. For instance, through a comparison of test
scores to a variety of other measures, an evaluator can determine
more precisely the aptitude, skill, or trait that a test can be used to
estimate and the limitation and specifications of test use. But the
Jungian multiple-comparison method of conceptual validation
corresponds even more closely to Campbell's (1966) "pattern
matching" and Trochim's (1985, 1989) "concept mapping"
approaches to validity, both of which are based on the premise
that the validity of a particular set of findings can be decided by
the match between the obtained pattern of the findings and a
hypothetical pattern predicted by theory and held together by a
meaningful "nomological network" (Cronbach & Meehl, 1955) of
conceptual meaning. "Concept mapping" has become a quantifi-
able, methodologically sophisticated evaluation technique for
both assessing program effectiveness and validating testing
instruments, and its practical value exactly parallels Jungian
amplification in its emphasis on holistic meaningfulness. In Jungian analysis, multiple symbolic images are interrelated into a complex, i.e., a pattern or map of individual symbols, the meaning of
which can be validated by correspondence to a similar archetypal
pattern found in cultural motifs. Similarly, in evaluation, multiple
experimental findings, test item scores, or interview responses can
be validated by correspondence to a theoretically predicted map of
the relationship between these same results, scores, or responses;
if the match is close, the theoretical map not only affords construct
validation, but also provides a meaningful explanation of the evaluation findings. Moreover, the variations which do exist between
the theoretical and the actual pattern of findings exemplify the
individuality of the program under study or the idiosyncrasy of the
instrument being validated. In this way, "concept mapping" provides information that is meaningful for a particular program or
research project and which will allow administrators to make
rational, program-specific policy decisions. The validity of an evaluation finding, therefore, rests on the specificity of its meaning for
particular workers, consumers, or clients, just as the specificity of
an analytical interpretation is an indication of how valid that interpretation is for a particular analysand.

The individual focus of both evaluation and Jungian analysis
is a primary aspect of conceptual clarification. In evaluation, a test

or measurement is not itself validated and then henceforth considered valid, but rather, the test is validated for a particular purpose in a particular setting with particular people (Messick 1989, Anastasi 1988). As Messick (1989) says, it is the inferences derived from test scores or observations that can be deemed valid or invalid, not the test or observation technique itself. This definition of validity as individualized relevance is not restricted to evaluation; Cronbach (1975) has pointed out that the validity of any hypothesis is dependent upon the individual circumstances under which the hypothesis is tested. In the case of qualitative data, this would mean that any interpretative hypothesis can be validated only through an assessment of the specific relevance of the hypothesis to the situation, circumstances, and individuals involved. In Jungian analysis, this individualized relevance corresponds directly to the process of amplification, wherein the collective, cultural aspects of a symbol are reinterpreted in personal, individual terms. As Shelburne (1988) suggests, analysis is a distinctly idiographic scientific method that leads to a "subjectively meaningful self-knowledge of the mythos" (p. 107).

It is important to note that an individual focus does not preclude a more general theoretical focus in Jungian analysis, but rather the general (nomothetic) serves to elucidate the individual (idiographic) meaning of a symbol and vice versa. Just as interpretations of individual case material are validated by finding analogous universal occurrences of the same symbolism in myth, religion, and art, so such archetypal material takes on subtle variations in meaning when viewed from the individual perspective. According to Jung (1931), such an interplay of theoretical levels facilitates self-insight in the analysand:

> In handling a dream or fantasy I make it a rule never to go beyond the meaning which is effective for the patient; I merely try to make him as fully conscious of this meaning as possible, so that he shall also become aware of its supra-personal connections . . . we need to have not only a personal, contemporary consciousness, but also a supra-personal consciousness with a sense of historical continuity. (par. 99)

In organizational evaluation, a similar interdependence between the general and the specific is apparent in the recent emphasis on metanalysis and the questions concerning the generalizability of construct validity (e.g., Anastasi 1986; Glass, McGaw, and Smith 1981; Jones and Appelbaum 1989; Schmidt et al. 1985). Any evaluation, while necessarily specific to a particular organization or program in order to be both relevant and valid, has implications as well for program and policy generalization. If the organizational system or program is indeed effective, then there is a need to determine if it would also be effective in different settings. And regardless of whether it was effective, there is a need to gain a deeper understanding of internal dynamics through a comparison to other organizations or programs of a similar nature. Ultimately, individual programs or organizations can be better understood through a comparison to prototypes identified through metanalytic research. As with Jungian analysis, the uniqueness of the individual (e.g., the organization) can be illuminated through a comparison to the general (e.g., organizational patterns). In this regard, both evaluative research and Jungian analysis are theoretical endeavors in the most sophisticated sense: each practice attempts to determine the individual meaning of empirical data through a careful delineation of relationships between specific situational variables which are themselves then related conceptually to more universal and fundamental theories of human functioning.

Conceptualizing the evaluative process as composed of three primary tasks (hypothesis generation, hypothesis confirmation, and conceptual clarification), and considering the correspondence between Jungian analysis and organizational evaluation in regard to these three tasks, we conclude that Jungian analysis is a more appropriate model for evaluation than is mainstream psychological research. Analytical psychology offers the evaluator a perspective that emphasizes the importance of documentation and conceptual validation, two phases of evaluation that are undervalued by mainstream researchers, while it distinguishes between demonstration of causality and inference validation, making it obvious that evaluation's *inferiority* to mainstream research in regard to the demonstration of causality is actually less important to organizational psychology than the *superiority* of evaluation in regard to the conceptual validation of empirical findings. Assuming the role of program analyst, the evaluator becomes more aware that his primary role is not merely to implement mainstream research in field settings, but rather to assist programs and administrators in understanding and improving their organizational functioning, a clearly therapeutic task that requires a perspective and an attitude very different from that of the mainstream research psychologist.

An Illustration

The methodological advantages of assuming a Jungian analytical perspective for evaluative research becomes self-evident in practice. Cathaleene Macias is currently directing a National Institute of Mental Health multisite evaluation of team case management for the chronically mentally ill, and because this evaluative research exemplifies the three primary tasks common to Jungian analysis and program evaluation, we will draw on the study to illustrate how analytical theory can be put into evaluation practice.

Following the Jungian analytical model, the hypothesis generation task of the case management project has been extensive. Throughout the project, there has been a concerted effort to document the implementation of team case management in the various mental health agencies and to answer the fundamental question, "What is team case management?" This broad question is being addressed more concretely by documenting the interactional processes of the team members, the utilization of high-functioning clients and paraprofessionals on case management teams, the leadership styles of the team leaders, and the case managers' attitudes toward their chronically mentally ill clientele. In addition, we are exploring the role of the teams within mental health agencies, agency policies concerning case management, and the facilities provided for the case management work. This documentation process is serving both to record the case management process for future replication and to generate hypotheses concerning the relative effectiveness of various styles of team case management for particular types of clients within particular settings.

Hypothesis confirmation, on the other hand, has been approached from a more traditional research perspective. The determination of the effectiveness of team case management is through an experimental research design. Chronically mentally ill clients have been randomly assigned by their community mental health agencies to either formal team case management or to only their usual informal case management by a therapist or day treatment worker. The progress of the clients in both the experimental (team case management) and control groups is being followed for a four-year period, including a period of two months before the entrance of the experimental group into team case management. The study is a longitudinal experimental study of client progress in team case management. The outcome measures used to assess client progress include level of psychological functioning, community adaptation, occurrences of life crises and problems, quality of family relationships, and autonomy/competency in daily living.

Following the model of Jungian analysis, conceptual clarification is also an integral part of this mental health program evaluation. The focus of our conceptual validation is the question, "What is a positive outcome for a chronically mentally ill client in team case management?" The question stems from our concern that our outcome measures of client progress may not be adequate when taken at face value for describing the progress of mentally ill clients. Because our research project staff includes clinicians and agency directors who have experience working with the mentally ill, we are aware that "progress" might be conceptualized as an overall improvement on several outcome measures, or simply as a stabilized existence, the relative absence of life crises, a minimal increase in personal autonomy, or even the prevention of further psychological deterioration. We are in the process of identifying indices of improvement for this client population. Like a Jungian analyst, we are relying on a variety of sources in our formulation of a "pattern" of outcome measures and other client variables which will describe progress for the chronically mentally ill. We are drawing on personal accounts from practicing service providers, on clinical case accounts, on published studies of effective interventions, and on theories of psychotherapy. We are also placing our research study in the context of other case management and mental health program evaluation studies in order to assess the relevance of our findings to other populations and other service implementations.

The reader should be aware that the documentation tasks and conceptual validation tasks are not usually extensive in evaluative research. From the perspective of the mainstream psychological research community, it would probably be sufficient to concentrate our research resources on the task of hypothesis confirmation alone. If we obtain a statistically significant overall difference in our outcome measures between our experimental and control groups in favor of the clients in team case management, then we can conclude that team case management is an effective way of providing services to the chronic mentally ill. However, the meaning of team case management effectiveness, whether demonstrated by a greater improvement or a lesser decline than in the control group, would not be sufficiently addressed by this simplistic approach, and the relevance of our findings for future implementations of team case management would be virtually unknown without the inclusion of a specific theoretical framework based on client characteristics, service idio-syncrasies, and organizational constraints. The application of a Jungian analytical approach to our program evaluation has allowed us to blend methodological rigor with theoretical signifi-cance and has guided our research toward the formulation of prag-matic recommendations for team case management implementation.

Conclusions

Evaluation is most certainly both a deterministic and an interpretative endeavor, but a distinction between these two ideol-ogies distorts the essential goals of evaluative research. The deter-ministic and interpretative tasks of evaluation are not exclusive nor simply complementary, but rather interrelate to provide the foundation for a rigorous, dialectical approach to applied research.

A comparison of organizational evaluation and Jungian psy-chology makes obvious the inadequacy of an experimental/deter-ministic versus interpretative/descriptive dichotomy for charac-terizing different forms of intellectual inquiry. The comparison reveals not merely the interpretative aspects of evaluation or the empirical aspects of analysis, but rather the fundamental rigor with which each practice approaches both interpretative and empirical goals. A reconceptualization of the role of evaluator as organizational analyst emphasizes the creativity needed for the evaluation task and makes evident the methodological sophistica-tion inherent in a well-planned, well-executed interpretative evalu-ation design.

References

Anastasi, A. 1986. Evolving concepts of test validation. *Annual Review of Psychology* 37:1–15.

_____. 1988. *Psychological Testing.* New York: Macmillan.

Campbell, D. T. 1966. Pattern matching as an essential in distal knowing. In *The Psychology of Egon Brunswik*, K. R. Hammond, ed. New York: Holt, Rinehart and Winston.

Campbell, D. T., and Fiske, D. W. 1959. Convergent and discriminant validation by the multitrait-multimethod matrix. *Psychological Bulletin* 56(2):81–105.

Campbell, D. T., and Stanley, J. C. 1966. *Experimental and Quasi-Experimental Designs for Research*. Chicago: Rand McNally.

Chen, H., and Rossi, R. H. 1987. The theory-driven approach to validity. *Evaluation and Program Planning* 10:95–103.

Cook, T. D., and Campbell, D. T. 1976. The design and analysis of quasi-experiments and true experiments in field settings. In *Handbook of Industrial and Organizational Psychology*, M. D. Dunnette, ed. Chicago: Rand McNally.

_____. 1979. *Quasi-Experimentation: Design and Analysis Issues for Field Settings*. Boston: Houghton Mifflin.

Cook, T. D., and Shadish, Jr., W. R. 1986. Program evaluation: The worldly science. *Annual Review of Psychology* 37:193–232.

Cronbach, L. J. 1975. Beyond the two disciplines of scientific psychology. *American Psychologist* 30:116–127.

_____. 1982. *Designing Evaluations of Educational and Social Programs*. San Francisco: Jossey-Bass.

_____. 1989. Construct validation after thirty years. In *Intelligence: Measurement Theory and Public Policy*, R. L. Linn, ed. Urbana, Ill.: University of Illinois Press.

Cronbach, L. J., and Meehl, P. E. 1955. Construct validity in psychological tests. *Psychological Bulletin* 52:281–302.

Della Piana, G. M. 1981. Literary and film criticism. In *Metaphors for Evaluation*, N. L. Smith, ed. Beverly Hills, Calif.: Sage.

Eisner, E. 1979. *The Educational Imagination*. New York: Macmillan.

Gephart, W. J. 1981. Watercolor painting. In *Metaphors for Evaluation*, N. L. Smith, ed. Beverly Hills, Calif.: Sage.

Glass, G. V., McGaw, B., and Smith, M. L. 1981. *Meta-Analysis in Social Research*. Beverly Hills, Calif.: Sage.

Guba, E. G. 1981. Investigative reporting. In *Metaphors for Evaluation*, N. L. Smith, ed. Beverly Hills, Calif.: Sage.

House, E. R. 1980. *Evaluating with Validity*. Beverly Hills, Calif.: Sage.

Jones, L. V., and Appelbaum, M. I. 1989. Psychometric methods. *Annual Review of Psychology* 40:23–43.

Jung, C. G. 1931. The aims of psychotherapy. In *Collected Works*, 16:36–52. Princeton, N.J.: Princeton University Press, 1954.

_____. 1934. The practical use of dream-analysis. In *Collected Works*, 16:139–162. Princeton, N.J.: Princeton University Press, 1954.

_____. 1935. The Tavistock lectures, III. In *Collected Works*, 18:5–182. Princeton, N.J.: Princeton University Press, 1955.

_____. 1963. *Memories, Dreams, Reflections.* New York: Random House.

Linn, R. L. 1979. Issues of validity in measurement for competency-based programs. In *Practices and Problems in Competency-Based Measurement*, M. Bunda and J. Sanders, eds. Washington, D.C.: National Council on Measurement in Education.

Loevinger, J. 1957. Objective tests as instruments of psychological theory. *Psychological Reports* 3:635–694.

Madaus, G. F., and McDonagh, J. T. 1982. As I roved out: Folksong collecting as a metaphor for evaluation. In *Communication Strategies in Evaluation*, N. L. Smith, ed. Beverly Hills, Calif.: Sage.

McCurdy, A. 1984. Establishing and maintaining the analytical structure. In *Jungian Analysis*, M. Stein, ed. Boston: Shambhala.

Messick, S. 1989. Meaning and values in test validation: The science and ethics of assessment. *Educational Researcher* 18(2):5–11.

Rossi, P. H., and Wright, S. R. 1977. Evaluation research: An evaluation of theory, practice, and politics. *Evaluation Quarterly* 1:13.

Scharnberg, M. 1984. *The Myth of Paradigm-Shift, or How to Lie with Methodology.* Stockholm: Uppsala Studies in Education.

Schmidt, F. L., Hunter, J. E., Pearlman, K., and Hirsh, H. R. 1985. Forty questions about validity generalization and meta-analysis. *Personnel Psychology* 38:697–798.

Shelburne, W. A. 1988. *Mythos and Logos in the Thought of Carl Jung.* Albany, N.Y.: State University of New York Press.

Smith, N. L. 1981. Developing evaluation methods. In *Metaphors for Evaluation*, N. L. Smith, ed. Beverly Hills, Calif.: Sage.

Stein, M. 1984. The aims and goals of Jungian analysis. In *Jungian Analysis*, M. Stein, ed. Boston: Shambhala.

Storr, A. 1983. *The Essential Jung.* Princeton, N.J.: Princeton University Press.

Trochim, W. M. K. 1985. Pattern matching, validity, and conceptualization in program evaluation. *Evaluation Review* 9(5):575–604.

_____. 1989. An introduction to concept mapping for planning and evaluation. *Evaluation and Program Planning* 12:1–16.

Wachtman, E. L. 1982. Storytelling: The narrative structure of evaluation. In *Communication Strategies in Evaluation*, N. L. Smith, ed. Beverly Hills, Calif.: Sage.

Wicklund, R. A. 1990. *Zero-Variable Theories and the Psychology of the Explainer.* Berlin: Springer-Verlag.

Cathaleene J. Macias *is a research psychologist and program evaluator at the University of Utah. She has studied Jungian theory from an epistemological perspective for many years and is currently writing a series of articles incorporating Jungian theory into mainstream research psychology.*

Father Gregory Santos *is a Trappist monk and theologian, a graduate of the C. G. Jung Institute in Zürich and a practicing Jungian analyst. He is completing a forthcoming book, to be published by Open Court, on the role of the feminine in the psychological transformation of a monk.*

The Complex in Human Affairs

Georgia Lepper

*Responsibility for and towards words is a task which is
intrinsically ethical. As such, however, it is situated
beyond the horizon of the visible world, in that realm
wherein dwells the Word that was in the beginning and is
not the word of Man.*

Vaclav Havel, 1989

The starting point of this article is really a return . . . to some
early Jungian concepts which entered into the general analytic
vocabulary and lost the dynamic of their original meanings. First
and foremost is the idea of the complex, with its origins in clinical
investigation and diagnostics. For Jung, "when you speak of
dynamic and processes, you need the time factor," and then there
was the struggle to "let psychology be a living thing and not to
dissolve it into static entities" (1976, p. 65).

My thesis is this: that the thrust of Jung's understanding of a
dynamic psyche comprehensible in terms of time and process
went beyond the concepts which scientific thinking of his day had
at its disposal. His concepts grasp basic premises of field and systems theory which occupy the mainstream of scientific thought
today. Lacking an environment of reflection and debate in which
his insights could take on form, he abandoned his original inspira-
tion, and dynamic concepts such as the complex began to be
treated as entities; the complex as an organizing principle became
the "mother complex" of popular parlance, and everyone knows
what that is!

What this paper proposes is an exploratory return to the concept of the complex as a dynamic process, to discover how its
subtlety might throw light on the understanding of the multidimensional dynamic system of the modern organization.

A key notion will be that of boundary and its role in the formation of a complex. Jung remarked, "The image of the world is a
projection of the world of the self as the latter is an introjection of

the world" (1976, p. 66). Decades later, systems theorist Peter Checkland, writing on "soft-system" problem-solving, notes that "perceptions of problems are always subjective, and they change with time" (1981, p. 155). I believe we can follow this line of thinking towards an understanding of how an organization and its members interpenetrate to create organizational complexes that are embedded in its dynamic systems, both technical and human, "hard" and "soft." These organizational complexes can bedevil the perceptions and problem-solving capacities of its members.

This paper will attempt an exploration of the relationship between the language and thinking of Jung and the language and thinking of systems theory. It will explore the complex as a systemic principle operating on the level of the group and the organization, as well as on the individual level. There will be four strands of inquiry:

1. Discussion of the concept of the complex as an emergent theory of meaning.

2. Complex as system—generating meaning through the processes of boundary formation and maintenance: emergence and hierarchy.

3. The emergence of meanings within the organization through the interpenetration of levels within the technical/social/individual matrix.

4. Applications—using awareness of complexes to deepen and develop a systems-level tool for a dynamic and process-based problem-solving diagnostic which emphasizes the role of the manager in the maintenance of an adaptive, multidimensional working alliance.

Jung arrived at the concept of the complex using the word association test, developed in 1897 by the German psychologist Wilhelm Wundt. Through the word association test, Jung established the existence of characteristic patterns in the responses of his subjects: the association experiments were "able to prove that certain restricting laws are in motion" (Jung 1905, par. 730). It is characteristic of the scientific language in which he was operating that Jung spoke of "restricting laws"—we might today speak of restricting *conditions* and of "constraints"—intrinsic limits within a formal system upon the degree of freedom of the elements which comprise it.

Through his experiments with the word association test, Jung was able to show the existence of blockages in the capacity to associate, which were measurable in terms of reaction time, and clusters of responses indicating associations of meanings which were not random but highly directed towards the experiences of the subject. Through further investigation with a galvanometer, he showed the presence of physiological reactions to certain of these clusters—increased respiration, heartbeat, etc. Jung came to understand several properties of complexes.

1. They can be discovered through means of language (e.g., the word association test), but . . .

2. they are implicated in profound physiological reactions, with the result that they are . . .

3. "feeling-toned": "we are speaking therefore of a *feeling-toned complex of ideas*, or, simply, of a *complex*" (Jung 1905, par. 730).

4. "The influence of the complex on thinking and behavior is called a 'constellation' " and the power of a complex-constellation is such that . . .

5. they seem therefore to have "a remarkable independence in the hierarchy of the psyche, so that one may compare complexes to revolting vassals in an empire" (Jung 1913, par. 1352).

Now I want to make a strong claim: Jung, in 1905, was postulating a systemic view of the complex as an emergent property of the living system, which includes the somatic, the psychic, the individual, and the collective as a series of emergent levels within a whole system (let us call it "the human system"). What was remarkable for Jung was not merely the existence of an entity called "the unconscious"; but rather the existence of a system which he called the collective and personal unconscious, out of which consciousness, with its particularly human characteristic, the quest for meaning, emerged.

The concept of emergence has its origins in the early part of the century with biologists struggling to find a disciplined means by which to explain the properties of the organized complexity which is the characteristic of purposive living systems, without recourse to metaphysical explanations such as vitalism and entelechy. Systems theory starts its inquiry at this point with the attempt to account for the properties of the whole through the concept of emergence: "the principle that whole entities exhibit properties which are meaningful only when attributable to the whole, not to its parts" (Checkland 1981, p. 314). The parts of whole systems form a hierarchical set of levels, and it is the objective of systems theory "to provide both an account of the relationships between different levels and an account of how observed hierarchies come to be formed: what generates the levels, what separates them, and what links them?" (Checkland 1981, p. 81). The physical and chemical properties of matter are a necessary but not sufficient condition of the properties of living systems; living systems are not reducible to physics and chemistry.

Here is the point at which we must begin to resist the temptation to think of the conscious and unconscious as two entities forming a structure which we conceptualize spatially as parts of the "mind," which is, in turn, more or less located in a brain and its nervous system. Rather, let's try to hold on to Jung's insight into psyche as a dynamic system of relations. The complex could then be characterized as an emergent property of what we have called the human system. Through its activity, the complex creates meaningful patterns that are formed on the one hand by the experiences of the individual, and on the other by patterns of invariance (constraints) imposed by the form of the biological and social matrix in which they are expressed. Jung named these patterns of invariance "archetypes," which he described as "a formative principle of instinctual power" (1947, par. 416). The complexes form a bridge between the syntax-based system of conscious thinking, which Jung called directed thinking, and the metaphorical form of thought, which he referred to as fantasy thinking. They link the personal and the collective through the behavioral/social matrix as it is mediated by emotions, feelings, and perceptions. Importantly, they form a link between the perceptual system and the directed human activity system. It is here that they may make their appearance as "revolting vassals in an empire." Often that empire is an organization.

The systems diagram of the complex (Fig. 1) makes several assumptions.

1. I am making the following distinction between emotions and feelings: emotions I take to be the behavioral pole and feelings the socially mediated pole of affect. Jung characterized this interpenetration of systems in the Tavistock Lectures: "It is true that feelings, if they have an emotional character, are accompanied by physiological effects; but there are definitely feelings which do not change the physiological condition. These feelings are very mental, they are not of an emotional nature" (1976, p. 31). I've represented this on the system diagram by separating them and showing them in dynamic relation. This is the thrust of Jung's intention. It makes a fundamental distinction which will help us see how this system cannot be ignored when judgments are being made in the "human activity system."

Figure 1. *Systems Diagram of the Complex*

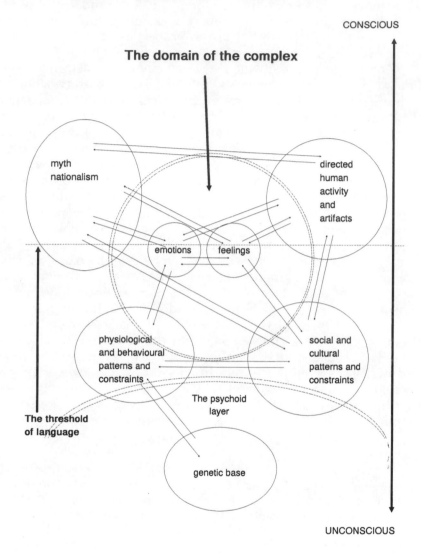

2. With the arrows, "conscious" and "unconscious" are to be read as *directional and temporal.* We will see what importance this has when we get to looking at the organization and its members as interpenetrating systems.

3. This systems diagram is a map, not to be mistaken for the terrain. As with the legendary Map of the Island, we may find no buried treasure there. It starts from a series of assumptions; it is made to be remade; it can be entered at any point, and its pathways followed in any direction. It is made to stimulate perceptions, initiate thoughts, create new pathways.

Jung recognized a hierarchy of levels in the production of the complex, ranging from the conscious, through the personal unconscious, to the deeply unconscious, embedded in the "collective psyche." Using the concepts of hierarchy and emergence, we have characterized a domain that locates the concept of the complex in a systems model. Jung described this domain as *psychoid*, and he said: "We must completely give up the idea of the psyche's being somehow connected with the brain and remember instead the 'meaningful' or 'intelligent' behavior of the lower organisms, which are without a brain. Here we find ourselves much closer to the formal factor which, as I have said, has nothing to do with brain activity" (1952, par. 947).

In introducing the use of the term *psychoid* Jung was at pains to be precise: "If I make use of the term 'psychoid' I do so with three reservations; firstly, I use it as an adjective, not as a noun; secondly, no psychic quality in the proper sense of the word is implied, but only a "quasi-psychic" one such as the reflex processes possess; and thirdly, it is meant to distinguish a category of events from merely vitalistic phenomena on the one hand, and from specifically psychic processes on the other" (Jung 1947, par. 368). What Jung is alerting us to, and warning us against, is the danger of reification. The "psychoid," like "energy" and "information," "cannot be directly perceived or represented" (Jung 1947, par. 436). Rather, it is like "the invisible, ultra-violet end of the spectrum" (Jung 1947, par. 417); we can discover it only phenomenologically through the study of its effects. As a concept, it is useful to the extent that it enables us to describe and understand the nature of the psyche more deeply.

Used within these constraints, the concept of the psychoid is an attempt to address the relationship between levels within "the community of body and psyche." The term *psychoid* describes the proto-psychic system by which somatically embedded instinctual "information" is "stored" in the form of archetypal patterns, to be replicated and fleshed out through the forms of culture and language, into individual and collective structures, which we call complexes and myths. By extending this conception to the active study of the organization, we follow Jung into a world where boundaries extend beyond the intuitively "natural," and the production systems we construct may usefully be understood as coextensive with the psychic properties of their builders. To manage an organization as if it were a simple linear system of causes and effects, as for example, management information systems so often assume, can generate a system of falsification.

A company—it was a founder-managed family business—was sold out to a holding company, hungry for acquisitions. It was a company which had operated profitably for three decades in an expanding market, with limited competition in a specialist field. However, its attractiveness for acquisition signaled the environmental changes that had not truly been addressed within—rapid growth of market, and competition, from the European Community. Childless and devoted, its founder-chairman and his wife lived in an apartment above the factory. The terms of the takeover gave him three years of involvement, but at an executive, rather than operational, level. Search for new markets was to be his prime responsibility.

The holding company, while generally satisfied with the profitability of its acquisition, felt, however, that "it wasn't going anywhere," and there was concern about "poor quality control," ascribing this primarily to the inadequacies of the managing director. Contact with the company began at this point: the holding company's manager-in-charge approached a management consultancy to look for a replacement. Before the search began, the consultant suggested assessing the managing director to determine whether there were problems there which could be solved, and this is the point at which I became involved. I conducted a full-day assessment with him, working with his natural anxieties and looking with him at the whole company and his feelings about his position within it.

What I encountered in my interview was a person in great distress. He felt he was in the grips of a process he could neither understand nor control. He had joined the company as a youngster, fleeing from the expectations of a demanding father by ignoring a career in the professions and entering business. He had been groomed and developed by the owner of the company, a favorite son, it felt. He now found himself servant of two masters: the manager from the holding company, who could not leave him to manage, and the founder-chairman, who could not let go and who demanded an ongoing relationship with him and the daily workings of the business. Small wonder he couldn't exercise his managing function! In my report, I advised that we look at the company as a whole, before trying to resolve the problems by sacking the managing director.

Here comes the moment of danger, for the management consultant, no less than for the manager: that of being transfixed by the images and becoming a player in the drama. My client wanted to be saved. This is the point at which I could become the representative of the lost "good" father and take my place in the power battles being enacted, for "an active complex puts us momentarily under a state of duress, of compulsive thinking and acting, for which under certain conditions the only appropriate term would be the judicial concept of diminished responsibility" (Jung 1934, par. 201).

To understand Jung and the power of his conception, it is vitally important to locate images as the *psychic representatives* of archetypal patterns which emerge through and take form within the dynamic psychoid process. This applies equally whether the social process or the individual is under investigation. Archetypal images are the emergent properties of a system: not the images in themselves but the form they take in the context of the environment is what gives them the dynamic of their meaning. Let me illustrate with a metaphor: consider that most elusive of systems, the cloud. Happily, or threateningly, passing us by, it is shaped by the prevailing conditions—relative temperature, humidity, and air currents—in which it is formed. We love to watch the ceaselessly changing patterns it makes. Its state, and the potential for change into another state, remain a statistical probability; precipitation a possibility. At a *critical boundary* its conditions will leap to a new state, in which the cloud is transformed: it will snow or rain; there may be thunder or lightning, hail or sleet. Depending on the season, on the differential in temperature between, say, a polar air mass and a warm oceanic air mass, it may be spring rain which aids germination, or storm and flooding which destroys crops; etc.

Jung wrote: "The archetype represents *psychic probability*, portraying ordinary instinctual events in the form of *types*. It is a special psychic instance of probability in general, which 'is made up of the laws of chance and lays down rules for nature just as the laws of mechanics do'" (Jung 1952, par. 964).

What I am proposing is that in order to make sense of the operation of a complex within an organization, we must consider the formal properties of the system of the organization as crossing the boundaries of the material and the psychic. Generated by the invariant (archetypal) patterns within the human system, the organizational complex reveals itself to us in the form of images. As consultants, and managers, we can use those images as a point of entry into the dynamic system of meanings which operates below the surface of the "objective" structure of the organization.

So with my company: were I to enter, through the image, the system which it clothed, the matter and the manner of my entry would change the conditions I was to observe, so any pretension to some kind of ideal of objectivity would be not only impossible but illogical. Approaching a complex through the power of the word and the image is an act of power in itself and to be addressed with humility. The arousal of strong emotions, the inevitable pull into the complex-constellation, in the direction of the unconscious, provides us both with our strongest tool for uncovering the nature of the system in operation and the most dangerous moment of entrapment.

An intervention was subsequently planned, and I had the chance, with a colleague, to assess the other managers. The following picture emerged.

The company, a manufacturer of specialist electrical lighting equipment, originally formed in the fifties, had been an owner-managed business ever since. Husband and wife, childless, both played a dominating role, even as the business grew beyond the "family-sized" organization of about forty employees. By the 1980s, the company had 280 employees, but the management style remained inappropriately very much in the paternal style. Most of the managers had been recruited out of school, in the fifties and early sixties; few had had any formal training. Newer managers included two European refugees—one from war-torn Germany, the other from Eastern Europe. Ability was insufficiently rewarded and underdeveloped. The core of the management staff had been no less than fifteen years with the company, and all, for one reason or another, were extremely dependent upon "RJ," as he was referred to with exasperated but affectionate feeling. All were agreed both that the managing director was in an impossible position and that he was treating them badly—he was inconsistent and could be bullying. All agreed that the main problem was "quality control." This despite general agreement that their engineer, the Eastern European refugee, was (and assessment verified this) exceptionally talented and "wasted" upon such a small company.

The complex operative in this system, sensed first and foremost on a "natural" emotional level, was of the father, and the gathering around him of a group of adults who had, for one reason or another, high dependency needs, providing for each other protection against the uncertainty and unfairness of the natural order. The childless couple invented a family—the employees who, "guaranteed" a measure of security and predictability, remained, grumbling and discontented but unable to separate and move on. In the calm environment of their specialist niche in the industry and isolated from the pressures of competition, they survived and carried on. The mildly repressive management regime that had been in place all those years, which one could represent as the simple structure form of organization (Mintzberg 1983), was sustained through the operation of the embedded complex-constellation. Within the prevailing conditions of the environment, this structure with its system of meanings was sufficient for the company to function.

The change in the critical boundary (the acquisition by the holding company) disturbed the homeostasis. The "cosy hearth" inside-outside boundary image that had prevailed was transformed into an "us-them" boundary image, and the takeover became, as well as external reality, an image of the intensifying complex-constellation operating in conditions of instability: there was the experience of real danger. The production of meanings precipitated through the dynamic system of the complex was transformed utterly by the changes in the conditions, and with it, the perception of the meanings of actions and activities of persons long known to each other changed, too. People experienced themselves as *fighting for their lives*. Under these conditions of distress, "the unconscious is heightened, thereby creating a gradient for the unconscious to flow toward the conscious. The conscious then comes under the influence of unconscious instinctual impulses and contents. These are as a rule complexes whose ultimate basis is the archetype, the 'instinctual pattern' " (Jung 1952, par. 856).

Now we can see the destructive activity of the complex in the dynamics of the organization: pushing the entire system in the direction of the unconscious, it is reflected throughout the system of communication and feedback employed by the founder-chairman, who keeps his "children" within his direct control, thereby inhibiting the kinds of exchange of information and the gathering of meanings about the "real-world" system (production control) necessary to correct mistakes and improve delivery—activities which we would locate in our map as tending in the direction of the domain of directed human activity and artifacts.

A different system *was* being served, and this was in the direction of the more unconscious and the power of the archetype, in the service of the needs of a group of people whose individual histories linked them into the particular constellation of that system through the emotional-feeling axis at its heart. As such the complex served a benign, if one-sided and antidevelopmental, purpose which, if not strictly "businesslike," provided for its participants' material and psychic needs well enough in that particular environment. The major change in the environmental conditions, represented by the takeover, provided a push in the direction of the unconscious, because the intervention of the agent of change (the new management) did not take into account the whole of the human system. Although not a ruthless kind of man, the manager-in-charge got trapped by and enacted a power role within the increasingly psychoid environment. Caught in the slide away from the conscious, he lost his capacity for feeling-informed judgment and reacted in a reflex mode, which, in effect, transformed the complex-constellation, for a time at least, into its malignant form of "power" complex, at which we shall look more deeply in another example.

Just taking the bare outlines of its predicament, we can see how the organization functioned at the deepest, psychoid level, as "a community of the body and the psyche": the psychic end of the spectrum and the material end of the spectrum are inseparable. The new management's intervention is the material system, based upon balance sheets and business plans, without looking into the underlying meanings of the dysfunctioning in the organization as a whole, inexorably pushed the system in the direction of the unconscious, entangling new managers in the process. The information upon which the holding company was relying—financial accounts for various sections, measures for delivery targets, production control, complaints from various members of staff—did not equate to meaning. Without a model from which to consider the organization as a whole, a model which could include both the material and the psychic as the elements of "quality control," the intervention simply drove the system in the direction of increased splitting, disintegration, and further away from the potential of meaningful and effective action.

Information is not meaningful in itself. It is through the management of meaning, not merely information, that the real-world expression of the formal ("rational") systems we create can be understood. Through his researches and his discovery of the dynamic properties of the psyche and its systems of complexes,

Jung has shown us a different direction for making sense of often random-seeming and contradictory real-world human activity. He has shown us that it is possible to investigate and discover *meanings* generated through the levels within a dynamic model of human processes. To understand our organizations and the contradictions therein, we need to understand how people make meaning.

The intervention of the consultants (a program of executive coaching followed the initial period of assessment) resulted in a transformation of the perception of the managing director within the organization: seen to be effective, he became effective. Computerization of delivery and production was undertaken—an increase in the self-worth of the managers led to a demand for and acceptance of change and training. The founder-chairman, through a series of counseling sessions, was helped to separate and begin the process of retirement. Understanding the *meanings* embedded in the complex was critical to the unblocking both of the organization and the individuals within it, and the return to profitable activity.

Organizations throughout both the public and private sectors are currently experiencing radical change, and this company provides an unusually clear example. Driven by technical change generally—telecommunications, internationalization, information technology—the organization with a clear boundary, a simple market, a clear sense of identity, is rapidly becoming a memory. Takeovers might be seen as a cause of this process—or an effect of this process—or they might be seen as another aspect of psychoid processes operating at a deeper level within society. In the following example, a public-sector organization experienced a similar dilemma, and its problems revealed themselves through a different complex-constellation.

Under the influence of major legislation transferring fiscal responsibility directly to the managers of colleges and schools, a local authority pursued a policy of merging its further education colleges under single management, while keeping viable buildings in service, so that, effectively, the new college would be run over three separate sites. The consequence of this was that existing management, both academic and support staff, had to apply for their own jobs, or others, and compete with colleagues. I was asked to consult to the colleges through the transition period, helping individuals with problems arising in their personal and professional lives, and anticipating problems that might arise as the new college was formed out of the old.

While this process was to be considered a merger of two equal organizations, and the staff were to be kept on their present salaries regardless of their post in the new college, the experience was very much one of takeover. Of the two, "Ridenham" was an old, established technical college, representing a tradition of blue-collar skill-training and attitudes—despite the fact that in recent years the majority of its students were from ethnic minorities, this being a borough that had absorbed a large portion of the immigration of the 1950s and 1960s. Most students were British-born children of the original immigrant groups, but there were also more recent immigrants with degrees of difficulty with English. About four years ago, a new, management-trained principal had been appointed, and staff who had been working in the same ways for decades found themselves under pressure to change. Many left. The remaining staff, and managers, became a closely knit and effective working group, with a high degree of loyalty to their new principal and dedication to the generally popular principles of "quality control" and "accountability" through modern management systems.

Purpose-built within the last decade, the second college was established with a different and more radical brief—to reflect the changing times and needs of the community. "Avesley" College attracted a young, highly idealistic, dedicated, and hard-working staff, who felt, and were encouraged to pursue, the need for social change. This college developed an outreach approach, looking to attract the disaffected and "unteachable," the mentally and physically handicapped, and those whose language difficulties discouraged them from participating in education. Issues of accountability, examination results, and outward "success" were steadfastly given second place to the pursuit of outreach work, despite which, over the years, uptake at the new college was poor, student numbers remained low, and the college was perceived as a "failure."

My counseling contact with individuals and observations at both colleges elicited a confusing picture of two cultures being "merged" in the interests of urgent material considerations, while one college felt that it was "being swallowed up" and "destroyed," and all its felt successes—a system of values that had redefined "achievement"—devalued and rubbished. One member of the staff at Avesley commented that "they would become the rubbish bin for all the problems the new college does not want to have." Staff at Ridenham perceived Avesley as "soft," "seventies idealism," "female," and "black." There are realities here: Ridenham's technical past means there is a large number of male technical teaching staff; Avesley has actively pursued equal opportunities policy and has a high proportion of black and female staff. Equally there are contradictions: the perception of Avesley as "soft and ineffective" was particularly virulently expressed by an otherwise concerned, liberal-minded, female teacher at Ridenham, while real concern for the plight of their staff was consistently expressed by "macho" engineering staff members! At the same time, I experienced encounters with male staff members at Avesley as frightening and dangerous, despite the low-key nature of my brief and approach, and I was perceived as an enemy. One department head would not say anything, stating that he did not want to be part of this process, not even to the extent of saying why, "because that would be taking part in it, wouldn't it, and I don't have to, do I?"

I began to feel that I was getting ensnared in a complex and tried to grapple with the feelings it was arousing in me: intense feelings of empathy for people in both colleges; one day a sense of hopelessness and helplessness; another, anger and fear. One day I would want to be on one "side," another day on the other. One day I would have an acute sense of the feelings of failure at Avesley—another, feel cross with the endless political wranglings they imposed upon themselves and me.

Jung wrote that "archetypal images [take] possession of our thought and feeling, so that these lose their quality as functions at our disposal. The loss shows itself in the fact that the object of perception then becomes absolute and indisputable and surrounds itself with such an emotional taboo that anyone who presumes to reflect on it is automatically branded a heretic and blasphemer" (1947, par. 413). The image at the center of the conflict was that of race, and this was the one thing that it was almost impossible to talk about. So I did.

One day, waiting in the reception area, I had a clue: a staff member came into the office area—clearly a powerful hub where people greeted each other and exchanged gossip informally—and observed that the rubber plants in a display planter were dusty. They were clearly marked: "Do Not Water—These plants are cared for by the Floristry Dept" (a traditional Technical School training activity). The staff member proceeded to comment on how much she disliked rubber plants—they were dark and the leaves are too large—at the same time as she went up to observe their dust-covered leaves, crooning at them, "Poor things, you are all neglected, let me clean you up," and proceeded carefully to wipe all the leaves clean.

Jung comments: "Let us turn to the question of the psyche's

tendency to split. Although this peculiarity is most clearly observable in psychopathology, fundamentally it is a normal phenomenon which can be recognized with the greatest of ease in . . . projections" (1937, par. 252), the psychological mechanism by which psyche creates and maintains the boundary between self and other, and through this, between different categories of things. For Bateson, "in fact, the unit of psychological input is difference" (1972, p. 481). It is the precondition for communication, consciousness, differentiation, and, ultimately, problem-solving.

Deepening his notions about the psyche's tendency to split, Jung goes on to note that it "means on the one hand dissociation into multiple structural units, but on the other hand the possibility of change and differentiation" (1937, par. 255). Staying closely with Jung's central metaphor of the spectrum, the psyche's tendency to split results not in two alternatives—differentiation or dissociation—but in a spectrum of levels, within which a process can move dynamically: "Psychic processes . . . behave like a scale along which consciousness slides" (Jung 1947, par. 407). Events and interventions within a system can move in the direction of dissociation or in the direction of differentiation. It is through this fundamental dialectic exploration of *difference* that the possibility of differentiation, and the evolution of consciousness and meaning, becomes possible. The means are through the (often painful) experience of dissociation, not simply as an intrapsychic event, but as an event that can be seen operating throughout the human system, through its psychoid processes. In this way, we can see the process of splitting as an essential dynamic and, by extension, revise the notion of the psychoid processes not simply as a negative force to be contained, avoided, escaped from, but as a dynamic and complex source of meanings and development.

Through the exploration of complex-constellations, we can connect the understanding of boundary and its central place in systems theory with the development of psyche within the human system. We can follow the way in which the struggle with *difference*, and its slide between the potential forms of dissociation and differentiation, can be represented multidimensionally through the active study of a human system. Central to this search is the struggle toward the management of information about the complex in operation, through experience within the emotion-feeling axis and its transformation into meaning-making: the capacity to reflect, to distinguish between levels and make use of information of all kinds, and to enable communication and feedback to flourish.

My observation alerted me to the degree of splitting which was being experienced in the college and to the necessity of struggling to maintain a critical attitude to my own feelings and emotions—empathy on the one hand with the intense emotions being aroused and, on the other, awareness of the dangers of dissociation and the ways in which that psychoid process can be projected onto the screen of racial difference.

Over and over again, staff at Ridenham asserted that "it would all work itself out with time." It was becoming apparent to me that staff at Ridenham, genuinely dedicated to providing good education, not purposefully racially motivated or biased, were caught within a process that split off and dissociated any recognition of the feelings of fear, anger, and failure experienced by those at Avesley, so that they could be thought about, recognized, or attended to. The effect of this was that they behaved more and more as if there were nothing but technical and material problems to be sorted out—realistically, everyone pointed out the need for intersite services and early opportunities to meet new colleagues to plan next year's curriculum changes—with little appreciation of the level of pain and distress experienced by the staff at Avesley. There was a sense of bewilderment about the power blocs that were beginning to form. The principal exclaimed, "When I ask them what they want, I can't even understand what it is or how I could give it to them."

On the last day of the old colleges' life, staff at Avesley planned a farewell social evening. Feelings were strong. During the day, the flag for the new college was sent from the site at Ridenham and raised hours before the farewell party was to begin. An understandable administrative misadventure: though there was acknowledgment from Ridenham that it was an error of judgment, it was perceived by Avesley as proof of all its beliefs and fears of annihilation.

I believe that Ridenham responded to the radical changes in the educational and economic environment with a kind of complex-formation which Jung described as "one-sidedness": "by concentration of the will . . . certain capacities, especially those that promise to be socially useful, can be fostered to the neglect of others" (1937, p. 122). In its drive to change and modernize, and to meet the challenges of pressures in the environment, Ridenham has "grown," gone past the constraints of its traditions, in a way current values and attitudes within the culture reinforce; it has

achieved the "socially useful" in the terms of the prevailing culture, and the staff are genuinely and deservedly pleased with the
quality of their service.

In its anxiety to succeed and flourish in its new environment
and to achieve the desired mission—"quality control"—Ridenham
evolved a "success-complex": not-success (the pain of loss, the
pain of failure, the pain of the unwanted) was not able to be experienced within that constellation, and the perception at Avesley,
that "it would be the rubbish bin for all the unwanted problems of
the college," was painfully accurate: Avesley was carrying all the
pain and failure for the new college already.

Returning once again to the notion of the spectrum, the splitting, most noticeable in observations, was a symptom of the
strengthening force of the psychoid processes pulling the entire
system in the direction of the unconscious, away from differentiation and toward dissociation. In both organizations, fear and
anger, distrust and pain, *as pieces of information*, were not available for use in order to create meaning. Increased splitting
decreases the potential for information to be exchanged over a
boundary and be transformed into usable feedback—the useful
return of information that can modify, reflect upon, and change
the perceptions of individuals. Once splitting is institutionalized,
these constraints become built into the social and technical systems within the organization (Menzies 1975).

Departments that perceive each other as enemies across
demarcation lines, rather than a flexible boundary, will have deep
effects on the communication of important information—and
quality control. This is how the complex takes its hold. In the case
of Ridenham and Avesley, the fiscal and social fiction of a "merger" is experienced and perceived by the organizations in a very
different way, which has to do with their histories and the very
different places they occupy in the social matrix. A complex was
constellated, represented in the image of the takeover. "Being
swallowed up" should alert us to a slide in the direction of the
unconscious which will heavily impose the constraints of dissociation and the "all or nothing" forms of splitting. The distress begins
at the (relatively conscious) level of identity with, and commitment to, two organizations with differing cultures, where common
values can be held by white and black, male and female staff members alike. It is only a small step to project the "takeover" onto the
racial screen, where the images, reified, will push the system inexorably toward dissociation. The strengthening of psychoid processes is already in operation, and the familiar forms which the

constraints of this level will impose are already taking shape: black staff members caucus, using it to try to regain a sense of power in the situation; individuals with high power needs take up battle positions within the growing schisms, invested with informal but highly charged authority to do battle for those who perceive themselves as the underclass; students divide along racial lines within teaching groups. An informal power structure is formed, and energy which could be invested in the directed activity system of teaching and learning—the maintenance of an open boundary—is expended in internal conflict (Hirschhorn 1988).

On the individual level, the dissociation is experienced in a variety of physical and psychological symptoms of distress and in defensive complexes that misinform others about the true state of affairs. Panic is experienced by others as threat: I felt intense fear when first meeting the group of male staff members at Avesley, which undermined my capacity for empathy and pulled me in the direction of splitting and projection. Once established, this psychoid level of organization will quickly represent itself in institutional forms. Subgroups form, acquire a history and culture of their own, and before long take on the impenetrable and seemingly eternal forms that we call "political reality" (consider, as an example, the history of the Berlin Wall).

In the slide into psychoid processes, emotional arousal can impose constraints on the perception of difference of, for example, the rights and values of others and the capacity for empathy, to "put oneself in the other's shoes." Pulled away from their interactional and social function, the emotions are expressed more and more as reflexlike action. The feedback relation between emotion and feeling is disturbed, and feeling-informed judgment, which could serve differentiation and work on the real-world problems *and creative potential* of multiethnic, multicultural, multilevel education, to which as individuals the staff are genuinely dedicated, is blocked.

Entering into the meaning-system through the images of the complex-constellation is a process of revelation that gives us a field in which to operate—to be gripped by and attempt to manage the forces tending in the direction of the unconscious. It gives us the opportunity to make interventions that tend toward consciousness, toward differentiation and communication, and toward tolerance—the necessary and sufficient conditions for the operation of whole systems of communication and feedback which are effective. This is quality control.

If it is to address the system as a whole, the task of management development, in addition to providing the technical and fiscal tools to assess and make use of information about the operations of an organization, must also enable and empower managers to comprehend and manage the information inherent in the psychic system of the organization, to move between levels of knowledge and comprehension, to transform information into meaning and effective communication. Where managers can tolerate the uncertainty necessary to unfold meanings within the working organization and evolve working practices around them, rather than imposing solutions whether they be in the form of "management development plans," "management information systems," or "quality control programs," the dynamic properties and potential of complexes can be managed and used, rather than simply suffered.

A plan to help the new community college is currently being evolved, based on a suggestion made to me by the member of staff who expressed the feeling that the site which was Avesley will become the rubbish bin for the new college. She suggested that all the staff of the new college be included in a "bottom up" process, with the help of neutral outsiders, that would generate a "mission statement" which everyone could then feel ownership of and identity with. Such an exercise is now under way, based upon the natural groupings within the new management structure, and we hope that it will enable all members of staff to express their hopes and needs for themselves and their students and enable the new college to move in the direction of differentiation and communication, pointing the way forward, so that the expressed needs of the entire community can be heard and served.

References

Bateson, G. 1972. *Steps to an Ecology of Mind*. New York: Ballantine Books.

Checkland, P. 1981. *Systems Thinking, Systems Practice*. Chichester, U.K.: John Wiley and Sons.

Hirschhorn, L. 1988. *The Workplace Within*. Boston: M.I.T. Press.

Jung, C. G. 1905. The psychological diagnosis of evidence. In *CW* 2:728–792. London: Routledge, Kegan Paul, 1973.

_____. 1913. On the doctrine of the complexes. In *CW* 2:1349–1356. London: Routledge, Kegan Paul, 1973.

_____. 1934. A review of the complex theory. In *CW* 8:194–219. London: Routledge, Kegan Paul, 1973.

_____. 1937. Psychological factors determining human behavior. In *CW* 8:232–262. London: Routledge, Kegan Paul, 1973.

_____. 1947. On the nature of the psyche. In *CW* 8:343–442. London: Routledge, Kegan Paul, 1973.

_____. 1952. Synchronicity: an acausal connecting principle. In *CW* 8:816–968. London: Routledge, Kegan Paul, 1973.

_____. 1976. *The Tavistock Lectures*. London: Routledge, Kegan Paul.

Menzies, I. E. P. 1975. A case study in the functioning of social systems as a defense against anxiety. In *Group Relations Reader 1*, Arthur D. Colman and W. Harold Bexton, eds. Washington: A. K. Rice Institute Series.

Mintzberg, H. 1983. *Structure in Fives: Designing Effective Organizations*. Englewood Cliffs, N.J.: Prentice-Hall.

Georgia Lepper trained at the Society of Analytical Psychology in London, where she conducts a private practice as an analyst and consultant.

Depth Consultation

Arthur D. Colman

In this paper I propose a marriage between Jungian analysis and organizational consultation. The purpose of the pairing is to develop a depth collective psychology and consulting process in order to help collectives, by which I mean groups, organizations, and other forms of human association, to individuate.* The need is clear. For two decades, depth psychologies have focused theory and method on individual development without a complementary emphasis on development in the collective. Rather than focusing on the ways in which groups and organizations may affirm individual development or the way individual growth may contribute to organizational development, I will take as my subject collective development per se, including broadening the concept of individuation, currently applied only to individuals, to include individuation in the collective as well. In particular, I am interested in exploring how concepts and methods from analytic psychology used to help individuals in analysis might also be applied to help collectives through consultation.

I will address two groups of readers: Jungian analysts and other practitioners and students of analytic psychology who, with the important exception of typology theory, often know little about organizational consultation (and have by and large acted as if they have little to contribute toward its study); and organizational consultants and organizational leaders who in general know little of Jung's depth psychology and have little sense of its potential in their work. For the past twenty years, I have had the good fortune to keep one foot in each camp. I am a Jungian analyst working primarily with individuals and also an organizational consultant trained in the tradition of Tavistock group relations and now practicing what I call depth consultation with a variety of client organizations from the business, education, political, and mental health fields (Colman and Bexton 1975, Colman and Geller 1985). I find

---

*The paradoxical use of "individuate" to describe a collective process is at the heart of the rest of this paper.

that the way I fill each role is powerfully informed and energized by the other; both of these activities draw their wellspring from a common source, an appreciation of the impact of the collective unconscious on individual and collective systems. Unfortunately, I have few colleagues who share my interest, and even fewer who have experience in both fields. I am writing this paper, in part, in the hopes of interesting more of my colleagues from both disciplines to explore this new area.

At the heart of Jung's theory is the individuation process, which he defines as a polarity between the individual and collective. His classic statement is this:

> Individuation is the development of the psychological individual as a being, distinct from the general collective psychology. Individuation therefore is a process of differentiation having for its goal the development of the individual personality. (Jung 1921, par. 757)

Individual development is everything here; the individual is the diamond to be liberated from the collective "rough." For Jung, adaptation to the collective psychology is a paradoxical and preliminary step to embarking on the individuation process which requires separating one's own values out of the compromising group matrix (Jung 1921, par. 761). Once the individuation path is taken, the group is left behind. Although passing reference is made to the individual's duty to create "equivalent value" for the society, Jung's major focus was always on the development of the individual apart from the collective and apart from the development of the collective (Jung 1916, par. 1096).

Many practitioners of depth psychology have continued this perspective. For example, I once posed this question to a revered analyst and revered teacher: "How does individuation serve the collective?" and received the following apochryphal answer from her: "If I walk alone on the beach intent on my own individuation, then and only then do I truly serve others. Service to others begins and ends in my own development!"

Undoubtedly if enough people took her perspective to heart, our society would be greatly improved, if just for the presence of so many developed individuals in our midst. Yet groups are not simply the sum of their individual members nor are individuals ever really separate from their significant groups. Sometimes the individual walking on the beach is on a journey that will benefit self and others, too, and sometimes he or she will be unwittingly caught in a group archetype; that is, those heroic solitary walks may serve the group needs to exclude or scapegoat, even as the individual is seeking integration.

Long-term separation from the collective can rarely ever be the aim of individuation; that would deny our humanity, our sentience as human beings. Rather it is one of the temporary paths some people use to learn more about themselves away from the influence of others. Nor can individuation of the individual proceed without a concomitant developmental process in the collective. From an ethical point of view, individuation defined outside of its collective context is a travesty, because it separates individual development from the suffering of others. From a psychological point of view, individuation separate from the collective is flawed, because it leaves the shadow out of the process by allowing the projection of personal shadow into the collective scapegoat and then turning one's back on that scapegoat and calling it, as Jung does, a product of a "lower level of consciousness" or "mass mind" (Jung 1950, par. 225).

The collective, after all, is no more or less than ourselves in relationship. However we may twist and turn to assert our separateness, there is no escape from the reality of each individual's involvement in the darkest behaviors of our human collective. In group relations theory, there is a concept known as "group in the mind" which expresses the ever-present group consciousness of individuals even and especially when they are most isolated and functioning most separately from others. This ongoing "group in the mind" or group consciousness seems to me as much an aspect of human consciousness as is awareness of our individual consciousness.

The "mass mind" is us; we are as much collective as individual entities; surely both parts of us must develop for us to live full lives. It is no accident, then, that the great models of individuated men and women have devoted themselves to helping the poor, the homeless, the diseased, the suffering—*our* collective victims.

Individuation theory has had and continues to have a powerful impact on depth therapy. I believe that individuation theory expanded to include collective process, including unconscious collective process, also has the potential to make an important contribution to organizational development and the individual/organizational development interphase. It is a perspective little tried, for although there are many disciplines that deal directly with the psychology of the collective, with a few important exceptions, these disciplines, and their practitioners, both academic and pragmatic, do not relate their work to the unconscious collective, to origins, myths, complexes, and the ways these elements manifest in organizational structure and process. Neither a culture of collective exploration nor a consulting methodology to assist such an exploration has yet developed parallel to the ethos that fuels individual exploration in depth therapies. To achieve this, we need a perspective which assumes that the collective unconscious operates in and through groups and organizations as well as in and through individuals and that the two are connected.

How would such a perspective operate through the consultation process? When I consult with these principles in mind, I start off with the same assumption that informs my exploration of an individual seeking help in analysis. I assume that the organization has integrity beyond its individual members, much as the individual has integrity beyond the ego or dominant complex that claims first voice in the analytic process. I also assume that every organization is capable of consciously and unconsciously developing in order to manifest its deepest identity, what could be called its organizational self.

The organizational self, like the individual self, is what that organization seeks to become, the unfolding of its potential, its inexorable movement toward integration and wholeness. Like the individual self, it is anchored in its birth process, reality and myth. The early enfolding of the organizational self is always filtered through the task system which defines its identity and survival. Erik Erickson wisely pointed out that identity formation is always as much a function of who one is not as who one is (Erickson 1972). An organization develops, much like a child, by fashioning a provisional identity that excludes and represses those parts which are troublesome and dystonic. Early in most organizations' lives, there is a need for a quality of cohesion that denies the complexity and confusion inherent in origin and task. Projection and repression is used in the service of furthering this cohesion; the price is exclusion of dissident elements and a loss of wholeness. In the individual, these excluded elements are coalesced and personified in what Jung called the shadow, that part of us that is deeply unacceptable to the ego. Confronting and reintegrating the shadow is, from the point of view of Jungian analysis, the *sine qua non* of individuation. So, too, with organizations, whose excluded parts hold the creative and change-producing elements without which stagnation is all but inevitable. Like the adult who must reclaim and acknowledge these discarded and repressed parts in order to feel whole and real, the mature organization must also struggle to include what has been left out, pushed out, denied, and ignored, in order to function at the highest level. Thus, from the point of view of the collective's as well as the individual's development, the shadow—individual and collective—must be acknowledged and reclaimed for the self to operate fully and transformatively.

In depth consultation, then, as in analysis, I assume that the client's path of development will include confrontation with the scapegoated parts of the organization. This approach differs from most kinds of consultation in focusing attention on these excluded parts as a critical element in the general aim of exploring unconscious collective process. From this perspective, my central task as consultant is to define these scapegoated elements as well as the scapegoating process and give meaning to both as they manifest in the functions and goals of the organization. The consulting contract includes client acceptance of this perspective and a willingness to join with me in this exploration—no matter where it leads.

This consultation contract is much like the contract between individual patient and analyst, an agreed exploration of shadow and other unconscious elements to enhance meaning and self definition. For example, organizations, like individuals or nations, are often unconsciously driven by their myth of origin. During my work with the client organization, I might explore their particular myth of origin, their birth or rebirth history, parental images, utopian visions, etc., in order to bring the meaning of these elements into the organization's consciousness, much as an analyst might explore origin and other unconscious motifs with his or her analysand for the same reasons. My experiences of doing this kind of work as either depth consultant or analyst are remarkably alike in basic ways. Of course, there are technical differences, e.g., differences in pace and timing. For example, organizational consulting tends to be less leisurely than analysis and may require more aggressive interpretation. Still, similarities outweigh differences. In individual work, the analyst elicits history, dreams, fantasy, relationship, and transference material to help the analysand explore his or her unconscious world of complexes and processes; the organizational consultant elicits similar material from individuals, subgroups, and intergroups within the organization in order to develop a map of the client's unconscious world. Individual analytic work proceeds on an inner psychic stage across which the figures of the unconscious play out the hoped-for psychic transformation; the analyst stands, one foot on that stage and one foot in the wings, anchoring the developmental process. In depth consultation, the consultant takes up the same boundary and anchoring position except that the players are real members of the organization and the consulting work is helping to sort through these patterns until the central myths are clarified and their meaning for the organization better understood.

From the analyst's and consultant's points of view, working with individual or organization is like working with siblings who share the same parent. The collective pattern of behavior in the organization, the dream of an individual, the outward play of an organizational myth, the inward play of an individual myth, all have common roots in the collective unconscious. Individual analysts or organizational consultants who are committed to depth exploration locate themselves at the border of the imaginal space of either system, listening, exploring, and interpreting the stuff of the unconscious, be it dream, fantasy, ritual patterns, myth, interpersonal drama, inter-organizational rivalry—all elements of the deepening search for meaning and transformation.

And always, in both systems, there is the missing element, the excluded part, the personal shadow, the collective scapegoat, both standing in the way of that search and containing its central meaning. In organizational life, the scapegoat holds the hidden corruption, the unspeakable scandals, the dark side, much as the shadow constellates those elements in the individual. The scapegoat and the scapegoating process often hold the unconscious problem of the organization, that which must be confronted and reintegrated if change is to occur.

All organizations work hard, consciously and unconsciously, to protect both the scapegoating process and their chosen scapegoats. This is in the nature of the archetype of the scapegoat, "the one who has been made to take the blame for others and suffer in their place." An organization will not easily give up a well-worn pattern of projecting its most unacceptable parts onto an available victim. Part of the art of consultation is how to ferret out the manifestation of this scapegoat archetype without losing one's client! Consultants and "whistleblowers" know too well the great danger of meddling with an entrenched scapegoating system. In the Bible story of the scapegoat, the man who takes the scapegoat into the wilderness is in great danger:

> And he that let go the goat for the scapegoat shall wash his clothes and bathe his flesh in water and afterwards come into the camp. (Lev. 16:21)

In practice, the man who speaks the truth about the scapegoat often shares its fate.

In my experience, the most common reason for developing a dynamic of scapegoating in an organization is fear of confronting real and imagined difference in the collective (Colman 1989). If the challenge of diversity becomes great enough to threaten what is seen as the cohesion, unity, and, ultimately, the survival of the group, the group will defend itself by invoking the scapegoating process. Or, put another way, groups, like individuals, are always in pursuit of wholeness and, like individuals who reject shadow elements of themselves by projecting them out into the environment, the group will create victims rather than face dealing with diversity and difference.

Typically, consultation requests usually carry within them this scapegoat issue although almost always defined from the victimizer's point of view. Thus, there is a defined "problem," "without whom" all would be well (or at least better). For example, on one occasion, I was asked by the literature department of a large midwestern university to consult around a "difficult" assistant professor who was denied tenure despite obvious academic excellence. The denial related to a particular "impropriety" in his behavior, an alleged slanderous remark toward one of his fellow tenure seekers. The department was afraid that he might protest the department's action. On another occasion, I was asked to consult to upper management of a governmental agency whose *esprit de corps* was being "undermined" by the agency's clients, "misguided" citizens who "misapprehended" the agency's policies and now were threatening to sue the agency. On a third occasion, I was asked to consult to a small business because one of the partners, who had a particularly important technical skill, was acting in a way that jeopardized the whole operation yet refused to change his behavior. In all these examples, the organization as a whole is faced with a challenge from an important constituent part—junior faculty, consumer citizens, and a powerful partner. In each case, the leadership perceives threat to its wholeness and its authority. Consultation has been requested because the scapegoating hasn't worked; the scapegoating process, developed to rid the organization of its dissidents, has aborted and the bloody remains are still in evidence and threaten the organization with infection. From the excluding subsystem's point of view, the dissident individual (group, department, or even nation) is seen as a pathological entity, the isolated problem. A trial without argument ensues; the verdict is already in. The tenure candidate is a loser but could make trouble; the consumers are misguided but could undermine policy and funding; the partner is acting inappropriately but could break up the company. All that is required is a consultant who, as an outside authority, will sanction the exclusion and recommend what is needed—reeducation, treatment, or even annihilation—the final solution. The man needs therapy for his aggression; the citizens are misguided and need further education; the partner is pigheaded and must learn to give in to the needs of others or get out.

In practice, the individual is rarely an innocent in the organizational process. Groups choose their victims well, and most victims have a way of volunteering for the job. The consultant brought into a scapegoating situation is inevitably asked to accept the organization's point of view and divert attention from the system's problem to the "disturbed" individual. It is quite a temptation, since the organization, not the scapegoat, is paying the consultant's bill! But whatever the balance between individual and organization, the individual who has been selected for victimhood will rarely be able to hold his or her own. The power of the organization or majority culture to create victims for its own psychological purposes is the power of the many over the few. Only very courageous or foolhardy individuals or subgroups can stand up to a powerful victim-creating process. To help an organization, the consultant must refocus attention on how the need for a scapegoat and the choice of victim is a diversion from the deeper collective issues.

The tactical problem for the consultant is how to gain sufficient trust within the organization to redefine the scapegoating system as a part of the organization's troubled process rather than its cause. The consultant faces a problem similar to the analyst with a patient who defines his or her symptom—anxiety, nightmares, a compulsive affair—as the problem without which there would be no problem. In individuals, where symptoms are part of a larger problem, shadow elements are breaking through the ego's defensive edifice, an attenuated structure based on an incomplete view of itself. But often it is easier to embrace mendacity and medication than to consider the symptom as pointing to a larger problem. The analytic, explorative mode depends on a willingness to search for meaning in the excluding and isolating patterns. Then

PSYCHE AT WORK

the symptoms are useful; they forcefully pose the problem of false integrity and point to what has been defensively excluded and what now must be redeemed.

Depth consultation requires the same mutual willingness to search for meaning in the excluding, scapegoating pattern. For the organization, the presence of a noncompliant scapegoat is like anxiety to the individual; the dynamic of scapegoating in organizations is a particularly efficient "medication," a "final solution"; for when it works, the unwanted parts can be permanently expunged and, like the biblical scapegoat, exiled to the wilderness never to return. That is the hope at least, but as the Israelites found in their sojourn in the wilderness, the excluding ritual had to be repeated yearly to have even minimal cathartic effect on the collective. And as Saul found when he tried to extrude a dissident David from his ranks, scapegoats have a way of turning up with large armies (or a bevy of lawyers) in pursuit of their definitions of justice.

I want now to turn to two consultations in which the dynamics of exclusion and scapegoating are prominent.

Consultation #1

I consulted to a top California management group—sixteen men and women—of a government agency concerned with conservation. The agency was embattled by a well-organized citizen's group who were opposed to the way government leadership carried out its mandate and made policy. I was asked by the agency director to help develop more successful approaches to the problem than the management group had thus far been able to devise.

I met with the entire group for a weekend retreat. I soon discovered that the director was convinced of the "goodness" of the way he and his management were performing. He said esprit was high and performance had improved in response to the current stress. He felt policy was well thought out and relevant to task. He was sure the agency was capable of changing its ideas and process if needed; that was not a problem, witness the successful incorporation of affirmative action hiring policies amply demonstrated by the women and minority present in the room. "This group," the director proudly told me, with affirming nods from the people in the room, "is like a good American family. We care about our own, and we take care of our own. And we have tried-and-true family ways of changing things when they need changing."

Obviously, a great deal was being left out. I have learned over many consulting efforts that whenever family metaphors are used to describe organizations, it is likely that the exclusion dynamic is particularly insidious. Hallowed family platitudes often hide a multitude of family sins, including incest, sexism, and "black sheep" victimizations, to mention a few. Organizations are not families, and those that claim to be are usually profoundly afraid of their secrets and their differences. I listened sympathetically for a long time, considering how to intervene and discarding every intervention that came to mind. My silence was irritating to the group. They were not paying me a good fee to be a noncontributor. They continued to speak about their cohesion and shared values, their ability to integrate one and all into their "family." When and whether I would join was the unspoken question of the group.

When it was finally made overt by one of the leaders, I made my move. "If everything is so good," I chided gently, "then who are the public that seem to disagree with your policies? Why don't they feel part of your family? Who might they represent here? Is anybody feeling left out of the family here and now in this room, the way those citizens feel left out of your decision-making process and your decisions?"

At first, there was polite but hostile silence to my remark. This was followed by even more fervent demonstrations of harmony and familyhood. But as I persisted in asking the same series of questions in a variety of ways, the group turned on me with more open anger. Apparently, they had gotten the wrong consultant. I obviously didn't understand, either, any more than the citizen's group and other detractors understood. Perhaps only family members could get it right. "Well, if that's true," I said, "then where does that leave those of us who aren't family—like the citizen's groups who aren't family, perhaps don't want to be family, but still want to get some of their needs met. Doesn't any one here identify with them rather than this family?"

No one did, which led to more rancor with me, diluted only by the congenial surroundings and good food. My questions and their patience were wearing thin. Some kind of breakthrough had to occur soon or I would be out of a job and the agency would be even more isolated than before. Searching for a chink in the armor, I asked the women present if they really felt part of the family (which seemed to me to be increasingly defined as an "old boy" network). "Yes indeed," one exclaimed, "we are just that and proud of it." There was a chorus of assent from most of the women, who went on to explain that those women who had made it in the agency were indeed daughters and wives of men who worked or had worked in the agency! "It is a big, happy family," they chided back. Didn't I see that now?

When I wondered about what such a kinship hiring pattern meant in a government agency—was only "family" to be trusted?—the group again defended itself. It obviously made sense to hire people who knew the job and were "blood-loyal," as one put it. But the silence that followed this rejoinder was less smug than before. Something was wrong; everyone could feel it. There was a piece missing, and attempts to get on with other business fell flat.

"Is everybody here really a part of this wonderful family?" I asked, more cynically than I wished. "Am I the only one who has another family to go home to at night?" I looked significantly at each person in turn and then shut up. This was the moment of truth, the one on which the consultation would probably turn.

To my great relief, a black woman stood up and faced the group. "Hell no," she exclaimed, "I'm not a part of this family. I've got my own family. I'm working here because the money is good. I'm also here to do what I can to stop the rest of you from stealing the public land for yourselves and your fat, white 'families.' And there's no way you're going to get rid of me for saying this. You need me and you know it. And this consultant is my witness, even if he is a honkie."

After a stunned silence, a young white man with longish hair stood up. "This isn't my family either. No way. I want to change things, bring in some new-age values. The citizen's group is right about some things. It's going to change around here whether you guys like it or not."

Gradually others in the group followed their lead in speaking up, some still identifying with the family, others opposing it in one way or another. There was a lot of mourning the loss of the "good old days," which, as so often is the case, turned out to be less halcyon than legend claimed.

The rest of the weekend was a long amplification of the theme of the need to learn how to let in difference, change, new people, and new ways. While the exclusionary dynamic continued to emerge at times of greatest disagreement, I could now consult to it and find some joining voices. While I had no illusions that the organization as a whole would drastically change its view toward outside criticism, a small inroad had been made, including some understanding of the problem, and more consultation was likely. The seed for future change had definitely been planted.

My interventions were based on the hypothesis that the excluded or scapegoated elements of an organizational system carry its individuating potential much as the shadow carries that potential in the individual. This agency's reaction to criticism from the citizen's group was to exclude their views and create an even more paranoid island called "family." Certainly this response was counterproductive to their task. It seemed likely to me that the outside group struck important unidentified views and feelings within the agency itself, whose "family romance" effectively excluded criticism and difference in its members, let alone those it served—the public. The citizen's group could not be negotiated with effectively until this undercover dynamic inside the agency was brought to light. In the intense atmosphere of a weekend group retreat, exploring what different views from a citizen's group might symbolize and mirror in the management group was potentially explosive. Once the challenge to the family fantasy was out in the open, once the "black sheep" were brought to light, the agency leadership would have a better chance to develop its leadership on more realistic grounds and find a new myth that better fit its present and future.

Consultation #2

I was asked to consult to a large organization that provides many highly valued services in health, education, and business within its target community, a multinational group, composed of first-generation immigrants and first-generation U.S. citizens. It is typical of similar organizations which serve immigrants from a geographical area such as the Pacific Rim, Central America, or the Middle East, in which internecine struggle is a fact of life. During the past ten years, many of the homeland countries have been at war in serious conflict with one another; many people have died in these wars. Many of the staff and clients are refugees from these wars. In effect, this background ensures that staff subgroups feel like enemies; in some cases, only their transplanted geography prevents them from being in a live war. And yet, within the United States, as has happened to so many immigrant groups before them, these virtual enemies are lumped together into a single organization and client system. In particular, funding is dependent on a racist assumption that lumps people together on the basis of skin color or facial characteristics. They are treated by government as if they are homogeneous, a single ethnic entity whose members can identify with and serve one another, when in fact their diversity is extreme and saturated in intergroup violence. Thus the scapegoating dynamic is already present in the relationship with the larger culture. One could predict that the leadership of such an organization would have an impossible and intolerable task, that any functional system which represented integration in the face of such violent opposition would come under attack.

The stated problem for which consultation was requested was recurrent instability in the organization's leadership. Two previous directors, both highly qualified and acceptable to staff at their hiring, had been fired or resigned in the past two years. The current director, L., was equally well qualified but he was also now being pressured to leave after only six months on the job.

When I first met with L. to consider our consultation contract, he suggested intensive work with the staff group. In view of the inflammatory nature of the problem, I proposed a careful diagnostic program through a series of meetings with key personnel, to be followed by meetings with various subgroups of staff before dealing with the staff as a whole. But the next day there was another major leadership crisis; the entire staff demanded a meeting with the director in the presence of a consultant. L. told me about this request, and he confirmed that he was being asked to resign. It was not the ideal way to begin a consulting job.

The meeting began with a dissection of L.'s personal and leadership characteristics, emphasizing his authoritarianism and his incompetence. Some of the group began to infer that he was also clinically paranoid and thereby unfit to lead. All these accusations found few "hooks" in the face of L.'s competent and judicious behavior during his short tenure as leader. L. pointed out that similar defamations had also been leveled at the previous directors. This defense was met with redoubled attacks; at one point, the group asked me, now labeled as a psychiatrist rather than organizational consultant, to "certify" L. as insane. When I demurred, suggesting that such a pronouncement was beyond my role, the fight leadership in the group seemed to give up all rational pretense. One of the informal leaders of the staff group put it bluntly: "Even if L. is mentally fit," he said, "and even if L. is a decent leader, he still has to be sacrificed. There is just too much tension with him around. He must resign."

My authority to consult to this meeting was extremely limited. I was a stranger in the group and had developed little reservoir of trust from either director or staff. Still, I needed to speak to the issue; I would probably not get another chance. So I consulted directly to the scapegoating process by interpreting what seemed to me to be the most overt politic of the group, that the leader was being used as a convenient lightning rod to project anger more appropriately focused on the intergroup and international conflicts within the staff group, as well as the racism implicit in their funding sources.

There was little discussion of my point; it was a premature interpretation born of impotence rather than ripeness. I knew that the intergroup rivalry was so acute that even focusing on the outside bureaucracy, the universal scapegoat in industrialized society, was unlikely to be heard. They were afraid of agreement on anything, thereby risking violation of profound ethnic and national loyalties. The only acceptable common target was the leader himself, who symbolized their taboo interconnections. He was available as the unifying scapegoat because getting rid of him, as they had gotten rid of leaders before him, would perpetuate the chaos. They epitomized, in microcosm, the social structure of denial, the use of real and symbolic human sacrifice, and the victimization of the innocent to circumvent responsible confrontation with extremely difficult realities.

The process I was observing was indeed archetypal. L., as leader/scapegoat, had become an enormously useful vehicle for the collective shadow of this group, uniting the various warring subgroups in ritual murder. Guilt would come later, but for now, the scapegoat archetype and the ancient dynamic of human sacrifice left no room for reason and rationality. The scapegoat holds the pain and suffering for the group, the pain and suffering which the group can no longer handle within its own boundaries but must project and expel from its midst. The scapegoating process must be swift and merciless; the humanity of the victim must be denied. Anything less would elicit sympathy and support and the possibility of more-explicit examination of the conflicts between member and member, subgroup and subgroup, which in this organization would move quickly into ancient and modern blood feud. These issues were indeed explosive and would have to be approached with great care. The staff was not ready to do this and so the leader/scapegoat had to go.

All the staff seemed united in this process except for one man. M. was a business student interning with the organization. Like L., he was more identified with the organization as a whole than the internecine struggles of the subgroups. Soon after my comments, M. spoke out forcefully in the group. He said he agreed with what I had said; he, too, felt scapegoated in this organization whenever he openly identified with the organization as more than a collection of ethnic subgroups. After his speech, the staff turned on M. with a fury almost equal to its attack on L., but he countered by repeating his interpretation and suggested that the irrational fury of the attack was more evidence of what he was saying. Eventually, the group turned from him to the more-satisfying massacre of L.

In a previous paper, I discussed the general issue of scapegoating in organizations by amplifying a short story by Ursula LeGuin entitled, "The Ones Who Walk Away from Omelas" (Colman 1989, LeGuin 1975). Omelas was a town that paid for its utopian life-style by consciously structuring the scapegoat dynamic into its politic; one child was kept in misery all the time as a receptacle for the collective shadow. The system worked well for most citizens; there were only a few "walkaways" who could not live in such a victimizing system and had to leave despite Omelas's material, aesthetic, and spiritual advantages. In LeGuin's story, these "walkaways" lived out the classic hero's journey, leaving their homeland to search for a better place where they could live their lives with more integrity.

There is another kind of walkaway, however, a kind of individual, not represented in LeGuin's story or in most other heroic plots, who rejects the system but acts in a different way toward it. These individuals, who I call "interpretors," do not leave; instead, they live on the boundary of such systems. They speak out against the system's injustice while taking responsibility for their part in its perpetuation. Individuals like this, the best of our artists, prophets, and healers, neither accept a comfortable place in the system nor put themselves beyond the human need that creates it. They locate themselves on the boundary of the scapegoating society which is every society, one foot in the wilderness and the other in the town square. The interpretor stance is dangerous to the individual who assumes it, particularly if there is no institutionalized acceptance of the role. As reformers and "truth-sayers" have learned throughout the ages, those who protect the scapegoat, those who speak out against injustice, run the risk of accepting the scapegoat's place. Students, because of their liminality and their

youth, have often been able to speak from that place of truth—
many societies use students that way—although the tragedies of
Kent State and Tiananmen Square suggest no absolute immunity.
M., an interpretor type by nature, was able to talk directly to the
difficult issue confronting the group; he had less to lose than the
paid employees and knew he could count on the support of his
university and its teachers. Still, in the throes of an active scapegoating process, it takes great courage to speak out against the
group norm and risk the danger of deadly contagion.

Neither my comments nor those of M., however, made a significant difference. The scapegoating forces were already too
strong. When the meeting ended, L. was all but excommunicated.
But with the last shreds of his authority, he did authorize and pay
for a consultation report. L. was fired a week after the meeting.

I heard nothing from the organization for five years, until I
received a phone call from M. He introduced himself as the new
director, the third since L. had been fired. While going through the
papers of his predecessor, M. came upon my report gathering dust
in a file cabinet. He was interested in my elaboration of the scapegoating phenomena and wanted to learn more about the model I
was using and also what I might suggest to ensure some longevity
to his leadership. Could we talk in *my* office? Emphasis his!

This request began a five-year, bimonthly consulting relationship that, by all ordinary measures, has been a great success.
The organization is now known nationally as a model for working
efficiently in a multiracial, multilingual setting. The greatest danger to M. is the parade of headhunters that pursue him.

What has changed? In our initial strategy session, M. said
that the scapegoating system was still intact. He was sure it would
destroy him if not held in check. My consultation report had given
him an intellectual understanding of the powerful dynamic and
also some hope for the future. We wondered aloud together about
growth and creativity, if the organization did not have to divert so
much of its energy for the costly and painful biyearly crucifixion
and could concentrate on the reality tasks of development and
service instead. But how to change that? Another direct interpretive assault on the scapegoating dynamic seemed doomed.
Instead, we decided to work indirectly to weaken the collective
need for fragmentation that underlay the continual transformation of leader into scapegoat. We outlined possible targets for this
effort: developing staff skills and organization-wide *esprit* through
in-house and external educational interventions; formulating new
hiring policies which would seek out individuals committed to

strengthening the organization at its center; restructuring the organization in ways that both took into account the need for some functional separations of dissident subgroups but also emphasized new tasks and systems which united and integrated these subgroups, i.e., projects which required nationality and language integration. We wanted to recognize the implications of the profound intergroup differences present in the staff, and we also agreed to add connecting elements which would decrease the threat of increasing integration. In essence, M. and I filtered all organizational change with an eye to weakening the collective scapegoating dynamic.

Five years earlier, M. had shown that he had the courage to risk saying the unsayable; now he also had the position of leadership to effect organizational change in a patient and noninflammatory fashion. He understood that staying in his job almost certainly required these changes and, unlike his many predecessors, he had the advantage of a concept to explain the leadership scapegoating behavior and a consultant who would work beside him and support him. This last element turned out to be critical and not just because of the information and perspective I could provide. Something more insidious happened, which was to remake our consultation in an unexpected way.

Let me describe what I mean. M. and I met in my spacious office in Sausalito, an affluent suburb near San Francisco. In contrast, M.'s organization was located in an impoverished area; its offices were plain and cramped. My consultation fee was high compared to his own and his staff's salaries, as well as the salaries of most of the organization's clients; staff was aware of these fiduciary contrasts. On occasion, we had held retreats in my offices. At these times, although I was treated with great deference, there were always veiled references to luxury, money, status, and racial differences between the consultant and the organization's staff.

From time to time, I felt vaguely uncomfortable about these fiscal and spatial arrangements. However, I did not decrease my fee nor even hold down regular increases. On three occasions in the five years of consultation, I insisted on coming to the agency site itself to see the staff in their own habitat. Twice the appointment was canceled, and on the third, much of the staff was mysteriously absent. Neither was I ever able to attend the banquets, fund raisers, or other organizational events that have been used to celebrate its growth and success. Perhaps most important, I continued to be always the only ethnic outsider employed by the organization.

In the course of several years, it became clear to M. and me that part of the reason for the success of our work together and its effects on his tenure as leader was the way our consultant pair had become the new scapegoat for the increasingly successful organization. Despite our gradual changes in personnel and structure, the inter-ethnic antagonisms continued to be fierce, even escalating, fueled by worsening international relations. Nor had there been internal "insight" work within the organization that might have buffered this ever-present disruptive dynamic. The scapegoat was still an essential requirement for this organization to cohere, much as the scapechild had been an essential requirement of life in LeGuin's city of Omelas. In effect, the staff group accepted M.'s leadership even when his policies moved the organization toward integration of differences, but they did this by projecting their negative feelings onto the "outside" consultant and the consultative relationship. Together we were viewed as a leadership pair split into good and bad. He was the brilliant, rational, risk-taking hero while I was the dark, mysterious, greedy, shadowy overlord, the white devil, as M. once heard a person refer to me in the bathroom. M. was viewed as strong enough to handle my potentially corrupting influence; his ability to do so probably added to his charisma. With M.'s tacit support, I established the valence for my "enemy status" quite unwittingly through choice of site, money arrangements, the secrecy of our work, my isolation from others, and the lack of other Caucasians.

In this organization, the pressure to find a victim has not altered but the identity of the victim has changed. The consultancy process had become a scapegoat-in-the-mind for staff, much as fired leaders and institutional chaos had been the scapegoat-in-fact five years before.

What is wrong with this outcome? Don't such projections go with the territory of consulting much as transference goes with the territory of therapy? Who, after all, was harmed by such an arrangement, especially since the organization and its leader were evidently thriving? The transfer of the negative projections away from the leader had allowed M. to survive as he carried out policies of integration. Without the consultancy as lightning rod, his job would have been continually in jeopardy.

Moreover, the scapegoat-in-the-mind is quite different from the scapegoat-in-fact. The consultancy system was much like scapegoating in families or small groups in which the victim is more "incast" than outcast. Families rarely expel their problems—the prodigal son is allowed to return—as are other black sheep or victims, because they are needed to maintain the psychological equilibrium as well as fill other family roles and functions. There was no overt damage to me or to M. similar to what happened to the five fired leaders before him. On the contrary, as individuals, each of us has gained greatly from the consultation process, and the organization has benefited from the improved leadership skills of its director. But there were costs that are not obvious. There was considerable cost to M., who learned little about dealing with the negative part of the authority vested in his role and so may not have been fully creative in his leadership. There was a similar creative cost to the organization as a whole and to some subgroups by continuing to deal through mechanisms of projection rather than exploration. In fact, M. had consulted with me about the way several of his best staff, outspoken and risk-taking individuals, were isolated and ostracized when they offered ideas and programs that required inter–ethnic group cooperation. Scapegoating is never without cost. The effect of leaving out any element of a system always has repercussions in parallel process throughout the rest of the system; M. felt muzzled, and his best personnel were constrained from acting in venturesome ways. Moreover, the consultancy, while serving a "helpful" symbolic function as alter-scapegoat, was thereby limited from providing information or interpretations that could well be used by the organization.

Perhaps this arrangement was the most that could be attempted with such an embattled organization. These and other costs may seem part and parcel of my role and small compared to providing a vessel to contain the chaos and destructiveness that existed before M., I, and his organization began our dance together. It is very hard to imagine not having a scapegoat in this tension-filled system. The utopia of Omelas or this consultation always depends on its scapegoat, just like the "utopian" vision of a "perfected" man or woman depends on the projected shadow.

I believe that all consultants who work in depth will inevitably be contaminated by the scapegoat/scapegoater archetype. No matter how carefully they work, and at what pace, they are outsiders who say the unsayable, who speak the truth. They shame those who know; they anger those who don't. They are like the proverbial messengers who bring bad news and are punished for it. Even if their work and information improves the situation, their presence is an embarrassment. Consultants will need to contain this group anger, usually at some personal and professional cost. This may mean limiting what they will accept as their goals. It will also mean making peace with liminality in the system, much as the analyst must accept a similar separation from the most important living systems in which patients are embedded.

Unfortunately, once M. and I had uncovered and analyzed the scapegoat role we were inadvertently playing in the organization, the consultation itself was altered and could not go on as before. New insights create new dynamics which create new insights. The next steps in the organization's individuation process often ride on what is done with this expanding awareness; when critical organizational insights cannot find new mechanisms of expression, development stagnates.

In this case, the risk focused in M. and his role. What M. knew about the consultation (which he valued a great deal) became more and more frustrating to him personally and stultifying to his leadership role. M. began to complain to me of a lack of challenge in his job; he felt less creative as a leader and less creative as a man. He became more aware of the degree of stagnation that was accepted by his staff in their programs, their unwillingness to take chances and risk change. M. now felt he should have brought the scapegoating dynamic back to the staff at various times in the past, but he was unwilling or unable to take the risk now. He was afraid of reversion to the too familiar "kill the leader" posture. He did not want to endanger the organization's progress or risk his future career. And he was no longer the rebellious student hero. He talked about his new child and the house he planned to buy in a prestigious neighborhood. Perhaps he had reached his own personal limit as a leader in this phase of his life, but he was unable to face his limitations in our weekly conversations. Eventually, he accepted an offer to leave his position for another leadership job with better pay and a less-volatile staff group. The organization hired his assistant to take his place; she is far less able than he and will also be less threatening as a change agent. I was not asked to continue my consultation.

In individual work, the shadow, including that part of the shadow constellated by the scapegoat, must be integrated by the person, or individuation will be limited. So, too, with collective work. Individuation within a collective requires a willingness to take responsibility for exploring the meanings of its collective shadow—its scapegoats and scapegoating process. A mechanism must be established to minimize and interpret the individual and collective shadow projections that feed the scapegoating process. M. and I took the first steps to contain what had been a profoundly dysfunctional pattern of scapegoating all leadership. But the interpretor function, a mechanism for truth-speaking about the intergroup rivalries and their effect on the organization, was never adequately developed. Despite M.'s leadership position, the consultancy did not really alter the intergroup scapegoating dynamic that had destroyed five past leaders. The first part of the consultation clarified the problem and also readied the organization for change through education and restructuring. But the insight function remained split off in M. and I; it never penetrated into his staff, his board of directors, his secretaries. Organizations often hire their consultants as leaders to take this next step. Others find a person or persons—the internal interpretor—to continue this vital work. M.'s organization may yet take this step but had not done so when he and I left.

In individual analytic work, the most personally meaningful and conflictual parts of the psyche are projected into the analytic container to be worked on and, when possible, transformed. The analyst's office, his or her personage, and the dyadic amalgam are gradually brought into the psyche of the patient and transformed into figures which have archetypal and personal meaning. These figures, such as wise old man, witch, shaman, totem animal, or a special familiar mentor or teacher, present themselves in dreams, fantasy, and imagination and may be called forth at critical times for conscious and unconscious internal dialogue. In organizational consultation, a similar internalization of the process occurs and may lead a person or subgroup within the organization to take up the consultative function. Sometimes it is a wise and experienced person who is outside the chain of command and who becomes an informal advisor to the chief executive; or the staff may use one department or another to provide internal consultation; or management may learn to use periodic retreats to move deeper into their creative process. Formal consultation externalizes this meaning-generating function when the organization needs to give it special prominence, especially in times of transition and crisis. Organizations under stress that have developed a pattern of excluding and denying their dissident elements rather than including them as part of the developmental process may need an outsider to loosen the boundaries and provide face-saving potential. But eventually the consultative function, with new knowledge of scapegoats and scapegoating, must be reabsorbed into the body of the organization as an ongoing source of guidance.

Partially as a result of this experience, I have made it a priority in my work with organizations to try to develop this internal interpretor function as the consultation unfolds. A first step is to develop a consultation relationship with the organization which models the kind of internal work required of its members and the organization as a whole. Working with important groups within the organization rather than just with the leader or other key personnel is particularly helpful. It is surprising how often an interpretor emerges from the membership, someone like M. who is able to speak from a perspective of the collective. Education about unconscious collective process, such as that provided by Tavistock group relations conferences and workshops about group archetypes which I have recently developed, are useful in developing individuals and a collective culture that values exploration and inquiry into its own process. Hopefully, with time, the impact of consultation and education is enough to develop internal autonomous interpretor systems which will provide an ongoing, valued, and self-perpetuating interpretive function for the organization.

It is my impression that depth consultation, consultation which deals with organizational development and organizational individuation through exploration of unconscious collective processes, is becoming more and more acceptable to modern organizations struggling to deal with greater diversity, complexity, and a more-competitive marketplace. For example, I have recently taken part in planning sessions for leadership training programs in California in which the reality of ethnic diversity (in ten years whites will be an equal minority with Asians, Latinos, and Blacks) is the main concern. Few of the consultants and trainers present believed that anything less than providing upcoming leadership with tools that move toward transcending differences, holding opposites and polarities, and dealing with group, intergroup, and inter-ethnic processes in depth would be useful in dealing with the new multicentered, multi-ethnic California. In a similar vein, many professional and business gatherings are asking for process facilitation as part of the program. I was recently asked to provide such a function by organizers of an international political conference containing legislative representatives from the Soviet Union and the United States. They wanted here-and-now, on-site depth consultation to help participants gain knowledge of the unconscious and covert intergroup complexes as they develop. Most political leaders now realize that complexity, diversity, and the greater risks of war increase the risks of ignoring or excluding any nation in the international collectives. Perhaps soon they, too, will be more willing to accept a broader definition of consultation than simply providing facts and tactics. Is it possible that in the near future, political bodies will want access to their unconscious collective as part of their decision-making process? I believe so, if we can learn to provide it.

Despite these hints of new developments, most organizations in trouble are still unwilling to undertake a depth exploration of the difficulties. Usually, rather than deal with potentially explosive conflicts and complexes, organizations, even more readily than individuals, resort to exporting their problems through firings, mergers, splits, and other structural changes which deny and obfuscate threatening shadow processes at work. Consultation, when allowed, is usually more like behavioral therapy than analysis. Strangely, "psychological" organizations, i.e., mental health clinics and therapy training institutes, which focus on individual development, are often less willing to accept consultation when they are in trouble than organizations such as businesses which are ostensibly less psychologically oriented. Perhaps the former are more aware of the danger of unconscious life. Receiving help requires the same humility and acceptance of woundedness as giving help. Organizations that are afraid to receive help, to learn about themselves in all their parts, including those parts that are excluded and victimized, are in trouble, just as individuals with the same constrictions in sharing and receiving help are in trouble. In my experience, *outside* consultation is usually the best way to begin exploring the collective roots of systemic problems in organizations. However, organizations can be remarkably self-protective even when their competence, even their survival, is at stake. After all, wars have been fought rather than submit to the scrutiny of an outsider. Alternative internal approaches must be tried and may be useful when resistance is too great.

If one is a part of a collective that scapegoats and is afraid to look for help outside itself, learning more about collective process in general may be of some help. In such cultures of denial, and this can occur in even the most enlightened collection of individuals, members can also try to develop self-study groups, internal interpretive systems whose input may be less threatening than an outside voice. This difficult process is analogous perhaps to the kind of self-analysis that both Freud and Jung carried out on themselves (with such mixed results).

For example, one organization that I belong to has been beset by scapegoating issues since its formation. Most members appreciate the problem but for reasons of unity and self-protection are afraid to bring in an outsider to help explore the issues. In this context, some of us have begun two projects with the long-term goal of increasing the individuation potential in the collective.

First, and least threatening, we developed an internal publication, called *Connected Works*, whose editorial policy is to accept all contributions from members with minimal editing. These "individual contributions" are then conceptualized as "collective associations" about the organization as a whole. Much can be learned from such a projective instrument. For example, one of the most important regular contributors remains anonymous despite the fact that our organization prides itself on openness and on taking personal responsibility for behavior. There was a move within the membership to stop "anonymous" contributions as if one could erase the condition that makes a signed contribution too dangerous. By holding to the editorial policy, an interpretation to the collective was effectively made. The membership was forced to confront the anonymous interpretor figure and ponder our censorship of "truth speaking" and tolerance of scapegoating as a way to solve its difficulties.

Connected Works functions pragmatically as a listening and communication post for the membership. But it is also an interpretor of the unconscious collective process of our institute. It is always a constant source of amazement to the editorial board how individual contributions are also group utterances, how contributions fit together, how common themes develop unbidden which reflect the organizational unconscious and the collective mind.

More recently, we have built on this process by forming an organization-wide study group whose task is to study the collective unconscious of our organization. This more-direct approach to our collective problems is far more controversial and threatening than a more-abstracted publication, although in form it is similar to other internal learning structures, such as "corporate universities," which function as internal consultants to their own parent organizations (Hampden-Turner 1990). The mere presence of such structures has a potent impact on a community. In my organization, the study group challenges the entire membership to give more than lip service to the concept of a collective unconscious which it espouses, as something in which we all take part, not some "mystical" synchronistic entity beyond our ken but a flesh-and-blood unit with coherence and identity. The study group has needed to develop a language and an analytic method to explore specific events as manifestations of this unconscious collective. We have begun by looking to our myths of origin, our group dreams and fantasies, as well as our internal process, as manifestations of the larger collective we represent and mirror. As might be expected, there have been some attempts by the organization to "sabotage" the group's work through unconscious scheduling slips and other classic resistances. However, thus far there is also a great deal of general support and interest in developing a richer perspective on who we are to each other and what we are enacting in and for the larger collective.

It is too early to know how well these "experiments in progress" will serve our organization and whether they will develop in other organizations as an alternative to the more-threatening "outsider" aspects of a consultant. It is clear that they serve a different function from the usual problem-solving committees, task forces, and the like, because they are committed to exploration and a search for meaning in collective behavior rather than geared to improvements and solutions. I hope that new forms of "depth" consultative approaches will develop to serve specific needs of organizations much as depth therapy forms have developed to fill individual needs. Most important to me is a renewed commitment to the psychological development of the collective, its individuation, for surely that is where our individual futures, as members of the human collective and the planet's collective, must lie. Perhaps it is in that commitment to help others, valuing others who share our cosmic home as much as ourselves, that Jung's concept of "equivalent value" will find its greatest meaning.

References

Colman, A. D. 1989. The scapegoat: a psychological perspective. In *Contributions to Social and Political Science*, F. Gabelnick and A. W. Carr, eds. Washington, D.C.: A. K. Rice Institute.

Colman, A. D., and Bexton, W. H., eds. 1975. *Group Relations Reader I*. Washington, D.C.: A. K. Rice Institute.

Colman, A. D., and Geller, M. H., eds. 1985. *Group Relations Reader II*. Washington, D.C.: A. K. Rice Institute.

Erickson, E. 1972. Play and actuality. In *Play and Development*, M. Piers, ed. New York: Norton.

Hampden-Turner, C. 1990. *Charting the Corporate Mind: Graphic Solutions to Business Conflicts*. New York: Free Press.

Jung, C. G. 1916. *The Symbolic Life. CW*, vol. 18. Princeton, N.J.: Princeton University Press, 1973.

_____. 1921. *Psychological Types. CW*, vol. 6. Princeton, N.J.: Princeton University Press, 1971.

_____. 1950. Concerning rebirth. In *CW* 9i:113–149. Princeton, N.J.: Princeton University Press, 1968.

LeGuin, U. 1975. "The Ones Who Walked Away from Omelas." In *The Winds of the Twelve Quarters*. New York: Harper.

Arthur D. Colman, *M.D., is an analyst and member of the teaching faculty of the C. G. Jung Institute, San Francisco, and clinical professor, Department of Psychiatry, University of California Medical Center. He has a private practice in Sausalito and is a frequent lecturer. He is author of* The Father: Mythology and Changing Roles.

Dealing with an Organization's Shadow Aspects

Kaj Noschis

Introduction

As a consultant I was asked to provide a psychological portrait of a smaller nonprofit organization (thirty-six employees). The request was formulated in a discussion with the organization's new director.[1] The organization is active in the field of prevention of drug and alcohol dependence in central Western Europe. Its main output is literature on prevention—leaflets, booklets, and research reports—as well as prevention campaigns through the media and in schools. The organization includes an information department, a research department, as well as a department providing consultancy on educational and employee assistance programs.

Financially the organization relies mainly on its own fundraising organization (90%) but it also gets some government subsidies (10%). Fund-raising campaigns are thus an essential aspect of the organization's activities.

When I was asked to draw a psychological portrait of the organization, the task was delimited to the following concerns:

- Finding ways of clarifying and improving the corporate identity as well as the image that the organization presents the general public;

- Making suggestions on how to lower the high figures for personnel turnover;

---

[1]Given the delicate nature of some of my conclusions, my deep appreciation goes to the director of the organization, who allowed me to share this material in public. We have agreed that I will take care in not identifying the organization. This paper is written with the intention of provoking comments on an approach to organizational analysis that, at this stage, probably raises more questions than it offers answers. However, my conviction is that it might prove heuristically quite fruitful.

- Making suggestions on improvements to the everyday working environment.

Approach

In my analysis, I have attempted to apply categories from individual psychology to an organization. This has certainly been done on previous occasions, and Jung himself did not hesitate occasionally to apply some of his psychological categories to entire populations. For instance, he discusses differences between East and West in terms of his typology or refers to capitalism and communism as being each other's shadow (Jung 1957, par. 544). I don't have a more convincing argument for making this leap from individual to organizational psychology than Jung had in moving from individual to group level. The way the reflection is developed and delivered is somehow intended to convince the reader about the legitimacy of the psychological analysis that Jung suggests. So, this will be my approach also in this paper. After presenting the type of data that I have had access to and that I have collected for the analysis, I will present the analysis itself. It is intended to make the point that by relying on some Jungian concepts—namely his typology and the figure of the shadow—we might gain insight into the functioning and difficulties of business organizations. The analysis ventures to indicate an outcome for issues that were uneasily dealt with within the organization's current framework.

Data Collection

For several months I had an opportunity to be a participant-observer in the organization's life (as a former part-time employee and for a further three weeks after becoming involved in this study). Thus, I was able to converse freely with employees during working hours and during breaks. My data partly consist of notes from my observations and transcriptions of discussions.

I have also been able to use data gathered by means of a written, open-ended questionnaire distributed to all employees. The questionnaire was handed out through the internal mailing system with the assurance that responses would be treated anonymously. Questions dealt with the employees' perception of the organization. Some questions explored the "image" that employees have of their organization, the "working climate"; others were related to a more-technical evaluation about the actual working environment and conditions.

In addition, the minutes of meetings at all levels of the organization throughout its history were at my disposal.

Notes from Informal Discussions

As a former employee myself, I was well known by several of my former colleagues. It was thus fairly easy to reach a degree of trust and confidence where employees would feel free to express themselves. In fact, I would move around the offices rather casually and use breaks and calm periods for sitting down and discussing "what was going on in the organization." My status, methodologically speaking, was that of a participant-observer, with my personal feelings of sympathy for the organization having an influence on data collection. Yet, this empathic approach to the functioning of the organization, together with the possibility of sharing the evolution of my own views, were probably essential conditions for the analysis.

Questionnaire

Although I was consulted for the analysis of data, the questionnaire was developed independently of my study. In fact, the director decided to distribute a questionnaire elaborated by the organization's Employee Assistance Program (EAP) department for use with other organizations. The purpose of this distribution was to gather data about how employees evaluate the functioning of the organization. Questions were obviously adapted for this purpose, but the general format of the questionnaire was the same as that of the tool used by the EAP department: fifteen questions dealing with the general perception of the organization, its functioning, its image and its structure, as well as with relations with others and more practical details about everyday working conditions. Answers—on four lines—could be typed or handwritten. All answers were guaranteed anonymity, but this became rather unexpectedly a major issue as the questionnaires were read by employees. Several employees felt that answering questions was something threatening; in fact, out of thirty-six distributed questionnaires, only twenty-five were turned in, despite reiterated assurances that none except for one person (from the EAP department and not from management) would have access to the answers. The questionnaire was also distributed with the assurance that results would be presented globally (categories with percentages and grouped "typical" responses) at a meeting open to all employees. It was agreed that I could consult the questionnaire results before this first general meeting, but in the same format as was to be presented at the meeting and accessible to everyone.

Minutes from Meetings

Among the documents to which I had access were the minutes of the weekly meetings of the directorate through the last decade. I also had the possibility of consulting all documents elaborated by management during the whole history of the organization. This documentation relates decisions and options and shows, generally speaking, the evolution from a paternalistic to a business-type organization. It is also apparent that technical concerns take over gradually with respect to the previously dominant ideological themes.

Jungian Concepts for Organizational Analysis

Once the data were in my possession, I decided to lean on Jung's typology for interpreting part of them. I became convinced that, by using Jung's typology, an agenda might be established as to how to achieve a more-balanced functioning of the organization. What attracted me to this particular typology was the relationship that Jung establishes between types, specifically, the opposition between conscious and unconscious functions, their compensatory relationship, as well as the definition of an inferior function, connected with the shadow side of the personality, as opposed to the dominant function.

Jung elaborated his typology by speculating on the diversity of human beings that he met in his practice. As is well known, the two attitudes defined by Jung are introversion and extraversion.

The two attitudes are intended to define general types and refer to the direction (inward or outward) of the movement of psychic energy. Jung later went on to say that both attitudes are to be found in each individual, the point being that one attitude was dominant with respect to the individual's relation to the outer world, while the other attitude was dominant with respect to the "inner world."

Jung later elaborated on this first typology by distinguishing the four functions—thinking and feeling as well as intuition and sensation, respectively (Jung 1921). The functions are intended to refer to the way that the individual chiefly adapts and orients himself or herself in the world. The two attitudes—introversion and extraversion—are intended to define more general types and refer to the direction (inward or outward) of the movement of psychic energy. Jung again argued that all four functions are present in everyone, but that, from childhood on, individuals are encouraged, by the environment at large, to develop one function at the expense of the others; thus this function becomes the dominant one. The functions are also ordered as opposite pairs: if the dominant function is thinking, then the inferior (most unconscious) function is feeling (Jung 1921, par. 588).

Another concept that I deemed interesting for my analysis is what Jung defines as the "shadow" aspect of personality. The shadow of the personality will be associated with "hidden" or "unacceptable" or "most primitive" (i.e., most undifferentiated) behaviors, thoughts, or feelings. In other words, the shadow is connected with the most unconscious components of our personality and thus also with the inferior function. The inferior function manifests itself through the shadow precisely in order to allow a process of integration to begin, on the condition that the individual is prepared to accept it as such.

The reader might object that I have now gone far too far into individual psychology and that it would be quite questionable to apply these concepts without further ado to organizational psychology. As I already said, it is only *post festum* that I hope to convince the reader of the feasibility of my leap from individual to group level.

In individual psychology the concern in dealing with typology is to identify the dominant function: to understand how the person is spontaneously apprehending the world. At the same time, this allows one to define the (opposite) function with which this apprehension is most undifferentiated or primitive. This identifying takes place by examining thoroughly the everyday functioning of that particular person, the way he talks and acts, his or her way of becoming interested in something, etc. Another way of identifying the dominant function is to use specially devised type indicators for this purpose and then to confront individuals with their results.[2] Yet, in talking with Jungian psychotherapists or with persons having training in typology, it often seems easier to build a typological portrait by first identifying the inferior function. It appears easier to define empirically in which respects the individual is functioning in the "most primitive" manner, where he or she is less differentiated in dealing with situations.[3] This procedure seemed also the most adequate for my purpose. It seemed at least possible to define the aspects in the organization's functioning that employees, as well as management, would be most "touchy" about, that they would discuss emotionally instead of being able to approach with a calm analysis. Methodologically speaking, it is obviously a weak approach, its justification coming only from the richness of the ensuing characterization. Once the dominant function is identified, the psychological task becomes an "integration" or, more modestly, the development of an awareness of the inferior function's manifestations and influence on the conscious functioning. In other words, the task is to confront the shadow. This, then, also became the sense of my proposal.

Analysis of Data

All through my analysis I infer certain conclusions from the data at my disposal. The argument resembles a psychological case study in the sense that I have, freely and without systematic rigor, used data from all my sources. Thus data are presented together with the analysis itself. Validity has been sought through discussions with employees during the duration of the work.

---

[2]I refer notably to the Myers-Briggs Typological Indicator or the Singer-Loomis Inventory of Personality.

[3]"Establishing one's inferior function may be a bit easier, for it is the area with which one has regular trouble" (Sabini 1988, p. 374). However, in this paper on "the therapist's inferior function," the author makes it clear that locating functions is a very complicated and lengthy matter. Our purpose in using typology is above all to have a heuristic tool at our disposal.

Expectations and Concrete Experience

From my discussions with employees, it became evident that, almost without exception, they had entered the organization with idealistic motivations and expectations ("to be able to help others"). Indeed, the recruitment process—advertisements and interviews—stresses that the organization is active in dealing with two major societal problems: "alcohol and drugs." Employees thus expect to have to work within this broad context. It is also in this respect that they will have to, or want to, define their own professional identity. Employees share an acknowledgment that the problems in the field are important and major societal issues. Yet, the daily work of the organization is not in taking care of alcohol- or drug-dependent people. The organization is working in the field of primary prevention, alerting people to the dangers of alcohol and drugs. Thus, employees must adapt their "helping" motivation to something more indirect, i.e., information with the aim of preventing people from becoming alcohol or drug abusers. However, this issue is not explicitly dealt with by the organization, as it could be, for instance, by showing in a tangible manner an articulation between preventive and curative work. Neither is there explicit evidence on the results of the preventive work done by the organization, nor a forum among employees for discussing efficiency issues related to prevention. It is a fact that it is genuinely difficult to measure the impact of preventive work. Quantitatively and statistically, alcohol and drug dependence diseases in all countries are closely related to the amounts consumed. Thus, if it is a "self-evident" choice for the organization to back political and other initiatives aimed at reducing alcohol and drug availability, it is more difficult to measure how preventive campaigns (for instance, the message being currently emphasized: "drink moderately") might have an impact on consumers. This is an important issue related to the organization's corporate identity. To an organization dealing with prevention, a more explicit stance on the impact of prevention would be important.

That this is a major issue in terms of corporate identity was also shown by the questionnaire results. Specifically, employees would note that they had a clear and satisfying idea about their daily tasks but that they did not know what the organization's more general positions were with respect to issues of importance and priorities in prevention.

On the other hand, if such issues have not yet been dealt with in a more direct fashion, it is also because the organization is not interested in stressing too much this preventive nature of its work. As the organization is mainly self-funded, it depends on large-scale fund-raising. The material used—letters, ads, etc.—voluntarily leaves scope for ambiguity about what the organization does: the fund-raising techniques are intended to move and to touch prospective donators emotionally by reminding them of the tragedy of alcoholism and drug dependence. The fund-raising activities implicitly suggest that the organization alleviates such tragedies. In other words, although it is not explicitly mentioned that the organization helps alcoholics and drug-dependent people, the persons exposed to the fund-raising campaigns are led to believe that it does. Fund-raising techniques currently in use within the organization are disapproved of by many of its employees. They have an uneasy feeling about how their employer raises the money used essentially to pay their salaries. But, even the management of the organization seems uncomfortable about this issue. It is deemed extremely important ("the persons in charge of fund-raising are the most important ones in the organization"), yet management is not ready to question current procedures. The main reason for this attitude is that "fund-raisers know that a message with emotional impact is the only one that can bring in money from donators." Both management and the persons in charge of fund-raising believe that there are no immediate emotions that can be related to prevention, whereas the alleviation of human suffering is touching a sensible chord in the general public. It is at this point that the connection between the message passed to the public and the effective work of the organization becomes loose—and it is so on purpose.

This is precisely what creates uneasiness among employees. This uneasiness is felt especially by newcomers, given their idealistic motivation for entering the organization. The problem is one of the organization as such, yet it is left to employees to come to terms with it individually. Thus, our data suggest that the longer the employees have remained in the organization, the more they will develop strategies explicitly intended to overcome this uneasiness or to put it aside. For instance, they may have contacts with therapeutic work outside the organization—especially when they are employed on a part-time basis—and in this manner "justify" in their own eyes the funding of their salary for the time they work on preventive tasks. They may also convince themselves that preventive work is more important than curative work or that both are equally important, and that it is merely because fund-raising for explicitly preventive work would be too difficult that things are the way they are. Or, they may adopt a more cynical view about the contents of the fund-raising campaigns: "that's how life is and if I were a public servant, it would be no clearer."

Yet, the struggle in finding an appropriate attitude affects the ability of some employees to remain loyal to the organization. The idealistic concerns dating from the time when employees originally applied for a job in the organization ("be able to help others") are put in jeopardy by the feeling of a contradiction between the work as it is and the funding of the organization. In fact, the work on prevention is not in line with what had been expected by the employee, although these expectations are "evoked" by the fund-raising appeals.

This is thus a problem of corporate identity that might also offer one explanation for the rather high rate of personnel turnover within the organization. Psychologically, this problem might also be called a major shadow aspect of the organization. We previously defined the shadow side as what is not explicitly acknowledged, as what is hidden or is primitive. The way the relation between fund-raising and preventive activity is dealt with within the organization fills these criteria. The issue is not dealt with in detail, and it is not really open to discussion. Fund-raising is deemed a top priority but is approached in a rather primitive way: the persons in charge "know best" and employees must comply. Yet, this is not at all how other important issues are dealt with within the organization.

Thus, I suggested that one should pave the way for a differentiation and an integration of this shadow aspect into the organization's official functioning by finding ways of stressing, at the group level, the importance of prevention. Without an explicit discussion on the subject, employees must tackle the question individually by finding some way of "coming to terms" with this shadow part of their professional identity; if they do not manage to do this, then they will leave the organization at short notice.

In order to make this suggestion on the integration of the shadow aspect more explicit, I relied on Jung's typology. In fund-raising, feeling, in terms of the messages used for reaching donators, is at the forefront. Yet, feeling within the organization's work is somehow confined to this arena. For instance, impact and efficiency issues that are crucial for influencing prevention are discussed and evaluated by the organization in an almost purely rational manner. Frequency, visibility, as well as acceptability for public and political opinion are discussed—without having much influence on ensuing fund-raising campaigns. "Realistic positions" are sought above all. Opinions that are felt to be guided by feelings about alcohol and drug policy, as well as by the emotionally loaded debate on this topic, are dismissed as inappropriate for a professional organization. This dismissal has become adamant in recent years, as is clearly visible from the minutes of the organization's management meetings. This uneasiness with feeling issues suggests again that we are dealing here with an undifferentiated and thus inferior function.

A confirmation of this hypothesis came also from the surprisingly strong concern of the employees that their answers to the questionnaire should be kept anonymous. The concern was expressed at the first meeting after employees had answered the questionnaire. They clearly had the feeling that their answers might be resented by the director and managers and that the ensuing emotional reactions might be quite forceful. This fear seemed quite out of proportion with respect to the questionnaire or to the context of its distribution and the guarantees given before employees answered it. So, this reaction also seems to confirm that feeling reactions are perceived as unforeseeable factors within the organization and are thus, psychologically speaking, quite primitive.

At this point, if we accept feeling as the inferior function within the organization, then in terms of Jung's view (Jung 1940, par. 292), through fund-raising, feeling operates autonomously toward consciousness. From this realization followed concrete suggestions about integrating aspects of the organization's shadow into its functioning.

Thus, I suggested that if a connection could be established between fund-raising and prevention on the feeling level, the organization would be moving in the direction of integrating its shadow side.

This introduction of a feeling dimension into prevention might be easier to achieve on an individual level first. I then suggested a seminar for employees where this question would be dealt with. Specifically, I proposed that the question "where does prevention enter my life and how do I deal with it" be discussed. The point was to be nonspecific about prevention and to consider it as one aspect of the many facets of life. Following this "grasp for consciousness," it might also be possible either to approach fund-raising differently (more consciously) or to elaborate another attitude toward it at the organizational level.

Facing the Psychological Heritage of the Organization

Historically speaking, the organization is an offshoot of a temperance society. In those early days (at the beginning of this century), alcoholism was seen as an evil resulting from degenerating morality. Thus, to be employed by the organization implied not only an interest for improving awareness and involvement against the use of alcohol, but also living a life that would be morally exemplary. However, the societal changes during the last decades with respect to the perception of alcohol consumption have also affected the organization. The name as well as the orientation of the organization's work have changed. The purpose is no longer defined as a "fight against alcoholism" but as "prevention of alcohol abuse." In fact, the last decade has witnessed several further changes in the organization's internal structure. Abstinence is no longer a requirement for collaborators, and the work of the organization is now defined in terms of up-to-date marketing and educational techniques. It is also seen as an articulation between standard academic research and the implementation of preventive measures. Collaborators have become employees performing technical tasks under precisely defined conditions and during specified hours. They are no longer idealists fighting for a cause with a strong moral conviction against alcohol.

Today, there is no debate within the organization about how employees should live their private lives in order to do good prevention work, whereas this debate was important some decades back, as shown in the early minutes of the organization's meetings. Nowadays, the private and work spheres are completely separated. Employees may consume alcohol or drugs according to their own judgment.

The current phase might, to some extent, be labeled a reactive phase in the organization's history. If, at an earlier stage, the employees' private lives had to obey precise (exemplary) rules before they would even be allowed to work in the organization, today everything happening outside the organization is considered the employees' private business. During the informal discussions I had, it became clear that many employees would in fact be interested in a debate on the question of the relationship between private and professional identity, whereas this is not considered a current issue by management.

One result of the questionnaire study, backed up by informally collected discussion data, is that there exists within the organization a concern about how the organization officially, and fellow employees privately, relate to alcohol and drug use and policies. There is a shared knowledge about the importance and reality of alcohol-related problems in the country, as well as about the way they are dealt with politically, yet there is a desire for a more explicitly defined stance at the organization's official level. If this were to be known, then employees could clearly situate themselves in relation to the often-expressed wish that the organization be tolerant as to its employees' personal stances.

There is, however, also a concern about the consequences of a clear-cut official stance, as this might leave some employees with problems in reconciling a personal view on alcohol and drug consumption with the one advocated by the organization. This concern could be somehow related to the past history of the organization and a fear of the resurgence of a sectarian group. Yet, it might also be a general characteristic of any organization that deals with themes that are necessarily also issues in employees' private lives. Thus, the present hesitation from management's side in risking a clear-cut position on alcohol and drug issues might also be understood psychologically as a reaction to the organization's previous policy. It might also be politically opportune, in a context where alcohol and other drugs are part of daily life yet where moral issues are left to the individual or to small groups, not to take sides too forcefully as a general organization working in prevention. Access to many "client" groups as well as to sponsors might depend on a "low profile" on "hot" topics.

However, this choice has its drawbacks for employees. "We don't really know what our employer thinks about the general policy matters that we are dealing with in our work" as one employee aptly summed up this difficulty. With the above data and considerations in mind, my suggestion for management was formulated in terms of moving beyond a reactive position. I suggested that managment become explicit, at least internally, on the organization's current political stances on alcohol and drug consumption—and that this position might then, depending on contingencies, be put forward to the general public. We further suggested that management make explicit for employees the possibility of being at variance with its own official positions; it should particularly state how public or private views need to be differentiated in social contexts. Consequently, as long as private views were not expressed in the name of the organization, it would be left to the individual whether he or she would consider his or her private views to be too conflictual with his or her employer's stances. This suggestion was intended to relieve some of the uneasiness felt because of the organization's unclear official views.

During the last decade, the organizational rules have required that employees use a compulsory clock-key system. Psychologically, the introduction of such a "measuring" system might be understood as a "cold, objective" procedure as opposed to the "hot, affective measure" relating to the degree of idealistic engagement for the cause defended by the organization. Currently, everyone is expected to turn his or her clock on when entering the office and to turn it off when leaving. Everyone is also expected to fill out a monthly card with the total amount of work hours indicated next to the amount of hours required; reasons for absence (travel, leave of absence, etc.) have to be given. Officially this is intended to instate a democratic work control system. The same objective criterion is used for "measuring" work for all employees, the amount of required hours depending only on the type of work contract signed. This is also meant to improve group spirit through personal exchanges at the workplace (as every absence from the office must be justified).

When asked to comment upon this system, the employees reacted in two ways. For several employees, mainly secretaries but also researchers, the system has a definite advantage in that "with the hours there are clear criteria for the quantity of work that one is expected to perform." On the other hand, other employees note that "the clock is there only for the façade and to give one a clear conscience. In fact one is free to justify one's absences at one's own will." Such statements imply that the use of the clock-key system is a way of avoiding the issue of one's working engagement as a shared concern. Officially, the clock-key system is intended to encourage sharing among employees. Practically, the employees are pushed into an individualistic attitude about how they relate to their work schedule and how not to introduce their private sphere into the workplace. In fact, the clock-key system favors a private versus a professional identity split. One may even suggest that, symbolically, the employee turning off his clock at the end of the day in his office carries, as a corollary, the message that all personal themes are entirely left to his private concern. During informal discussions with employees, it appeared that the clock-key system has one major drawback. One is forced into thinking about work in terms of hours although, in many respects, this does not make very much sense. You might in fact find that you do not "do enough" during office hours, that you cheat because you have not done enough hours, and you add "absence hours" for making up the required amount—or that you don't care about the quality of your work as long as you work the required hours. Whatever the situation, it puts undue emphasis on the "cold and objective" definition of working within the organization, when practically everyone has an idealistic motivation for being in this particular working environment. Thus, employees are almost compelled to consider their involvement in terms of hours rather than tasks, although officially this was never intended to be so. Management will constantly stress the tasks to be accomplished or those that have been accomplished. Yet, psychologically, the clock-key stands in the background when employees are measuring their work in terms of the organization's requests from them. My suggestion was to consider the withdrawing of the clocks, or to leave it to employees whether to use them or not.

I also tried to deepen the analysis by referring to Jung's typology and specifically to the two attitudes that he distinguishes. What is "psychic energy" in the case of an organization? I define it as what employees concern themselves mostly with while working. If concerns are related to adapting activities to the information coming from the external world (following market trends), then this is an argument for the organization's attitude being extraverted. On the other hand, if employees are more concerned about creating from within the organization something new to be proposed to the outer world (generating market trends), then this is an argument for an introverted attitude. However, as Jung wrote, both attitudes go together.

In the case of the organization that I am discussing, it became clear from the interview data that the emphasis was on the "in-house" events: these were the source of creative work, and employees would also emphasize the importance of the internal debate on most matters. Commissions, ad hoc groups, delegations, departmental discussions, in-house written communication, etc., take a significant amount of time and energy, as also noted (and appreciated) by the employees in their answers to the questionnaire. Another argument in favor of introversion is that management is attached to the clock-key system because it is concerned about having at its disposal a criterion for calculating and demonstrating to the board of directors the amount of work its labor force performs. The clock-key hours are deemed useful in this respect, although the total amount of work hours could obviously also be calculated more theoretically by multiplying the working force by the contracted working hours. Yet, management has the impression that this would not be "objectively" as "valid" a measure. Also, hours spent working inside the office are considered "valid" hours, whereas hours spent outside the office must be justified. This almost suspicious attitude with respect to the outer world seems a further characteristic of an introverted attitude. So also is the apparent neglectfulness about the image that the organization presents to the outer world, to the point of avoiding a clear image. To be introverted is to be frightened by but also careless about the outer world.

I thus concluded that the organization is introverted. In fact, there seems to be an awareness of a conscious introverted attitude, that is, that psychic energy circulates basically inside the organization itself or from inside toward the outside world. As a corollary, the unconscious functioning of the organization is extraverted. How can we understand and eventually confirm this? Within individual psychology, an extraverted unconscious amounts to "grabbing" all sorts of stimuli from the internal world and nourishing lively fantasies and speculations with them. Thus the unconscious will be filled with impressions that, in turn, nourish conscious functioning. Given this, I will consider the unconscious of an organization as what goes on inside its walls, what makes up for it being experienced by employees the way it is. In our case, employees are in fact grabbing all sorts of impressions from within the organization and nourishing their fantasies and speculations with them. Rumors about fund-raising issues are a case in point, and so are persistent rumors about continuous reorganizations of the departments. Their relevancy here is that they are in sharp contrast with the continuous efforts made by the organization to practice a "transparent" information policy.[4]

By suggesting that although the organization is devoted to contact with the outside world, it has an introverted attitude, I was able to show the following counterproductive tendencies:

- A tendency to be careless about the organization's public image, in fact about its corporate identity.

- A tendency to be "frightened" about the outside world, this particularly in terms of a fear of being exposed to critique or of having to take a position.

---

[4]The question might be raised of whether this is not the case in all or in most organizations. There are obviously always "rumors" within an organization, but their amount and importance may generally be thought to be in proportion with the degree of management's secrecy.

- Too strong an emphasis on in-house matters. This might give these too much weight and cause neglect with respect to public matters.

As to the counterproductive tendencies of the unconscious extraverted attitude, I mentioned the very rapidly developing "corridor rumors" about the situation of the organization; it is as if the contents of these rumors are increasingly valued by employees despite the great effort made to inform employees officially about all important matters.

To sum up, a psychological view of the evolution of the organization allows us to understand some of its characteristics today. These may be explained as being concomitant to a "reactive" phase in the organization's history. I was able to suggest some changes that were intended to achieve a more-balanced functioning in the organization's rules and procedures. By relying on Jung's distinction between introversion and extraversion, I was able to identify some of the organization's counterproductive tendencies. It is my hope that these suggestions will contribute in a positive manner to the organization's future work.

Conclusion

Applying to an organization a framework originally intended for individual analysis cannot be done without problems. I have tried to show the insights that nevertheless can result from this exercise. In particular, I believe that by relying on Jung's concept of shadow as well as on his typology it becomes possible to make explicit and to take further several considerations suggested by the data collected on the functioning of the organization.

My analysis has specifically focused on two themes. First, there is a generally felt uneasiness within the organization about its own fund-raising techniques. It is by viewing openly this uneasiness that a solution might come into sight. A psychological description of the functioning of the organization, by defining its "shadow side" and "inferior function," shows how fund-raising has remained an ill-defined part of the organization's work, in particular since it has no explicitly stated connection with the organization's main aims. Thus, "integrating" this shadow side here comes to mean formulating an openly acceptable relationship between prevention as the major aim of the organization and the existing fund-raising techniques. Specifically, by viewing prevention differently, a new attitude may be reached by employees about the fund-raising techniques which as such remain indispensable to the organization's financial existence.

Second, it is necessary for the organization to face its psychological inheritance. Here the assumption is that it is only by seeing the present situation as mainly resulting from a reaction toward the organization's own history that current peculiarities in its functioning can be understood. A definition of the organization's "conscious introverted attitude" makes it possible to pinpoint some counterproductive tendencies that should be dealt with.

Böhler, a Swiss professor of economics who repeatedly discussed the relevance of Jung for the business world (Böhler 1960, 1962), made several attempts to recognize the role of the unconscious within the context of economics. In particular, he argued that the rational organization of any business has an irrational basis (Schmid 1963). Becoming conscious of this basis is to have at one's disposal an additional strength. A psychological analysis, such as the one attempted here, aims at being a step in this direction.

Outcome of the Consultancy

Having finished my report, I have handed it to the organization's director as well as to the commission that is intended to take further the questionnaire's analysis. This commission has used this situation as an argument for requesting a permanent personnel commission that would participate in all major decisions concerning employees and in the definition of major policy options. The director has requested a complementary report from a business consultant. A strategy will then be formulated, based on the joint reports.

References

Böhler, E. 1960. Die Grundgedanken des Psychologie von C. G. Jung. In *Industrielle Organisation*, 182–197.

_____. 1962. Der Mythus in der Wirtschaft. In *Industrielle Organisation*, 129–160.

Jung, C. G. 1921. *Psychological Types. CW*, vol. 6. Princeton, N.J.: Princeton University Press, 1971.

_____. 1940. *Psychology and religion. CW* 11:3–106. Princeton, N.J.: Princeton University Press, 1969.

_____. 1957. *The Undiscovered Self.* London: Routledge and Kegan Paul, 1975.

_____. 1972. *Two Essays on Analytical Psychology.* Princeton: Princeton University Press.

Sabini, M. 1988. The therapist's inferior function. *Journal of Analytical Psychology* 33:373–394.

Schmid, K. von. 1963. Uber die wichtigsten psychologischen Ideen Eugen Böhlers. In *Kultur und Wirtschaft*, Festschrift zum 70. Geburtstag von Eugen Böhler. Zürich: Polygraphischer Verlag AG, 79–86.

Kaj Noschis, *Ph.D., is a Jungian analyst in private practice and personnel resources consultant based in Switzerland. He is editor of* Revue des sciences economiques et sociales *and* Architecture and Comportement: Architecture and Behavior. *He is author of numerous articles in environmental psychology and Jungian psychology and teaches psychology at the Federal Institute of Technology in Lausanne.*

A Dionysian Way to Organizational Effectiveness

Mia Nijsmans

Introduction

During the last decade the lexicon of organization theories has expanded. It includes, for instance, terms and concepts such as *storytelling, mythologies, culture, neurosis, climate, irrationality,* even *shadow* and *mentors*. Whereas these terms, preceded by the adjective "organizational," contained a rather pejorative or marginal meaning in the business and academic field in the past, they are bestowed with a different flavor and message these days. They have become quite eccentric, even fashionable. However, I believe that this vocabulary amplification is more than a trendy and passing wave. It may refer to more fundamental changes in thinking about organizations. It may be a sign of a paradigm shift.

The Apollonian Paradigm

Apollo, an ancient god in the Greek pantheon, is the god of reason and order, beauty and harmony. He embodies man's longing for clarity, structure, action, and form. He symbolizes the masculine and more conscious side, a detached rationality, and a belief in the absolute manageability of life (Stassinopoulos 1983, pp. 53–65). We are Apollonian people living in an Apollonian civilization where rationality is a premium good, a taken-for-granted virtue. This applies to organization theories as well. It seems, however, that the exclusive adoration of Apollo is fading a bit, not so much because managers or theorists don't like him anymore, but rather because he has lost his almighty and unquestionable status. The meaning of rationality has changed, and it has generated its self-destructive potential. Its shadow is recognized. The rationality monopoly is being questioned also within organizational circles (Ramos 1981).

Mainstream Organizational Thinking

The prevalent paradigm in social sciences is characterized by the concept of "functional rationality." Mannheim introduced the term for referring to the type of purpose-specific behavior demanded by an organization or society to attain the values and goals of the organization. Alternately, substantive rationality refers to individual behavior that is directed toward the achievement of personal goals and values.[1] The functional rational person allows the organization to make choices for him or her. They let themselves be guided within prescribed channels of social order.

Most orthodox thinking in social sciences and the related organizational and managerial fields centers around basic norms such as rationality, order, control, and predictability and starts from the assumption that the rational is real and the real is rational. However, this Cartesian axiom is being challenged by phenomenologists, psychoanalysts, and empirical findings or even day-to-day observations. In this paper I will point to the mythical quality of organizational rationality.

Organizational Myths

In a recent participant observation study of a Jungian counseling and training organization in London, I noticed that the purposive rationality models don't fit the everyday reality.[2] I explored how organizing occurred in terms of traditionally held organizational properties such as goals, structures, information, and effectiveness. Despite much sophisticated advocacy of organizational rationality in mainstream theories, I discovered that widely held

---

[1]Mannheim's concepts of functional and substantive rationality are described and commented on by A. Ramos (1980, pp. 140–167).

[2]This organization was the Westminster Pastoral Foundation in London, a large and complex therapy and training institute. It was predominantly inspired by Jungian and object-relations ideology. For an overview of these theories, I refer to Samuels (1985).

beliefs regarding these social constructs belonged to organizational "mythology" rather than to organizational reality (Nijsmans 1988). The following mythical assumptions will be explored:

• Decision making and information processing are rationally connected.

• Effectiveness is goal achievement.

The Myth of Rational Decision Making

Within the prevalent paradigm of functional rationality, decision making and information are assumed to be rationally connected.[3] Information collection, processing, and implementing are traditionally thought to be instrumental to decision making. This means, for instance, that people make decisions based on information they have previously collected and analyzed, that available information is analyzed before gathering more information, that the reasons for information collection are stated before requesting it, and that information which seems irrelevant to certain decisions will not be collected.

In practice, however, the link between decisions and information appears to be weak or "loosely coupled" (see Feldman and March 1977, Brunsson 1985, and Allison 1971). Observational data collected in my case study pointed to the disjointed relationship between decision making and information processing. Much of the information had little relevance to the decisions made. Much of the information was collected ex post facto in order to legitimate decisions already taken. Much information was not used in the decision-making process for which it was requested. And there existed a paradoxical situation in that no matter how much information was available, often more than one could handle or use, even more information was pursued. What I observed was a situation of administrative and clerical busy-ness of information gathering, apparently decoupled from substantive decisional or functional organizational outcomes. That is not to say that the retrieved data were never used, but that they were used for different purposes, perhaps by different people with different intentions, at different times.

---

[3]Extensive research on rational decision making and information is conducted by Janis and Mann (1977).

Information gathering, processing, and usage appears to be a time-consuming and elaborate system. If, as it turns out, it is not used in order to make more intelligent, rationally calculated choices, then what is the purpose and meaning of it?

The organizational search for always more information can be seen as a process of surveillance, of monitoring the environment for surprises, or for reassurances that one is in control. This monitoring has more an exploratory character rather than serving to test hypotheses or make immediate cost-benefit calculations. Often the significance of the collected information cannot be grasped in advance. Yet the data are collected and stored until further notice, as being potentially significant for future decision making or comprehension.[4]

The indirect link between information gathering, meaning and use of information, and decision making leaves us to wonder why such anomalies of unlimited data gathering flourish in spite of the predominant functional rationality paradigm in our Western culture. A plausible hypothesis is that information is seen as a symbol.

The theoretical linkage between information and decisions is framed within an Apollonian context where the value of intelligent and rational choice is paramount. The belief that more information leads to better decision making implies that having information in an organization is a good in itself.

Decisions ought to be presented, accounted for, believed in as reasonable, and therefore acceptable. Information has an important symbolic meaning. This symbolic meaning has been described by Meyer and Rowan as mythical and ceremonial, often independent from its immediate efficiency criteria or internal logic. They argue that the organization's tendency to become isomorphic with an elaborated institutionalized environment—incorporating prevailing rationalized concepts—increases its legitimacy and its survival prospects (1977, pp. 340–363).

The ritualistic processes of information in organizations can be seen as a representation of a basic social value, the ability to account intelligibly for rational decision-making processes. The symbolic meaning of information requesting, gathering, and providing explains, for instance, why clients were asked the same questions on the phone at the first intake session and in ongoing counseling. It explains why the same data were processed on various forms and why the same agenda items reappeared in multiple

---

[4]This storing of information resembles the therapeutic practice where information and data are kept as potentially useful.

committees without actually being solved. Such findings and questions lead us to yet another myth.

Effectiveness Is Goal-Achievement

Organizational effectiveness, like goals, rules, and decision making, is a persistent theme within the practical sphere of management as well as in theories (Goodman and Pennings 1977). Despite considerable research, the literature suffers from a lack of coherence. Campbell even refers to a "helter-skelter" situation produced by the most divergent perspectives on effectiveness (1977, p. 46). In the structural functionalist approach, effectiveness means goal attainment. Without elaborating on the concept of goals, it may suffice to point to its elusive nature. As it is often hard to specify and define goals, for they are multiple, self-interested, conflictual, changing over time, biased and so on, goal attainment as a criterion of effectiveness is presumably even more complicated and elusive.[5] Despite the ambiguity of the usage of the concept, there seems to be a broadly assumed consensus about traditional categories of organizational effectiveness. Steers mentions organizational qualities such as productivity, profit, work satisfaction, efficiency, flexibility, and, of course, basically, survival (1975).

The Concept of Effectiveness as a Tool

Evaluating the effectiveness of a service organization in terms of outcome is not only methodologically problematic, but also qualitative or occupational effectiveness cannot be broken down into figures. What constitutes "mental health" or an "individuated being," a "meaningful life" or a "therapeutic effect"? In spite of several research attempts, criteria for therapeutic effectiveness have not been established or agreed upon.

Within the organization, professional effectiveness was not openly talked about and for several reasons. The meaning of effectiveness in the traditional sense of goal achievement did not fit or coincide with the therapeutic culture and language. As the goals (or needs) of the clients were multiple, even contradictory at times

---

[5]This perspective is increasingly employed and integrated in recent organizational research by Scott (1981) and Lawler (1980).

and developing over time, they were only vaguely stated, e.g., "becoming" or "finding one's true self" or "individuation." The evaluative aspect implied in the conventional definitions of effectiveness therefore seemed not only impractical but also impossible given the multidimensionality of the therapeutic "journey." Not publicly talking about therapeutic effectiveness seems to underline Manning's argument that some organizations avoid the problem of effectiveness "by obscuring their functions in the rhetoric of sacredness (as in churches, education in general and private mental health organisations)" (Manning 1980, p. 219).

Failure or ineffectiveness was still a taboo. Counselors and trainees were careful not to talk about it in order to maintain a professional front. Even on occasions where "creative errors" or "learning from failures" were the specifically stated agenda, clinical staff were cautious in order not to lose face. Given the hidden nature of the job and its norms of confidentiality and care for the client (and one's self as a counselor), case presentations were mostly about "success" stories. After all, within the frame of reference of the evolving nature of the psyche, the constant flow and changing state of being, and the systemic assumptions that nothing can be left unchanged or unaffected, the therapy experience was thought to be effective, at least to a certain degree and at a certain time in a client's life.

But apart from professional effectiveness, organizational effectiveness was referred to in particular contexts and language.

Selling the image of the organization for financial or prestigious reasons to the public always involved references to organizational effectiveness. Depending on the audience addressed, effectiveness could be translated into different variables. For instance, when the organization addressed government agencies, local services, or hospitals, effectiveness was expressed in average fees, average waiting periods, attendance numbers, i.e., the enormous number of weekly clients who would otherwise seek help from national or local health services. If, on the other hand, professional bodies of therapists and analysts or academic institutions were addressed, effectiveness would be talked about in terms of diversification and level of sophistication of treatment provided by the service or training. Styles of intake models and allocation, styles of therapy, and name-dropping of prominent employees were other indicators of effectiveness.

It seemed that the concept of effectiveness was used as a tool. This idea comes close to the interactionist and phenomenological perspective on effectiveness. The latter perceives organizations as negotiated interaction systems instrumental for the satisfaction of personal interests. They are portrayed as "political coalitions," "games," "competitive arenas," "negotiated orders," and "garbage cans." In these models and metaphors, effectiveness is equated with the satisfaction of participants' interests, which is different from the criteria used in functional rationality theories.

"W(e)icked" Approach

A novel approach to effectiveness is suggested by Weick. His radical reappraisal is an attempt to "re-punctuate" the problem. Weick points to the arbitrariness of any set of punctuations, as punctuation simply means "chopping the stream of experience into sensible, nameable, and named units" (1977, p. 193). He introduced a rather provocative set of punctuations for looking at organizations:

> Specifically, I would suggest that the effective organization is garrulous, clumsy, superstitious, hypocritical, monstrous, octopoid, wandering, and grouchy. (1977, p. 194)

Weick asserts that "an organization can never know what it thinks or wants until it sees and says what it does." That accounts for the fact that organizations talk to themselves most of the time in order to clarify their surroundings and to make sense of previous events. The reversal of the classically assumed sequence of knowing and acting is crucial in his approach. Weick argues that some kind of talk and/or action occurs first and provides the display which may be used retrospectively for sense-making. In other words, the proposition is that organizations talk in order to discover what they are saying, act in order to discover what they are doing or wanting. And as organizations, certainly the organization I studied, display an enormous amount of time and energy in talking to themselves, "garrulousness" appears to be a worthwhile organizational feature to explore with regard to effectiveness.

Initially controversial properties of organizations such as being clumsy, wandering, octopoid, and grouchy are interesting in that they lift the screen of taken-for-grantedness off classically held beliefs about effectiveness. This "new wave" organizational thinking does not seem to claim either theoretical or empirical accuracy or generality. Instead, its value lies in a conceptual and perceptual provocation which breaks through current "tunnel vision" generated by much myopic functionalism adhered to by theorists and practitioners alike.

Where effectiveness is traditionally understood to be the qualitative outcome of purpose-specific activity, "new wave" organizational thinking emphasizes the non–purpose-specific character of effectiveness, its playfulness.

Weick borrowed the term *galumphing* from Miller to underline the organized playfulness in organizational activities. Play is a way of organizing activities not as a means to an end, but rather, "a crooked line to the end."[6] Play in this sense is a more means-oriented than a goal-oriented activity. The importance of organizational play or galumphing is that it allows for flexibility and adaptability. Complicating organizational processes often implies an elaboration of means. Organizational play allows people to create various responses to particular situations. It leaves space to broaden the actors' horizons or alternatives, not only in their search for solutions but also in their perception and definition of the situation. In that respect, organizations that complicate their "lives" may well come to be seen as more effective than the ones that keep more fixed and focused attention vis-à-vis their activities. In my study of the counseling organization, play and process elaboration seemed to be virtually second nature.

Playing Is Effective

Organizational "galumphing" or play matched the professional ideology in the organization. Staff and students alike were eager to quote or refer to Winnicott's "playing and reality," where, among other things, the importance of play was stressed as a natural way for self-exploration and finding one's "true self." Then how did the organizational members play? A favorite organizational game was talking, convening, sharing, and being in groups.

An initially possible counterindication of effectiveness was, for instance, the frequent reappearance of the same topics and items on committee agendas. Participant observation in the organization for nearly two years, and inspection of organizational

---

[6]Miller defined galumphing as the "patterned elaboration or complication of process, where the pattern is not under the dominant control of goals" in Weick (1977, p. 200).

records and minutes, led me to wonder why particular agenda items such as fees, record keeping, and research seemed to appear over and over again in multiple committees and meetings for years without actually being settled.

As "talking things through" was assumed to be a necessary means in order to "solve the problem," it was almost paradoxical that the more the issues were talked about, the more problematic they became. The escalation effect was that the next solution was thought to be found in sharing it in another committee, with yet a further escalating effect in the sense that each committee would take the issue to another group, and so on, until the problem permeated most of the organizational territory, nearly thirty committees.

When this level of becoming an "organizational problem" had been reached and most of its members had been given the chance or opportunity to "talk about it" and the problem still had not been solved or swept away, a working party was set up. The collective feature ascribed to proposals or information gathered in an ad hoc working party bore a "common good" or common goal character, thus transcending the idiosyncrasy of many individualized comments or critiques. The fact that suggestions, comments, or questions developed by the committee were an already negotiated outcome gave it a less aggressive or self-interested quality. It became more acceptable to the different constituencies within the organization. The democratic, professional, semivoluntary, and long-term nature of the ad hoc working party endowed it with moral identity. From a managerial perspective, the idea of a working party was an acceptable substitute for plain managerial control and decision making.

Other kinds of playfulness could be observed and experienced in the weekly community meetings for professional, academic, and administrative staff and students. They were set up as a forum to provide "time and space where many things could happen." In this sense, the forum was more akin to a playroom where the process, the people themselves, and their interactions, rather than specific ends, were the agenda. The goals and effectiveness of the community meeting were in the eye of the beholder. From a strictly rational, goal-means linearity, such a group encounter may appear to some people as a "useless tool." If, on the other hand, effectiveness has a repunctuated meaning, the playful process engenders positive long-term adaptability effects.

The effect over a period of time was that people in the organization learned about the multiple realities involved. It was an opportunity for and a process of identity construction. Although most of the items talked about were expressions, favorable or critical and all of them entirely fragmented, this allowed for a search for an "organizational self." Opposite views could be expressed. Old timers might credit the organization; newcomers may question it; part-timers may partially discredit it. This implicit differential thinking prevents one-dimensionality and facilitates an attitude of adaptability. The playfulness of confrontation, creative thinking, and reflection of past events engenders a sense of alertness toward the future and paradoxically toward the past, too.

Weick refers to play as "the reshuffling of the organizational repertoire" (1977, p. 206), an ability to recombine means into new sets. That seemed precisely one of the effects of the community meeting. Its participants (the population of the community meeting varied each week) played with ideas and perceptions and related certain feelings to certain organizational events. They linked personal experiences to future planning, connected their ideas of colleagues with missed opportunities or coming events, and so on. This playful "connecting" and associating prevents the possibility of groupthink in which one-dimensional thinking can lead to hazardous outcomes (Janis 1972). As with associative thinking in individual and group counseling, free association in the community meeting (or for that matter in most organizational gatherings) may generate novel insights and new alternatives and perceptions (but also new problems) that may not be discovered otherwise. In this sense, play and galumphing facilitate one's explorative field and horizon. It can be seen as a consciousness-raising exercise.

Randomizing Is Effective

Against the "findings" or proposition of the rationalists and the planners, Weick suggested that randomizing activities (he used the anthropological metaphor of superstition) could be organizationally effective. Analogous to superstitious decision making in some tribes, for instance, in order to decide on the direction of hunting for game, randomizing experiments have been conducted in more contemporary tribes of sociologists. Garfinkel, in his counseling simulation studies (1962), used the randomizing device of coin flipping. For each question a client asked, the counselor secretly flipped the coin for answering yes or no.

Although ethically questionable, the interesting finding of such randomizing experiments was to see how clients tried to make sense of replies which might have sounded peculiar at times. Yet the clients attributed to them a sense of coherence and reasonableness. The significance of such experiments and metaphor is that they facilitate adaptability so that people learn to think in different categories. In order to make sense of the situation in which they found themselves, the clients in these experiments needed to look at past experiences, events, and relationships from a different angle. Novel connections emerged and new perceptional vistas opened up as a result of the reshuffling of ideas and "facts." The study showed how, out of fragmented information, people embroidered a story that was meaningful to them.

As randomizing devices may break up well-established patterns of thinking, they provide an immediate platform for reflection and interpretation. Organizational randomizing occurs frequently not as the well-intended experiments of some clever sociologists but as the natural response of managers and organizational actors. In fact, if we consider randomizing activities as the counterpart of functional rationality, we notice that a considerable amount of organizational "coin flipping" takes place. This was the case in the institute I studied. Examples of such organizational "coin flipping" included the following questions and their materialized outcome:

> "Shall we have an intake stop or not?"
> "Shall we have an open group or not?"
> "Shall we have a researcher in the organization or not?"

If we locate these decisions on an imaginative scale, ranging from randomized to fully rational or planned, they would probably point to somewhere near the random pole. At the time of my research, the issue of imbalance between demand and supply of clients and counselors or therapists was a recurrent theme. The consequences of the problems were defined in terms of economic loss, uncertainty, and uncontrollability of the flux. The randomizing of the alternative of closing intake for several weeks was based on several actors' anxiety regarding a growing waiting period. How the "acceptability" of two months was agreed upon was, at least from a rational point of view, arbitrary: "two months felt good." Not only the acceptability of the waiting period, but also the introduction of a new policy, namely "closing intake" was a debated, yet undocumented and not fully explored, decision.

I am not suggesting that randomizing and arbitrary decisions were signs of bad management, nor of "ineffectiveness." On the contrary. As it turned out, the effect was that lateral thinking and a broadening of the stated problem emerged. Associative thinking and active imagination brought up questions like, How will an intake stop affect further referrals from doctors, hospitals, social services? How will it affect the internal administrative system here? As a social organization, can we afford to close intake? What is our identity? What kind of training curriculum shall we offer? And so on.

Parallel to counseling attitudes, organizational members kept an air of openness in their organizing activities. After a lot of galumphing debate, octopoid moving, and free association, the outcome of the process suggested a "let's do it and see what happens" approach. And such an approach is often preferable to counterproductive planning sessions where people worry about alternatives that never materialize. Activity, rather than contemplation, enables effectiveness in the sense that activity, no matter how random, arbitrary, or odd, provides material for reflection and alertness.

Wandering Is Effective

Classical theory with an emphasis on effectiveness as goal achievement bears a rather static quality. The phenomenon of processes as criteria for effectiveness has barely been touched upon. By repunctuating the problem, different criteria for effectiveness may be discovered. Satisfaction and pleasure in the participation of organizational processes might be as good as other categories such as profit, adaptation, etc.

The following quotation is provocative, fun, but certainly real:

> Organizations keep people busy, occasionally entertain them, give them a variety of experiences, keep them off the streets, allow them to socialize. If they do that, then they are effective. If the process absorbs time and energy and provides the pretexts for storytelling, that is sufficient. (Weick 1977, p. 216)

This is certainly a unique description of what organizations do. Nevertheless, it is a real one, because organizations do indeed wander. In the case of the counseling organization, there was enough empirical evidence to conclude that the organizational destination was not primary. What counted or became manifest was its wandering process.

As with the psychodynamic counseling approach, where destination sounds like a contradiction in terms, both structurally and purely processually, "destination" was a mythical predicament. As in clinical practice, the process is the destination. Growing, individuating, evolving is the pursuit of personal counseling and therapy. That is how the staff was trained. Hence, there was an implicit attitude of "not forcing things" but letting the experience "flow."

This internalized professional culture was reflected in daily morality. Endless hours of talk about apparently unrelated topics, in ever expanding committees or ad hoc working parties, were a case in point. The color of the paint in a reconverted room might become as controversial as the requirements for assessment or the annual budget. I am not suggesting that people in the organization did not have a value or priority system, neither that everything was equally important or trivial. Instead, I am trying to emphasize the more "irrational" aspect of organizational life as a real and nearly taken-for-granted component, not only in the clinical but in the organizational setting as well. People's feelings, doubts, hunches were considered equally meaningful along with their logical and rational performances. The wandering, the exploring, the circular was thus a virtually institutionalized feature which seemed to satisfy most members' needs and may therefore be called "effective." There was certainly an element of "pleasure in the process" that kept people in the organization. The need to belong, the need to share with one's colleagues, and the need to participate in organizational activities were recurring reasons staff members mentioned for staying in the organization. Such benefits compensated even for lower salaries than the ones they earned in their private practices. The generative social and organizational processes seemed to satisfy people's "higher order needs." They liked to be in groups, to participate in meetings, to wander. That's where the pleasure principle was prevalent.

The counseling staff meetings, where the counselors met monthly, and the weekly supervisors' meetings had a "sharing" character. Their members took a "free associative," open stance. Communication among peers generated further thinking and enabled a special "wandering" climate. New ideas were welcomed, personal experiences could be shared and connected, plans could develop. Some of the issues or clusters of thoughts could provide an embryonic state for more formal thinking and policy generation at different levels. In this sense, the wandering of many hours of talk and "being together" could crystallize into new approaches, alternatives, and novel combinations of an already existing means repertoire. Wandering prevented organizational sclerosis, and in that respect appeared to be "healthy." The consummatory act of participating in the dynamics left space for "displaying, learning, improvising, practising, risking, living, feeling and so on" (Weick 1977, p. 217).

In such meetings, wandering could perhaps be perceived as the agenda in its own right. Peer groups bounded by a specified time and place and convening chairperson turned out to be meetings that had a self-contained character. That is, they did not have any sequential link with previous meetings, neither did they prepare any following meeting. Each meeting started afresh. As in the counseling situation, it was up to the individual in the committee to bring in issues, questions, problems, experiences, feelings. Each new meeting meant new exploration, not a linear or instrumental approach, but a disjointed and circular one instead.

The wandering nature of many organizational meetings is supposed to be effective and healthy in the long run. Here, it served the function of self-exploration. Here again, anthropomorphizing was quite strong. In order to "grow" and to "be," a person needed to be able to express his or her anger and complaints. The complex nature of the individual psyche was translated and transferred to the organizational psyche. The individual psyche is constellated of opposites of consciousness and the unconscious, of a true self and a false self, of a self and a shadow, one-ness and separateness, whereby each pole needs to be recognized, confronted, and integrated in order for one to grow or to become who one really is. Analogously, the organization was thought to operate on similar levels. It ought to be able to express its "dark side." Learning about its shadow was thus a necessary condition for its own well-being. The wandering quality of many meetings provided such a journey toward self-discovery. Through dialogue and interaction, the organizational opposites of thinking and feeling, of good and bad, of real and false, could be explored. In the more structured and agenda-set meetings, too, wandering was the acceptable and "natural" style. The fact that some items kept appearing on the agendas for months or years made one wonder about style, nature, manifest and hidden functions of organizational meetings.

It seemed almost that people found some meaning in processing déjà vu events and problems. As in the clinical situation, problem solving was not the organizational house style. The ideological emphasis was on insight through therapeutic interaction between counselor and client. The "unnaturalness" of problem solving had permeated the day-to-day mechanics and processes of administrative systems and organizational affairs. Archaic filing, record, or administrative systems seemed to be merely auxiliary systems, reacting and responding to a situation but not solving it. Incrementalism in administrative procedures reflected the evolving nature of the professional culture.

My observational findings pointed to an attitude of "living with" the problem, "accepting" it, "owning" it, and finding ways of dealing with it. The most popular strategy was to talk so often about it that members got used to it. The problem became familiar and appeared less of a problem after a while. Therefore, problem solving and effectiveness were loosely coupled, too, and could not be equated. Noninstrumental talking and wandering took up a considerable amount of time and actors and provided the pretext for storytelling.

Wandering was an attempt to catch moments of order and stability and the flux of changing contingencies, inputs, and interpretations. The enjoyment of wandering in the process is an expression of consensual validation, namely the process of establishing or reestablishing a consensus of what was going on. People in the organization had to talk about situations and activities in order to discover what they were doing and had been doing so far. Talking about a new fee policy or the records problem or internal reconversions in at least three different meetings, often primarily consisting of the same people, could be seen as a process of checking the intersubjectivity level, restoring it, challenging it, and stretching it.

It would sound somewhat unusual if we referred to an organization comprising about one hundred staff members, most of them professionals, five hundred weekly clients, four different departments, and an ever increasing number of subgroups and mushrooming ad hoc working parties, as priding itself in its wandering and enabling conditions. Even internally, the wandering spirit demanded a more visible hand to define the organizational situation. Fixed time, space, constellation of members, agenda, reporting, minute taking, and distribution were the props used to restage the pleasure and playfulness of the wandering process into a controllable and predictable state of affairs.

The wandering feature in the organizational processes was noticeable in the "process language" people used. Organizational members used gerunds in describing what was happening in the organization. Verb forms, especially gerunds, described more accurately the constant flux and processual character of organizational activities. The more personalized language also prepared an atmosphere of temporariness and transience. This meant that situations were not defined once and for all, but preserved the quality of flux, changeability, and adaptability. And this keeps an organization moving.

The Dionysian Way

The description of a "Weicked" effectiveness in a complex Jungian organization in London may contain an odd or inadequate flavor for Apollonians. Its irrational or nonlinear character, as well as its deliberate unpredictability, makes it harder to find a place within a cognitive and controllable frame. However, by seeing such apparent "inadequacies" in a Dionysian light, one is more likely to stop evading them, and by accepting them, one can begin to transform them. What then means "Dionysian"?

Dionysus was the last god to enter the Olympic pantheon. He was the son of a mortal mother, Semele, and the god Zeus. The myths of Dionysus are dominated by an initial resistance to the god, in the same way that Western man refuses to recognize the wild and instinctive forces in himself. Freud threw a glaring light on this suppressed territorium of the unconscious. But it was particularly Jung who established the Dionysian as a basic structure of the psyche. What were seen as inferior, hysterical, or dangerous phenomena that needed to be tamed, controlled, and analyzed, began to be thought of as vital aspects of ourselves, to be brought into consciousness. The god's myths, politics, and psychology alike point to a common ground: however hard we resist, neglect, or oppose him, Dionysus strikes back. He is as real as Apollo's rationality and order.

Dionysus, the God of Opposites

Dionysus is the god of ecstasy, dance, and song. He is the loosener and the liberator. "He brings plasticity and flexibility into what is rigid and hard, he frees us from old bondages; he dissolves old claims; he lifts the age-old barriers which conceal the invisible and the infinite. And the infinite vitality that had been locked away wells up from the depths like the milk, honey and wine that spurt forth from the earth" (Stassinopoulos 1983, p. 100). He is the enemy of rigid dignity and self-control. He is also the god of madness, violence, and wildness. The luminous air that he inspires shatters all order and can lead either to an ecstatic creative experience or to hysteric destructiveness. He is the god of life, of soul, of emotions, and uses all means to prevent a stifling life. The most powerful symbol of the god and his twofold nature was the mask worn by the actors on stage (he was also the god of the theater). The wearer of the mask is himself and yet he is not. He evokes the mystery of a dual reality where what we see is not what is, and what is transcends what we see. This Dionysian duality of spirit confronts and questions all human certainties. Human reality instead becomes a flux of images and constructions that need continuous reappraisal. His inherent opposites of good and bad, of creativity and destruction, of life and death challenge the edge of alertness in order to pursue life in its full dimension.

Conclusion: Toward a Dionysian Culture

Wonderfully exciting as the god Dionysus might be, where and how does he enter our domain of organizational effectiveness? How can he be meaningful in our case study? And why can he perhaps serve as the latest god on the organizational Olympus? Possible answers to these questions assume or coincide with a different paradigm from the Apollonian or rational functionalist framework.

Handy, in his study of organizations, refers to several cultures, each dominated by mythical figures such as Zeus, Apollo, Athena, and Dionysus (1988, p. 108). Success or effectiveness of the culture depends on various factors: the history of the organization, the kind of task, and the kind of people working there. Some organizations will be more effective with a "club culture" centered around a charismatic Zeus; bureaucracies, on the other hand, may be more in tune with an Apollonian "role culture." Still others whose structure and mandate is more task force or project oriented will be better off with an Athenian "task culture." The Dionysian or "person culture" is often best suited for organizations of professionals. The Dionysian culture is different from the previous cultures where goals and purposes of the organization are paramount. In the person culture, the individual and professional talent prevails. The individual member "uses" the organization for his or her interests. That means that people working in such organizations don't like rules, commands, and prescriptions but prefer a minimal organization where individual professionalism and autonomy are valued. They use the organization in Winnicott's terms as a "facilitating environment" in order "to be."

The difference in culture is well captured in a game suggested by Handy:

> Ask someone what their job is. If they reply, "I work for X (naming a person), then they are probably in a Zeus club culture. If they reply, "I work for X organization," they probably belong to an Apollo culture. If they reply, "I am Y in X organization," then they think of themselves as a professional in an organization, i.e., part of an Athenian culture. If they reply, "I am a writer" (or architect and so on), they are likely to be a Dionysian. (1988, p. 102)

The replies in my case study—"I am an analyst," or "therapist," or "counselor"—seem indeed to point to a Dionysian culture, not only structurally, but also ideologically. One could say that the organization of loosely coupled Dionysians "works" when the talent of the individual is what matters and where he or she has the freedom and space to satisfy idiosyncratic needs. If an organization is able to provide that, it could be perceived as effective, even if it means playing, wandering, and randomizing. Because of the latter dynamics, alertness, adaptability, creativity, and lateral thinking are given space.

Thick descriptions of daily realities seriously question the all-embracing credo of organizational rationality. It becomes apparent that people in organizations do not behave rationally. The effective part of this particular Dionysian culture was that it allowed for irrational or nonrational aspects of people to evolve. It not only facilitated individual creativity and meaning but also organizational health. Both sides of Dionysus were taken seriously—his spurring and lavishing possibilities, but also his potential "dark side."

The new-wave language game, introduced by recent phenomenologists, may seem far from coherent and integrated, but then this disjointed view might resemble more accurately the actual nature of "organizing." The new lexicon, inspired by Weick, and further elaborated by the makers of an "emergent paradigm," addresses flux rather than order, multicausality rather than linearity, fragmentation instead of monolithic entities, rationability versus rationality, exploration versus laws, adaptability versus adaptation, and so on (Lincoln 1985). What all these themes and concepts have in common is their belief in and acceptance of the nonrational, the intuitive, maybe the more feminine, the bipolar Dionysian character of organizational interaction.

References

Allison, G. 1971. *Essence of Decision Making*. Boston: Little, Brown and Company.

Brunsson, N. 1985. *The Irrational Organization*. New York: John Wiley.

Campbell, J. 1977. On the nature of organizational effectiveness. In *New Perspectives on Organizational Effectiveness*, P. Goodman and J. Pennings, eds. San Francisco: Jossey Bass, pp. 13–56.

Feldman, M., and March, J. 1977. Information in organizations as signal and symbol. *Administrative Science Quarterly* 26:171–186.

Garfinkel, H. 1962. Common sense knowledge of social structures. In *Theories of the Mind*, J. Scher, ed. New York: Free Press.

Goodman, P., and Pennings, J., eds. 1977. *New Perspectives on Organizational Effectiveness*. San Francisco: Jossey Bass.

Handy, C. 1988. *Understanding Voluntary Organizations*. London: Penguin.

Janis, I. 1972. *Victims of Groupthink*. Boston: Houghton Mifflin Company.

Janis, I., and Mann, L. 1977. *Decision Making*. New York: Free Press.

Lawler, E., et al. 1980. *Organizational Assessment*. New York: Wiley.

Lincoln, Y. 1985. *Organizational Theory and Inquiry*. London: Sage.

Manning, P. 1980. *The Narc's Game*. Cambridge, Mass.: M.I.T. Press.

Meyer, R., and Rowan, B. 1977. Institutionalized organizations: formal structure as myth and ceremony. *American Journal of Sociology* 83:340–363.

Nijsmans, M. 1988. Phenomenology and organizational theories. Ph.D. diss., The University of London.

Ramos, A. 1980. Organization theory and the new public administration. C. Bellone, ed.

Ramos, A. 1981. *The New Science of Organizations*. Toronto: University Press.

Samuels, A. 1985. *Jung and the Post-Jungians*. London: Routledge and Kegan Paul.

Scott, W. 1981. *Organizations: Rational, Natural and Open Systems.* Englewood Cliffs, N.J.: Prentice Hall.

Stassinopoulos, A. 1983. *The Gods of Greece.* New York: Harry N. Abrams.

Steers, R. 1975. Problems in the measurement of organizational effectiveness. *Administrative Science Quarterly* 20:546–558.

Weick, K. 1977. On re-punctuating the problem. In *New Perspectives on Organizational Effectiveness*, P. Goodman and J. Pennings, eds. San Francisco: Jossey Bass, pp. 193–226.

Mia Nijsmans *holds a Ph.D. in sociology from the London School of Economics and Political Science. She has held research and managerial positions in various organizations including a political party, mental hospitals, and universities in Belgium and the Netherlands. She is currently associate professor of organizational sociology, at the Department of Public Administration, Erasmus Hogeschool, Brussels.*

Opening to
the Change Process

The Transcendent Function
at Work

Edwin E. Olson

Managers develop effective work teams using a number of approaches, including the informal, day-to-day activities of planning, organizing, encouraging interaction, influencing, and rewarding, and more formal, structured techniques. These formal methods include communication meetings, clarifying roles, improving interpersonal relations, solving problems, and organizational confrontation meetings (McAfee and Champagne 1987). In most of the informal and formal approaches, the manager deals primarily with information that is within the team's awareness—mostly motivational or performance issues. Even in experiential group training where the participants learn about group process, the focus is on behavior of which they are aware in the "here and now."

In the theoretical literature of group dynamics there are psychodynamic traditions that recognize the unconscious processes which drive many aspects of human behavior (Gillette and McCollom 1990). Most of this literature has been written principally in the psychodynamic and psychoanalytic tradition (Bion 1959, Diamond 1986, Hirschhorn 1988, Kets de Vries 1989, Kets de Vries and Miller 1984). Although the hidden and unconscious aspects shape how the leader and group members struggle for control or drive the group's commitment to its norms or structures, the unconscious factors are generally ignored by both managers and consultants. As a result, group processes become blocked or deadlocked, splits in the group develop, sides are chosen, and persons despair that the conflict or impasse will never be resolved. Often

Adapted with permission from the *Journal of Applied Behavioral Science,* "The Transcendent Function in Organizational Change," by Edwin E. Olson, volume 26, number 1, copyright 1990 NTL Institute.

group members do not have the courage to take the risks to deal with the underlying factors even when they become apparent.

To reach the deep levels of change, we need to understand and deal with the unconscious and spiritual dimensions of organizational change (Schein 1985, Levy and Merry 1986, Vaill 1988, Owen 1989). Johnson (1987) points out that our conscious dominant function under the control of ego "keeps God out," that is, new learning does not occur with our dominant function. However, the less-conscious inferior functions let us open up to new possibilities.

Jungian View of the Unconscious

Jung viewed the unconscious as a creative and vital resource for conscious life (Hall 1986, Morgan 1986, Wilmer 1987). Jung defined the unconscious both as mental contents which are inaccessible to the ego and as a psychic place with its own character, laws, and functions (Samuels 1986). In an organizational or group context, the unconscious may manifest itself through varied phenomena such as: myths or "essential stories" of the organization's origin, values, assumptions, and artifacts (McWhinney and Batista 1988, Schein 1989); metaphors whose imagery captures the unconscious (Katz 1983); underlying forces that create and fuel organizational conflicts (Smith 1989); and sudden revisions of a group's performance framework (Gersick 1988). The unconscious is "the other" that encompasses all that opposes the prevailing conscious view or value system. In conflict situations, whatever opposes one lives in one's personal unconscious; it is an "equal opposite" that locks horns with consciousness.

A Jungian perspective encourages one to work toward mending the split between the inner nonrational world of images and symbols which one experiences in dreams and fantasies, and the outer world of objects and people. Often a person believes that the outer world is the only "real" world until the unconscious world makes itself known through recurring dreams or inner urgings. Unlike the conscious, objective world that one creates through one's senses, one cannot shape the unconscious world. It just presents itself to us and offers one the opportunity to relate to it or to ignore it.

In individual therapy the analyst helps the client comprehend his or her own internal processes and make a bridge for understanding between consciousness and the unconscious. This is done by encouraging unconscious feelings, images, and projections to emerge in a creative process. An energy field is created in a therapy session that facilitates this transformation. Bolen (1984) describes an emotional field that is generated between her and the clients that affects the unconscious elements in both the therapist and the client. In the session, by staying with the polarities (e.g., involvement-/detachment) something new emerges. Bolen (1989) believes this process of change is represented by Aphrodite and Hermes, who symbolize the power to transcend boundaries and levels.

In this paper I will discuss the unconscious aspects of the transformative change processes in an organizational and group context and explain how Jung's understanding of the transcendent function is applicable at the collective level.

T-Group Example

My experience in facilitating a recent T-group (experiential training group) will provide an example of the unconscious aspects of group development and examples for discussing the transcendent function.

The T-group was part of a human interaction laboratory sponsored by the NTL Institute. My group had thirteen adults who met for five hours each day for one week. After the second day, I observed a growing split between those who wished to get into what they fantasized as the "real" work of a T-group by disclosing their feelings and personal issues and another subgroup who feared such disclosure and preferred to treat the group as a problem-solving seminar to discuss communication issues in their workplace. By the end of the second day the group was stuck in the polarity between the "feeling-personal issue" subgroup of about 3–4 people and the "thinking-workplace" subgroup of about 3–4 people. The remainder of the group were unaligned or undeclared. Both subgroups had attempted to steer the group in their preferred direction, but each time the process was blocked by the silent, nonverbal expressions of disinterest of the other subgroup. At the same time, other splits in the group became apparent such as "engineer" vs. "nonengineer" which began to be loaded onto the major split in the group.

As the facilitator I reviewed my options about dealing with the growing conflict. The options ranged from doing nothing to heightening the conflict by physically separating the two subgroups in a fishbowl arrangement, hoping that by experiencing the conflict more fully there would be movement. Before I could decide what to do, a nonaligned and quiet member of the group began to provide another nonaligned member with feedback about behavior he had observed earlier in the day. I could immediately sense a shift in the group. The group had been presented with a way of doing engaging work that was neither a rational workplace issue nor an emotional personal issue. In the collective unconscious of the whole group was the value of their current experiences. Both subgroups were in flight from the present reality by seeking resolution of a perceived workplace problem not directly involving other members of the group. The new awareness that began to come into the group's consciousness was the value of working with the here-and-now data they shared in common. The tension began to subside, more and more members leaned forward and joined the process. Within several minutes other members also began to deal with issues among the members of the group that had both affective and cognitive aspects.

At the conclusion of the session, I discussed what happened and pointed out that the group had shifted from being stuck between two polarities of workplace vs. personal issues to a new level where the group could focus on current human interactions which were related to the interests of both subgroups. For the remainder of the week there was no further reference to the two subgroups, and all members continued to work at both the feeling and thinking level as they covered a wide range of matters of concern—problems in their workplace, issues with spouses and children, and the here-and-now interrelationship data generated during the workshop. The group had become a safe place for many kinds of work.

Transcendent Function

The process of the T-group illustrates the operation of the "transcendent function" in which C. G. Jung's psychology links the unconscious and conscious aspects of the psyche. The tension between the opposite functions of thinking and feeling was held until a creative resolution occurred. The two opposites were not blended, but a transformation occurred as the group integrated unconscious material (its fear of the here and now) in its work. The thinking and feeling functions were in the unconscious of each respective subgroup. When a member who was not caught in that polarity began to work with material in the group's unconscious and avoided the either/or thinking of the two subgroups, others in the group began to see a new way the group could work, and it was transformed.

Jung saw the transcendent function as an autonomous regulator which emerges and gradually begins to work as the process of individuation (the process of change for an individual) begins to unfold (Humbert 1988). The psyche gradually finds equilibrium and orients itself after conflicts have occurred between the ego and the unconscious. In this process the unconscious factors rise to a level of awareness, and the person reacts with the ego's values and goals. According to Jung, the compensatory relationship of ego consciousness and the unconscious develops because consciousness must achieve a concentrated and directed focus and intensity; thus, the unconscious becomes, by necessity, the gathering place for those elements that one forgets, inherits (collective unconscious), or finds incompatible with one's consciousness. In the course of time and under suitable conditions, any of these unconscious elements might enter the "light of consciousness" (Jung 1916, par. 132).

The transcendent function does not refer to any metaphysical quality implied by the word *transcendent*. In this context, transcendent refers to the capacity to transcend the destructive tendency to move oneself—or to let oneself be drawn—toward one side of a polarity in the psyche. The transcendent function enables the two sides of a polarity to encounter each other on equal terms (Samuels 1986). The tension between the opposing sides is raised to a higher level (transcend) as the transcendent function reconciles these opposites by creating a synthesis. This synthesis takes the form of a metaphorical statement or symbol (Stevens 1982) and enables a person to experience a creative shift. The transcendent function allows a person to move from a one-sided orientation toward greater balance and integration. The transcendent function releases energy as the person comes to understand her or his inner strength, and a sense of peace emerges.

> At that point, it is as if you were to stand on a mountain top
> watching a raging storm below—the storm may go on, but you
> are outside of it; you are to some extent objective, no longer
> emotionally involved. There is a sense of peace. (Sharp 1988,
> p. 38)

The reconciling symbol experienced through the transcendent function adheres to neither side of the conflict. Rather, it unites them both and offers the possibility of an objective solution or a new attitude that transcends the original divided state.

Jung defined ego as the center of consciousness, but stressed that the ego is limited, incomplete, and less than the whole personality. The ego maintains the tensions of opposites until the psyche can manifest the transcendent function (Hall 1986). The ego then surrenders to a greater authority: the ordering principle of the personality that emphasizes both the conscious and unconscious, which Jung called the *Self*. If one's ego cannot maintain the tension and one makes a one-sided choice between two forces, the opposing force will become even stronger—and the tension will build again.

At the group level, as was evident in the T-group case, if the tension of the polarities is held between aspects which are in the unconscious of the group members, the group can shift to a new level of understanding of its purpose and its way of operating. Gersick (1988) found that group development follows a pattern of sudden formation, maintenance, and sudden revision of their framework for performance which she calls a "punctuated equilibrium." The sudden shift in the T-group, which can be explained as the operation of the transcendent function in the psyches of its members, is an example of the importance of the emergence of a new symbol or way of understanding which integrates the major split in the group. This new understanding must be voiced by at least one member of the group. When it appears to group consciousness, then the adoption by other members can proceed quickly. It may also be an example of the necessity of reaching a point of acknowledging that the position of the "other" is not understood before conflict can be resolved (Gurevitch 1989).

Edith Sullwold (1979) has described an experience in a planning group which captures the difficulty of concretely or rationally explaining how change occurs at a group level. The task of the group of thirty-five conference planners was to select a title for an upcoming conference. Not only was the group successful, but Sullwold reports that the experience profoundly changed her life.

The mystery remains—how did this event occur? Remembering the evening, I pondered over the ingredients. A sense of trust in silence, in the inner working of the spirit within that silence, was paramount. And necessarily there was an acceptance of the sense of order and lawfulness of spirit. And there was amazing patience with and acceptance of the individual, giving the persons and the ideas a large, unjudged space in which to exist. There was an important tension of differences, a tension that heightened awareness and stretched the understanding in such a way that the final resolution had a sense of grace and glory to it. These ingredients, trust, openness, nonjudgment, focus of tension, and an intent to resolve seemed to be the necessary conditions for the alchemy of change to take place. The knowledge of the process, of the grace of change, is contained within the experiencing of life itself, as happened to me in January. Every moment has the potential to bring me such knowledge if I can awake to the actual reality of a state of constant change. (p. 3)

In many respects the situation experienced by Sullwold and my experience of the T-group are similar.

The transcendent function may appear differently at the various stages of individual and group development. It allows the ego to make sense of new experience—at an early stage of development by using an emotionally charged symbol through projection and later in life with creative formulation and imagination (Moore 1975).

Organization Redesign Case

A large bureaucracy allowed one of its divisions to conduct an experiment to see if reducing the supervisory layer of management would improve organizational efficiency. The larger organization prized order, security, and hierarchy. The director of the experimental division valued involvement, creativity, and risk-taking. As a consultant to the experimental division, I facilitated a series of group meetings to identify the forces which were driving the organization to change and which were acting as restraints (force-field analysis). The staff longed for the certainty and security of having a supervisor while they also began to value their new autonomy, as scary as it was. Over a period of eight months, the group moved from a one-sided position of reliance on a supervisor to valuing their new sense of power. The balancing work of the transcendent function was assisted by the conscious experience of conflict. The group continued to hold both realities—their identification with the values of the larger organization and their new maverick identity. During our reflection on the conflict between the old and the new, there arose a new symbol for the group. They began to refer to themselves as the "007" division (as in the James Bond movies). They began to be proud of their role in a group which was pioneering a new path. The old consciousness (power and authority) is present in the new symbol, but now that power was located in one person, a supervisor; it was dispersed—they were all 007 agents. The new material from their unconscious (risk-taking and creativity) is also present in the life-style of a 007 agent. The conscious side was brought face to face with the counter-position of the unconscious. The resulting conflict led to the 007 division symbol, which united the opposed positions of individual power and group involvement. Jung referred to such a symbol as intuition or revelation, which cannot be consciously chosen or constructed (Jung 1973). My role as facilitator was to create confrontation meetings in which the group could take risks to surface the tension, to empower themselves, and to encourage the group to hold both sides of the polarity until a resolution would occur.

This case demonstrates the importance of holding the tension and discomfort until the psyche is stirred to manifest the transcendent function, permitting a symbolic solution to emerge (Hall 1986, p. 83).

Opening to the Unconscious

A person's own unconscious can manifest itself in many ways, such as through illness, personal myths, unexpressed fears, strong feelings that unexpectedly surface, metaphors that come to mind, images or visions, fantasies and daydreams, associations, and dreams. Those living fast-paced lives, however, often value assertive action and control of events and devalue the unconscious, which they consider as nothingness (Yandell 1987).

> A full schedule with constant activity initiated and controlled from above [the ego] leaves no space for anything to emerge from below [the unconscious], for anything to happen that has not been consciously chosen and decided. . . . Viewed psycho-dynamically, chronic hyperactivity is a motivated, habitual ego defense against the threatening unconscious; as long as I keep busy and distracted, or keep my muscles tight, I don't have to deal with what might come to mind if I didn't. (Yandell 1987, p. 95)

According to the Jungian perspective, the unconscious engages with consciousness in developmental stages. Humbert (1988) describes three such stages, in which one does the following:

I. Opens oneself to what may happen (*geschehenlassen*, i.e., to let happen);

II. Considers the emerging unconscious phenomena by remaining at a distance and being objective without becoming possessed by them (*betrachten*, i.e., to consider); and

III. Experiences the tension developing between conscious and unconscious as distance between them increases; the unconscious becomes more powerful and elemental, and self-confrontation occurs (*sich auseinandersetzen*, i.e., to confront oneself with).

Unconscious material gives the person the opportunity to come to terms with the "other" voice (Jung 1916, par. 186). Responding to unconscious material is like a dialogue between two persons "with equal rights, each of whom gives the other credit for a valid argument and considers it worth while to modify the conflicting standpoints by means of thorough comparison and discussion or else to distinguish them clearly from one another" (ibid.). Resolution may take much time and demand sacrifices from both sides. Jung says:

> Everyone who proposes to come to terms with himself must reckon with this basic problem. For, to the degree that he does not admit the validity of the other person, he denies the "other" within himself the right to exist—and vice versa. The capacity for inner dialogue is a touchstone for outer objectivity. (Ibid., 187)

The process of change involving the transcendent function is not simple. The center is the archetype of wholeness—the Self. Any attempt to control the unconscious or to find quick, easy solutions requiring no sacrifice will prove futile. The creative metaphor, the luminous symbols will come from a place deep inside and only after a struggle. The consultant's own transcendent function is crucial for allowing her or his own unconscious to link unconscious and consciousness and to making a bridge for understanding (Powell 1985). By helping unconscious feelings, images, projections, and nonverbal communications emerge, the consultant can keep the creative process alive.

Integrating Conscious and Unconscious

The transcendent function requires both unconscious material and conscious awareness to create a new position of unity (Moore 1975). Conscious understanding through intellectual concepts, words, and abstractions accompanies creative formulation through fantasies, symbols, and what Jung calls "active imagination" (Stevens 1982). *Active imagination* is an attitude toward the unconscious, one that opens both the image and feeling levels to sources of energy in the unconscious, enabling one to see what is happening (Williams 1984). In the process of change fostered by the transcendent function, one can see consciousness taking the lead at some times and the equally powerful unconscious taking the lead at others (Moore 1975). To illustrate the interplay of both the conscious and unconscious aspects of change, I will discuss a recent team-building session I facilitated.

A division reorganization created a new team of eight functional managers. Because their director had previously worked with only two members of the team, he decided to hold a team-building session to promote mutual understanding and to plan the team's new work processes. I had conducted team-building sessions with the director several years earlier and was asked to facilitate an off-site session. Prior to the meeting, I interviewed all the group members to learn their concerns about working with the team and to begin building trust in the process of team-building. Most were skeptical about needing to work as a team because the members had many independent responsibilities, and several had already had some conflict over work space and staffing issues.

To create a climate conducive to a deeper level of discussion among the team members, I began the session by asking each member to express "what gift you bring to the team." The symbolism of gift giving helped the members release latent positive feelings about each person's Self and unexpressed feelings about being a part of the new team (the group Self).

I next gave the participants the results of the Singer-Loomis Inventory of Personality (SLIP) they had completed prior to the session (Singer and Loomis 1984). The SLIP was designed by two Jungian analysts to measure the particular patterns of behavioral responses of an individual based on Jung's concept of eight psychological types: introverted thinking, extraverted thinking, introverted sensation, extraverted sensation, introverted feeling, extraverted feeling, introverted intuition, and extraverted intuition (Jung 1921). The relative development of these independent types for each team member is visually represented and compared to managerial norms and to the patterns of their own team.[1] The SLIP profile reveals which of the eight types are in the individuals' persona (the conscious, attractive side of the personality) and which are in the shadow (the less-conscious, "inferior" functions). The inferior function, which is largely unconscious, contains great potential for change if its contents are integrated into ego consciousness (Samuels 1986, p. 154).

After reviewing his or her own profile, each team member was paired with a colleague with a similar profile so that they could explore their self-images and feelings about their individual persona. To trigger consideration of the less-conscious functions and to help the team members experience the tension between the conscious and the unconscious, each was then paired with a team member with an opposite profile. This pairing put those members together who had the most interpersonal conflict. In most of the pairs, the tension was maintained long enough to activate the transcendent function in each person and to enable each person's ego to confront itself and the opposite reality of a colleague representing the less-conscious aspects of one's personality. When the pairs gave reports to the total team after the exercise, several team members expressed satisfaction about beginning to understand colleagues with whom they had been in conflict.

---

[1] The SLIP visually represents each team member's relative development of these eight independent functions and compares this to norms for a reference group of managers and to the patterns of the other team members. The author is adapting the Singer-Loomis Inventory of Personality (SLIP) for organization consultants and trainers.

The stages each individual went through during this session corresponded to the four components of active imagination described by von Franz (quoted in Dallett 1982).

1. Opening oneself to what may happen by setting ego consciousness aside so that the unconscious can enter;

2. Considering the emerging images, emotions, and fantasies from a distance, letting tension arise between the ego (the conscious) and the unconscious, and maintaining the tension—without choosing one side of the polarity—until the transcendent function is activated;

3. Allowing the ego to react by confronting the unconscious material; and

4. Drawing conclusions and bringing the new awareness into one's work and life.

The team-building session continued with summary feedback on the themes I had discovered through my interviews with the team, a group priority-setting activity for these themes, and a problem-solving session led by the director. During our processing of the problem-solving session, the director received feedback concerning his dominant intuition function and his inferior feeling function. He valued team members for their ideas (intuition), but he continuously avoided a commitment to increasing his involvement with their staffs (lack of extraverted feeling). The director initially rejected the suggestions which were offered, but the team urged him to remain open and avoid dismissing their requests out of hand. The team, in effect, was asking him to become conscious of the consequences of his one-sidedness. His strength of intuition was affirmed as he was confronted about the staff needing his attention. The nature of the interaction during these moments of tension yielded insights similar to those gained by staying in the "neutral zone" during life transitions (Bridges 1980). Stein and Stein (1987) use the term *liminality* to explain the period of flux and internal reorganization during which the unconscious vividly and forcefully appears.

> In the midst of the emotional flux and turmoil of midlife liminality, persons struggle with fundamental splits and dynamics of their personality and undergo internal structural changes that will affect their attitudes and emotional reactions permanently. The net result will be a transformation of consciousness. (Stein and Stein 1987, p. 295)

The director succeeded in staying with the tension in the room and experiencing as consciously as possible the conflict it produced for his managers and staff. Eventually, he made a sincere commitment to visit the work sites, to participate in "brown-bag" lunches, and to make himself more available to others. The following day he began the session by reviewing his commitment to meet with the staff and, upon returning to the office, scheduled site visits for the next six months—evidence that the transcendent function had been activated. The director had accepted the reality of his one-sidedness, and, paradoxically, his attitude was changed.

Smith and Berg (1987) note that when working in a group, the consultant often encounters "splits" that create two sides for major issues, values, factions, and perspectives. Midway during this team-building session, we explored these splits in individual counseling sessions, which focused on each member's inferior function as revealed by that person's SLIP profile. When we began the second half of the team-building session, each person disclosed to the group "how I could become a problem to the group." Sharing their vulnerabilities enabled the group to reduce defensiveness and close gaps in such areas as interdependencies, staff sharing, and communication styles. We ended the session by having each person answer the question, "What will the team be two years from now?" The outpouring of feeling and visions provided clear evidence that the whole group had reached a new level of understanding. The group members' vision statements used phrases such as: "focusing on issues," "helping each other," "sharing staff," "recognizing individual needs and abilities," "deciding for good of whole group," "attracting staff," "having fun," "doing first-rate work," and "giving honest feedback." The team-building session led to a significant change in the conflictual and individualistic attitudes the members had when we began.

In summary, the director of the team opened himself to expanding his personality by bearing the tension of integrating material from his less-conscious functions.

Individuation is the process of expanding the personality to include both opposites of a pair. The transcendent function can be born when one is willing to stand in the center of one's circle typologically and bear the tension of developing an inferior function. (Singer and Loomis 1987, p. 440)

The team members had taken the time to let unconscious material surface and had tapped the energy of images and emotions deep within themselves and in the other members who represented their psychological opposites. Through periods of silence, patience, individual reflection, disclosure, and open acceptance of one another, the team members had managed to sustain the tension of their differences. This tension alerted members to emerging symbols, language, values, and assumptions, and enabled them to let go of their individual positions (Sullwold 1987). The group developed a team identity, increased empathy, an awareness of its communal vulnerability, and greater spontaneity and trust.

Conclusions

The activated transcendent function can move a person from impasses by creatively bridging unconscious material and conscious awareness, thereby producing new images, symbols, and possibilities. If one can sustain the tension between surfaced unconscious material and consciousness, one can reach a new level of understanding—a nonlogical integration of opposing sides of a polarity. Ego consciousness listens to what the unconscious wants—without trying to control it—until a unifying position emerges.

Expending energy in efforts to avoid the unconscious aspects of one's organizational life limits one's perspectives. Marion Woodman says metaphorically that we keep ourselves going by keeping our boxes small—but smashing against these frail structures is the chaos of the unconscious "which is ready to bombard us like Niagara Falls" (Goodrich-Dunn 1989). The obstacles to dealing with the unconscious in an organizational setting include the following:

- Unwillingness to face the conflict;
- Reluctance to sustain the tension until a more comprehensive vision appears;
- Failure to give the "voice" of the unconscious enough value and time;

- Lacking the courage to enter into the cyclical process of taking risks, suffering defeats, and taking more risks; and

- Reluctance to obtain help and guidance in integrating one's less-conscious psychological functions.

To overcome these obstacles, both the client and the consultant must affirm and appreciate what their consciousness has negated. Consultants are often tempted to show results quickly by using existing organizational frameworks for "understanding" and "solving" a problem (Smith and Berg 1987), when they actually need to explore the links between the polarities in the client's unconscious as well as their own.

To bring forth aspects of the deeper unconscious, consultants must ask questions such as: "What were things like in the origin of this group?" "What are the things we believe about ourselves?" "What gifts do you bring to the group?" "What would be deemed blasphemies in the organization?" "What will we be two years from now?" By asking such questions consultants can build a bridge to understanding. By surfacing and affirming the polarities in themselves and in their clients, consultants can help stir and harness the energy of the transcendent function to transform organizational struggles into new ways of perceiving and thinking (Bernstein 1989).

This article illustrates the integration of unconscious aspects in individuals and groups. When working at the organization level—as in work redesign efforts—consultants can bring direct attention to unconscious phenomena by facilitating dialogue between members of diverse parts of the organization. They can surface and sustain the tension between opposing values in the organization until new structures emerge—if the clash of opposites has not been destructive and if organization members have not come to identify totally with one of the opposing positions (Bernstein 1989).

Jung used the word *temenos* to describe the psychological container shaped by the analyst and client during analysis which respected the unconscious processes, confidentiality, and trust required to foster transformation (Samuels 1986). Analogous psychological (and perhaps physical) boundaries need to be created in the life of groups and organizations to foster an active imagination process. The T-groups used in many of NTL Institute's workshops are good examples of creating a container in which confidence and trust can build. Some quality circles or self-managed work groups may be another example.

The transcendent function can operate wherever conflict and tension exist between opposing sides of a polarity. Because organizations are growing increasingly multicultural with respect to race, gender, age, ethnicity, and religious affiliation, polarities are expected to increase. The paradoxical tensions at multiple horizontal and vertical levels—within and among the consultant, the manager, the group, the organization—significantly increase the opportunities for these polarities to emerge. Such opportunities are essential to our tasks of individual individuation and organization development for which the transcendent function, when activated, will gradually do its work.

References

Bernstein, J. S. 1989. *Power and Politics: The Psychology of Soviet-American Partnership*. Boston: Shambhala.

Bion, W. R. 1959. *Experiences in Groups*. London: Tavistock.

Bolen, J. S. 1984. *Goddesses in Everywoman: A New Psychology of Women*. San Francisco: Harper and Row.

———. 1989. *Gods in Everyman: A New Psychology of Men's Lives and Loves*. San Francisco: Harper and Row.

Bridges, W. 1980. *Transitions: Making Sense of Life's Changes*. Reading, Mass.: Addison-Wesley.

Dallett, J. 1982. Active imagination in practice. In *Jungian Analysis*, M. Stein, ed. LaSalle, Ill.: Open Court, pp. 173–191.

Diamond, M. A. 1986. Resistance to change: A psychoanalytic critique of Argyris and Schon's contributions to organization theory and intervention. *Journal of Management Studies* 23(5):543–562.

Gersick, C. J. G. 1988. Time and transition in work teams: Toward a new model of group development. *Academy of Management Review* 31(1):9–41.

Gillette, J., and McCollom, M. 1990. *Groups in Context: A New Perspective on Group Dynamics*. Reading, Mass.: Addison-Wesley.

Goodrich-Dunn, B. 1989. The conscious feminine. *Common Boundary* (March-April), pp. 10–17.

Gurevitch, Z. D. 1989. The power of not understanding: The meeting of conflicting identities. *Journal of Applied Behavioral Science* 25(2):161–174.

Hall, J. A. 1986. *The Jungian Experience: Analysis and Individuation*. Toronto: Inner City Books.

Hirschhorn, L. 1988. *The Workplace Within: Psychodynamics of Organizational Life*. Cambridge, Mass.: MIT Press.

Humbert, E. 1988. *C. G. Jung: The Fundamentals of Theory and Practice*. Wilmette, Ill.: Chiron.

Jaffe, L. W. 1990. *Liberating the Heart: Spirituality and Jungian Psychology*. Toronto: Inner City Books.

Johnson, R. A. 1987. *Ecstasy: Understanding the Psychology of Joy*. San Francisco: Harper and Row.

Jung, C. G. 1916. The transcendent function. In *CW*, 8:67–91. New York: Pantheon.

_____. C. G. 1921. *Psychological Types. CW*, vol. 6. Princeton, N.J.: Princeton University Press, 1971.

_____. C. G. 1973. *Letters*, 2 vols. Princeton, N.J.: Princeton University Press.

Katz, G. A. 1983. The noninterpretation of metaphors in psychiatric hospital groups. *International Journal of Group Psychotherapy* 33(1):53–67.

Kets de Vries, M. F. R., and Miller, D. 1984. *The Neurotic Organization*. San Francisco: Jossey-Bass.

Kets de Vries, M. F. R. 1989. *Prisoners of Leadership*. New York: John Wiley.

Levy, A., and Merry, U. 1986. *Organizational Transformation: Approaches, Strategies, Theories*. New York: Praeger.

McAfee, R. B., and Champagne, P. J. 1987. *Organizational Behavior: A Manager's View*. St. Paul: West Publishing Co.

McWhinney, W., and Batista, J. 1988. How remythologizing can revitalize organizations. *Organizational Dynamics* 17(2):46–58.

Moore, N. 1975. The transcendent function and the forming ego. *Journal of Analytic Psychology* 20(2):164–182.

Morgan, G. 1986. *Images of Organization*. Newbury Park, Calif.: Sage.

Powell, S. 1985. A bridge to understanding: The transcendent function in the analyst. *Journal of Analytical Psychology* 30(1):29–45.

Samuels, A. 1986. *A Critical Dictionary of Jungian Analysis*. London: Routledge and Kegan Paul.

Schein, E. 1989. Conversation with Edgar H. Schein by Fred Luthans. *Organizational Dynamics* 17(Spring):60–76.

Sharp, D. 1988. *The Survival Papers: Anatomy of a Midlife Crisis*. Toronto: Inner City Books.

Singer, J., and Loomis, M. 1984. *Interpretative Guide for the Singer-Loomis Inventory of Personality*. Palo Alto, Calif.: Consulting Psychologists Press.

Smith, K. 1989. The movement of conflict in organizations: The joint dynamics of splitting and triangulation. *Administrative Science Quarterly* 34(March):1–20.

Smith, K., and Berg, D. N. 1987. *Paradoxes of Group Life.* San Francisco: Jossey-Bass.

Stein, J. O., and Stein, M. 1987. Psychotherapy, initiation, and the midlife crisis. In *Betwixt & Between: Patterns of Masculine and Feminine Initiation.* L. C. Mahdi, S. Foster, and M. Little, eds. LaSalle, Ill.: Open Court.

Stevens, A. 1982. *Archetypes.* London: Routledge and Kegan Paul.

Sullwold, E. 1979. Mysteries of change. *Spring* 47(92).

Vaill, P. B. 1988. *Appreciating Organizational Spirit.* Paper presented at the Symposium on Executive Appreciation, Case Western Reserve University, Cleveland, Ohio.

Williams, S. K. 1984. *The Practice of Personal Transformation: A Jungian Approach.* Berkeley, Calif.: Journey.

Wilmer, H. A. 1987. *Practical Jung: Nuts and Bolts of Jungian Psychotherapy.* Wilmette, Ill.: Chiron.

Yandell, J. 1987. Wasting time—the something of nothing. *Psychological Perspectives* 18(1):82–97.

Edwin E. Olson, *Ph.D., is an organization development consultant and therapist in the Baltimore-Washington, D.C., area. He is a former professor of information science, management, and organization behavior. He has written numerous articles on organizational change. His current work focuses on team development and issues of quality and diversity in organizations.*

Toward a Theory of the Self in the Group

Medora Scoll Perlman

Most organizational life happens in groups as people at all levels come together to plan, organize, carry out, and review the work of the organization. To outsiders or those unfamiliar with organizations, the work group's persona appear in glossy annual reports, everyone sitting around the table smiling. To insiders and consultants, the picture is quite different. Meetings of work groups are frequently full of conflict, frustrating, boring, inefficient, and ineffective. For every few moments of productive task orientation, there seem to be many of wandering irrelevancy, time-consuming and unresolved arguments, frustrating failure to bring the group to meaningful consensus or closure.

To examine psyche at work, therefore, requires attention to the problems of psyche in groups, and to attempt to penetrate the mysteries of group behavior, it is necessary to develop hypotheses about the nature of group unconscious life. The Jungian analytical perspective would seem to be a natural source of such hypotheses, yet it is hard to ignore Jung's attitude, and that of many Jungians, toward group life.

> The bigger the group, the more the individuals composing it function as a collective entity, which is so powerful that it can reduce individual consciousness to the point of extinction, and it does this the more easily if the individual lacks spiritual possessions of his own with an individual stamp. The group and what belongs to it cover up the lack of genuine individuality, just as parents act as substitutes for everything lacking in their children. In this respect the group exerts a seductive influence, for nothing is easier than a perseveration of infantile ways or a return to them. (Jung 1959, par. 891)

This passage describes group life as a threat to individual consciousness, arguing that the pull toward group life is only the pull of infantile regression. Jung's attitude, as expressed in this passage and many others like it, has kept many Jungians from exploring collective psyche. Yet individuals in our society increasingly work in groups; large organizations composed of groups are a reality of modern life. In fact, much of the work of the world is done in groups.

Other depth psychologists, while often sharing Jung's perspective, have used principles of depth psychology to explore group psychic life. One such approach is group relations theory, embodying the work of Bion, British psychoanalyst and follower of Klein. Bion and others present a powerful picture of the pathology of group psychic life. It is the thesis of this paper that they have made a significant contribution to our understanding of group unconscious life, but that their vision, as was Jung's, is limited by biases about group life which originate in a view of the world which may be described as patriarchal.[1] To reframe Bion's creative insight, using the perspective of Jungian psychology, and examine the unconscious assumptions of group relations theorists allows us to see not just the pathology but the positive potential of the phenomena he describes, with the hope of liberating the creative power of the group.

In examining group life, Bion (1959) attempted to work phenomenologically, unencumbered by theoretical frameworks. He theorized that in every group assembled for a purpose there simultaneously exist two groups, one, the work group, and another, which he named the basic assumption group (the Ba-group). The work group, task-oriented, cooperative, mature, and rational, has the characteristics Freud attributed to the ego. The second group, the basic assumption group, produced by powerful emotional

---

[1]While the terms *masculine/feminine* or *matriarchy/patriarchy* are used to describe the contrast in worldviews that is now being so widely explored, neither they nor any others are totally satisfactory. Eisler (1987), for example, incorporates the ideas of domination and partnership in her terms *andocracy*, describing a society characterized by domination by men, and *gylany*, describing a society in which the sexes are linked rather than ranked in a domination hierarchy (as opposed to what she calls actualization hierarchies). For purposes of this paper, and recognizing the difficulties involved in choosing any of the available alternatives, I will use the term *patriarchy* to describe a worldview which comes out of a Western cultural history dominated by men and ways of seeing, thinking, evaluating, and behaving that are rooted in the archetypes of masculinity and the father rather than those of femininity and the mother, as those archetypes have been experienced and understood in that culture.

forces, exists as a shared fantasy in the minds of the individuals in the group. Bion and his followers extensively document several varieties of Ba-group behavior, generally characterized by high levels of anxiety, rapid shifts in direction, and an inability to focus on or accomplish a task or consistently to follow leadership as it emerges in the group.

Bion and his followers argue that individuals experience the group in fantasy as the mother, at the point in infant development where the maternal image is unstable. The individual regresses to the paranoid/schizoid position described by Klein and the primitive defenses associated with that position, primarily splitting and projective identification.[2] When Klein describes the splitting that characterizes the paranoid/schizoid position, she is hypothesizing that the infant handles the conflict engendered by experiencing the mother as both good, that is, loving and nurturing, and bad, that is, inevitably associated with discomfort, frustration, and pain, by splitting her into two mothers and clinging to the good one. With normal development, the infant synthesizes the good and bad aspects of the mother image, learning that people can be loved in spite of their faults, that the world is not all black or white. Klein asserts that each of us carries remnants of that primitive psychological state, ready to be reexperienced when conditions are right (Klein 1959). The group relations theorists hold that when the group exhibits Ba-group behavior, the members of the group have regressed psychologically to the stage Klein describes as paranoid/schizoid and are resorting to the psychic defense mechanisms of that stage.

Eishold (1985), a group relations theorist, reframes Bion's conclusions from the perspective of later developments in psychoanalytic theory.

---

[2]*Projective identification* is a term first introduced by Klein in 1946 to describe the following sequence of events in an infant: first the infant employs the defense mechanism of splitting to keep "good" internal objects (the loving parts of the self) separate and safe from the "bad" internal objects (the aggressive parts of the self); then the infant experiences the split-off objects as being lodged in someone else; and finally the infant feels intimately bound up with, identified with, the recipient of these projections, needing to feel close to the overidealized other in the case of "good" projections or needing to stay in contact with or control the other, in the case of "bad" projections. The recipient of these projections feels coerced into playing a role that fits with the projections of the projecting other (Gorkin 1987).

The problem thus is one of adaptation, establishing emotional contact with the group members, an adaptation that cannot take place without regression because we lack other means of relating to an aggregate. . . . To put it crudely, the group is mother, but before mother was experienced as a person entirely distinct from other significant members of the family constellation . . . with this recollected object world to draw upon from the depths of early experience, the person wishing to join the group can perceive the group as a group and he can hope for the condition of being joined to it. (Eishold 1985, 39)

The regression and accompanying anxiety can also be accounted for as arising from the disintegration of the psychic structures in the ego and superego. The self image begins to come apart under the influence of regressive object ties, posing continual threats to self-esteem; members become vulnerable to confusion, embarrassment, and shame. In addition, the effort that the ego always makes to integrate its self-image with its ideals and actual behavior, and reality with fantasy and impulse, cannot be sustained in the group setting. This experience gives rise to a panic coming out of a faltering, disintegrating self losing its very capacity to right itself (Eishold 1985).

From either perspective, group members are experiencing very painful feelings, particularly associated with their desire to belong, and feeling their usual adult capacities to be unavailable to them. Patterns of group behavior begin to emerge as members assume roles in the group, particularly leadership roles, becoming "real" objects for the group members, in order to limit, momentarily, "the chaotic turbulence of infantile fantasy" (Eishold 1985, p. 40). Each individual will have a certain innate psychological predisposition, Bion calls it "valency," which will determine the individual's readiness to enter into combination with the group in making and acting on basic assumptions (Rioch 1975b). For example, a member will have a valency toward being a leader on whom the group wants to depend, or a leader that will lead the group in fleeing from the task, perhaps a scapegoat, an obstructor, or a soother, all depending on the power of the group's unconscious fantasies and the member's capacity to be sucked into the necessary role.

Group relations training, based largely on Bion's theories, began in 1957 in a two-week residential conference organized by the Centre for Applied Social Research of the Tavistock Institute of London and the University of Leicester. In 1965 the approach was transplanted to U.S. soil with a Group Relations Conference sponsored by the Washington School of Psychiatry, the Yale University Department of Psychiatry, and the Tavistock Institute (Rioch 1975a). Events based on what is now called the Tavistock group model vary, but the model utilizes essentially large and small study groups. The task of the groups, in the classic model, is always the same, to study the behavior of the group as a group in the here-and-now (Rice 1975).

Groups are staffed by consultants, who comment on the behavior of the group to the members. The consultant establishes time and space boundaries, entering the meeting room and stating the task of the group at the precise moment when the group is scheduled to begin and leaving the room at the moment the group is scheduled to end. Otherwise, during the time the group is scheduled, the consultant sits with a neutral expression, not responding to any comments or questions directed to her, and offering comments, sometimes metaphorically, on the behavior of the group as a whole, not on or to individuals.

The participants have come to the conference to learn about group behavior and their own leadership behavior in groups. The task of the group is to produce group behavior and to study that behavior. What surprises the participant who comes to the experience without prior knowledge is how profoundly distressing it is. The task is paradoxical, the participants are strangers who don't know or trust each other, stripped of their outside identities by the requirement that the group stay in the "here and now." If, as Bion theorizes, entering into group life involves a profound regression under any circumstances, these threatening circumstances create an even more profound regression. The consultant in the classic model is strictly enjoined from alleviating the anxiety produced; participants are deliberately left to struggle with it on their own. Under the circumstances, massive amounts of basic assumption behavior are reliably produced.

The individuals involved in a Tavistock study group feel the powerful feelings of anger, sadness, abandonment, envy, competitiveness, and fear of retaliation associated with Klein's paranoid/schizoid position. Group members split off unacceptable feelings, and other group members, according to their own tendencies, become seized by the projections and act out members' split-off feelings, frequently to be scapegoated or taken care of by the group. The group members' need to defend against the anxiety precipitated by this infantile regression, by creating a leader and conditions of safety, creates the group phenomena that Bion describes (Eishold 1985, Gustafson and Cooper 1985).

Eishold hails Bion's "binocular vision" of the group, the understanding that one eye has to be trained on the surface, where the group acts as an assortment of individual and uncooperative group members, and the other on the group purpose, the level on which nothing is more important than the need to belong, as "an unparalleled contribution to the understanding of group life" (Eishold 1985, p. 43). "That . . . the regressive perception of the group as a maternal entity allows the group to be perceived as a collective entity that can be joined . . . is a point that has impressed many subsequent theorists" (ibid.). Eishold modifies Bion's vision by that of later object-relations theorists who see the infant as gradually able to organize a sense of a good maternal object as well as a bad one out of recurring fragments of experience. Thus, in their regression, group members have access to both good and bad objects.

From the perspective of Jungian psychology, what the group relations theorists describe as regression could be reframed as an inevitable constellation of each group member's mother and child complexes. Those complexes are composed of each group member's personal history of mothering and childhood, as well as the archetypal mother and child. Group members will tend to experience either the good mother or the bad mother pole of the archetype, since they are regressed to a stage of development where the capacity to integrate the poles of the archetype consistently into an inner image of the real mother has not yet developed, what Klein calls the paranoid/schizoid position.

Another way of looking at what the group relations theorists describe is to focus on the group members' need to belong. The need to belong is one of the most fundamental human needs. As the group relations theorists see it, the act of joining a group triggers memories of the first and most profound experience of belonging, that of the earliest relationship to the mother, with all of its primal yearnings and fears, as well as the defenses against those fears. Or, as Whitmont (1961) puts it, from the Jungian perspective, the group numen, because of its encompassing aspect, is the numen of containment in the mother.

Jung and the group relations theorists paint a bleak picture of group psychic life. The emotional life of the group is chaotic and powerful; members suffer a loss of boundaries as they are buffeted by the group's emotional currents. Anxieties about belonging needs are triggered, producing painful fears of attack and abandonment. The adult selfhood a member brings to the group seems to disintegrate. The group looms as a powerful entity, threatening to overwhelm the member's individuality. From this perspective, uniqueness and creativity are at risk in a group. Many writers talk about being hopelessly torn between the need to belong and the fear of annihilation of the self, as Eishold does here.

> Society is an association of diverse groups and our need to belong to at least some of these groups is as profound as our need to sleep and dream. And yet, what we give up to belong! Some of us have more to give up than others, to be sure— certainly from the perspective of society that stands to lose precious contributions of wisdom. We cannot evade the dilemma involved in joining. (Eishold 1985, p. 48)

This view of the vicissitudes of group psychic life is seriously flawed in its one-sided focus. For example, Eishold notes that both good and bad maternal images are available to members but assumes that bad mother experiences predominate. He rejects the idea that as group members regress to the earliest experiences of mother the group can become a good maternal image, fostering a sense of basic trust. He sees only an impossible dilemma.

But must we make the painful choice between belonging and being ourselves that Eishold poses? The way Jung and the group relations theorists answer that question, in fact, the very "either-or" way that they frame it, comes out of certain assumptions about what it means to be an individual, a self, and how selfhood is achieved. The insight of Bion and others that the group evokes at an unconscious level the personal and archetypal mother is powerfully influenced by our cultural assumptions about selfhood and mothering, which are inextricably mixed together. Because mother is our first and most powerful experience of the feminine, patriarchal attitudes toward the feminine play a key role in shaping the perspective expressed in their writings.

At this moment in history, our ideas about selfhood and how it is attained are being reexamined. We are realizing that the patriarchal view of the self which has dominated our thinking is only one view. A basic premise of this view is that selfhood requires separation. Selfhood begins with separation from mother and continues with defining oneself as separate from others and from the natural world. As feminist theologian Keller (1986) points out, the assumption that selfhood requires separation is rooted in language: "The Latin for 'self,' *se*, meaning 'on one's own,' yields with *parare* ('to prepare') the verb 'to separate.' For our culture it is separation which prepares the way for selfhood" (p. 1).

Selfhood, in this view, is centered around what Whitmont (1984) calls the "heroic ego," which values consciousness over the unconscious, order over chaos, individuality rather than the collective, one god rather than many, one way of seeing things rather than a plurality. As Whitmont suggests, the archetype dominating this view is that of the hero. Separation is essential to the hero's quest for self, described by Campbell (1949) as essentially of one fundamental pattern "separation–initiation–return" (p. 30).

The hero must accomplish his great deeds alone, returning to the collective, the group, only to bestow the boons he has won in his solitary quest. The assumptions underlying this archetypal pattern are those which dominate the writings of Jung and the group relations theorists: that the individual can individuate only alone; that the fruits of one's creativity can be bestowed on the collective, but only after they have been won in solitary effort.[3] From this perspective groups are not creative, only individuals are, and the individual risks loss of individuality and selfhood whenever he associates with a group. As Colman describes it, the most important moment for the group member comes when he breaks free of the group

> The individual after gradually becoming immersed in the group and feeling himself powerfully wedded to the group corpus, suddenly breaks free from this group consciousness with an accompanying acute, exhilarating sense of his own uniqueness and originality. Such experiences often have mystical or spiritual overtones; the individual is discovering and creating himself for the first time. (Colman 1975, p. 42)

But, something more than an imperative to separation is operating in this perspective. There is anguish involved in this separation, a sense of something terribly lost, of being on the horns of an impossible and deeply painful dilemma. We need to belong, says Eishold, as surely as we need to sleep and dream, yet, what we give up to belong! As Turquet (1985) describes it, the individual leaving the group faces "loss of a sense of unity, cohesiveness, camaraderie, or being part of something bigger than himself . . . to meet loneliness and isolation, to face alone Camus's

---

[3]While Jung protests otherwise in his writings, saying that it is not possible to individuate in isolation, it is clear that he does not mean that it is possible to individuate in or with what he calls "the collective," rather that individuation is always a process of claiming one's unique self in opposition to the pulls of the collective, which would always tend to make the individual like everyone else.

'Absurdo,' to know things that cannot be shared" (p. 86), but the alternative to that loss is death in the group, as a nonconforming group member, as a failed leader, or by abandonment.

If, as the group relations theorists and others have discovered, group membership triggers early and powerful feelings associated with the first experience of belonging, the mother, and it is that archetypal image which dominates the experiences of the members and the group psychic field, then it becomes clear that the archetypal image informing the work of the group relations theorists is that of the wrenching, irrevocable separation from mother which the patriarchal ego assumes to be the *sine qua non* for growth as an individual. But is it?

At this point it becomes necessary to consider what Keller says about the patriarchal idea of the separate self, that from the vantage point of an ego bent on separation and preeminence, the mother must be killed, that "separation and sexism have functioned together as the most fundamental self-shaping assumptions of our culture" (p. 2). For heroism and matricide are inextricably linked together in our cultural imagination, beginning with the ancient fragments of the Babylonian creation myth in which the hero, Marduk, kills and dismembers the mother, Tiamat, forming the world from her flesh (Jung 1956, par. 646). The little boy forming his masculine identity must not only push away from the outer mother, he must destroy the vestiges of her inside him and all that which would link him to her, his belonging and dependency needs, his vulnerability, his weakness, his softness. To do otherwise, in a culture which denigrates and devalues those needs associated with the mother and the feminine, would be to forfeit his place in the world of men.

Depth psychology tells us that what is pushed out of consciousness goes into the unconscious, where it remains in threatening and destructive form. As Campbell says, describing the hero Perseus's slaying of Medusa:

> Mother Nature, Mother Eve, Mother Mistress-of-the World is there to be dealt with all the time, and the more sternly she is cut down, the more frightening will her Gorgoneum be. This may cause her matricidal son to achieve a lot of extremely spectacular escape work; but, oh, my! What a Sheol he will know—and yet not know—within, where his paradise should have been. (1965, p. 153)

The group relations theorists come down firmly on the side of the mature, task-oriented work group, the group equivalent of the heroic ego. Belonging needs, needs for nurturing and support, needs for connection are all described as characteristic of members of the Ba-group; the group in which members experience and act on, and act out, those needs is labeled as regressed and infantile. The more those needs are denigrated by consultants to study groups, the more they are pushed into the purgatory of Ba-group life, the more they threaten to rise up and overwhelm the group and the individuals in it, who flee from the group rather than face, in Turquet's terms, death at the hands of the group. The more needs and feelings threaten to overwhelm the group, the greater the need to repress them, to insist that the group focus on its task. For, in the world of the heroic ego, the task is everything; needs and feelings only get in the way.

> One of the major aims of the conferences is to contribute to people's ability to form serious work groups committed to the performance of clearly defined tasks. Whether or not members of such groups feel friendliness, warmth, closeness, competitiveness, or hostility to each other is of secondary importance. It is assumed that these and other feelings will occur from time to time, but this is not the issue. (Rioch 1975a, p. 9)

The group relations theorists express the predominant worldview of the patriarchy which has been difficult to challenge, for "with a worldview one just sees; one does not challenge the eyes with which one sees" (Keller 1986, p. 2), but, particularly in the last twenty-five years, feminist writers argue that the patriarchal view sees only half the world. The patriarchal developmental litany intones the celebration of separation, autonomy, and individuation, but it is supported by the invisible but essential context of connection, protected by the feminine recognition of the ongoing importance of relationship in the male life cycle (Gilligan 1982). Women have carried men's basic needs for belonging, for affiliation, those needs too dangerous to carry in consciousness for a male in the patriarchy (Miller 1976). In reality, relationship and self are unimaginable without each other. "We know ourselves as separate only insofar as we live in connection with others, and . . . we experience relationship only insofar as we differentiate other from self" (Gilligan 1982, p. 63).

Why must we choose between self and relationship, between belonging and being ourselves? Is there another perspective from which to view that relationship of mother and child, that relationship evoked so powerfully in groups? True, it is necessary for the developing child of either sex to differentiate from mother, more so for the boy than the girl, but freed of the patriarchal imperative to repress all of his inner feminine, would the male child's differentiation need to be so matricidal? It may be hard to know with any certainty at this post-Industrial Revolution time in our history, when, as Bly (Bly and Thompson 1985) points out, fathers have become so absent during the early childhood period. Chodorow (1978) asserts that in a male-dominant culture with relatively absent fathers a boy feels that in order to attain independence and masculine self-identification he must overcome fundamental feelings of dependence, overwhelming attachment, and merging with his mother, developed during the intensive and exclusive early years, a task made more difficult in many cases by his mother's desire to seek in her relationship with her son an emotional bond which is missing in her relationship with his father.

But some of those who study child development are suggesting that if we see self and relationship as existing and developing simultaneously, rather than as opposite ends of a polarity, a very different picture of development emerges. Infant psychiatrist Stern (1985) argues, contrary to prevailing theories which hold that the infant spends his early months in a state of merger with the mother, that a sense of an "emergent" self is present at birth, that infants are "predestined to be aware of self organizing processes" (p. 10). Furthermore, each stage in the development of a sense of self takes place in the context of a corresponding domain of relatedness, "as new behaviors and capacities emerge, they are reorganized to form organizing perspectives on self and other" (p. 26). "Each new sense of self defines the formation of a new domain of relatedness" (p. 34). Thus the development of self is seen as occurring within the context of relationship.

Similarly, the psychologists at the Stone Center at Wellesley look at the mother-daughter relationship as the existing model for a theory of relationship as the basis for self-experience and development, arguing that there is no inherent need to disconnect or sacrifice relationship for self-development (Surrey 1984). Through the development of mutual empathy and mutual empowerment, the mother-daughter dyad attends to the well-being of each other and the relationship between them. The notion of "separation-individuation" is replaced with a notion of "relationship-differentiation," "a process which encompasses increasing levels of complexity, choice, fluidity and articulation within the context of human relationship" (Surrey 1984, p. 8). The Stone Center psychologists call this relational experience of self "self-in-relationship."

Following the lead of the Stone Center psychologists, what might we become aware of if we understand the self and the group to be simultaneously developing experiences, what we might call the self-in-the-group? Bion and the group relations theorists have demonstrated quite convincingly the presence of the "bad" mother in the group and the impact of her presence on group behavior, but perhaps her presence is assured by the techniques used by Bion and consultants in Tavistock study groups. Perhaps these particular kinds of interventions are utilized by consultants to Tavistock groups because of unconscious patriarchal assumptions about mothering and the feminine. If, instead, we explore the possibility that self and relationship are mutually enhancing rather than mutually exclusive, if we acknowledge the legitimacy of needs for support, belonging, and nurturing, then the archetypal mother and child in the group could open up new creative possibilities, rather than closing them down. Then the fact that the mother is inevitably constellated in the group could become an opportunity rather than a curse. If the presence of the good mother in the group were encouraged, the resulting child could become not childishness, not infantile behavior, but something entirely different.

> The "child" is born out of the womb of the unconscious, begotten out of the depths of human nature, or rather out of living Nature herself. It is a personification of vital forces quite outside the limited range of our conscious mind; of ways and possibilities of which our one-sided conscious mind knows nothing; a wholeness which embraces the very depths of Nature. (Jung 1951, par. 289)

When groups are at their best, they become more than any one individual in the group could become. They bring together all the knowledge, experience, and talents of their diverse constituent members to produce fresh creative ideas, new energy which vitalizes the group and the members of it. Those creative solutions, that new energy, is the hoped-for result every time a work group comes together. New possibilities come not out of the assembled egos, but from some place quite beyond ego control. Such results cannot be produced on demand, they come only as the result of a process, a process that cannot be regulated, only nurtured and facilitated. To realize the birth of the child that is always potential in a group requires the mother.

What does the good mother in the group look like? While the group relations theorists often see only the presence of the bad mother in the group, one significant exception is the work of Gustafson and Cooper (1985). In a paper entitled "Collaboration in Small Groups: Theory and Technique for the Study of Small-Group Processes," Gustafson and Cooper argue that groups will exhibit either phenomena consequent to conditions of scarcity, in which case the group members will participate in the regressive experiences described earlier in this paper, or phenomena consequent to conditions of safety, in which case the group members are able to participate in the free flow of illusion necessary for learning about group life. Since Bion developed his theories, psychoanalysts have learned something about how to foster collaboration between analyst and patient. The provision of an adequate "holding environment," involving the physical arrangements of the room and the analyst's calm and understanding, are now assumed to be necessary for the patient to tolerate the painful exploration of old injuries and be willing to learn from exploring them and the fantasies that arise in the analytic setting. To be fruitful, study groups require their members to be willing to immerse themselves in fantasy about the group, to involve themselves in painful archaic relationships for purposes of study. Given the maternal nature of the necessary holding environment required by the group members' regression to infantile states, nothing is more traumatic than abandonment or intrusion, what the authors describe as the cardinal characteristics of the bad mother. They view Bion's interventions, as he himself describes them, as abandonment and intrusion errors, which, in their experience, lead to basic assumption groups "of great tenacity," group dispersion, or group rebellion (Gustafson and Cooper 1985, p. 145).

Gustafson and Cooper cite the work of Balint in working with groups of doctors meeting to discuss patients as establishing that group members will have "the courage of their own stupidity" in the group, feeling supported by the other members, if the leader is able to establish the right conditions of safety. Balint explains that collaborative group norms follow from the leader's behavior in allowing everyone to be themselves, to have their own say in their own way and in their own time, with the leader speaking only when something is really expected of him and, instead of prescribing the right way to deal with the problem under discussion, opening up possibilities for group members to discover the right answer. The authors also cite the work of Freire in his *Pedagogy of the Oppressed* (1970), who describes a problem-posing technique used in Latin America with rural peasants in order to avoid imposing on them an urban "director culture" which, in defining the terms of communication, results in complete suppression of their own experience. This approach avoids intrusion; the primary emphasis is placed on the group members' communication of their own reality.

The collaborative study group model proposed by Gustafson and Cooper seems to be one in which the consultant consciously takes on the "holding environment" attributes of the good mother, not intruding on the group's process, yet not abandoning the members, either. If "conditions of safety" can be analogized to the presence of the good mother and "conditions of scarcity" to the presence of the bad mother, then their work suggests that the capacity of group members to be productively collaborative will be profoundly influenced by the nature of the archetypal mother present in the group field.

How can this idea be translated into terms useful to those who work with groups in organizations? One possibility is to see the containing presence of the mother as either carried by the leader, whether male or female, or by group members themselves, depending on the nature of the group. All groups need the environmental aspects of mothering, attention to details about convening the group in an orderly way, a place and time conducive to facilitating attention to the group's process, adequate supplies, fundamental creature comforts. Mature groups composed of experienced members may need little more in the way of good mother from the leader, if the group norm is for each member to treat other members', their own, and the group's process with respect, that is, each group member takes responsibility for keeping the good mother present in the group.[4] The less experienced and mature the group, the more the good mother will be required from a leader, with the least experienced and least knowledgeable

---

[4]A fundamental attribute of the good mother is empathy. Mutual empathy in dyadic relationships and in groups involves the experiences of feeling seen by the other, seeing the other, and experiencing the other as feeling seen (Surrey 1984). For the good mother to be present, it is crucial that group members feel supported enough to be willing to share their own reality, experience having their reality accepted, and be able to accept the reality of others.

groups requiring, in addition, some good father, in the sense of teaching and assistance with the task.

Even so, in the work group environment, as in the study group environment, group psychic life is still going to be chaotic, powerful feelings and acting out behaviors are still going to occur, for if the group relations theorists are correct in suggesting that the group inevitably triggers the primitive psychological states of early infancy, the presence of the good mother can help contain and mitigate these chaotic psychological states but cannot make them go away. Traditionally, the primary means of dealing with these disruptive phenomena has been to respond out of a patriarchal model of leadership, analogous to that of the heroic ego subduing the unruly unconscious, which may restore order, but seriously limits the possibilities that the group's process will produce the hoped-for child, for it is only when the ego relinquishes its iron control that unconscious can produce its treasures.

Here, again, it appears that looking through a patriarchal lens limits our appreciation for the potential of group psychic life. Jung and the group relations theorists agree that the individual experiences the chaos of group psychic life as threatening and potentially destructive. All the descriptions of group psychopathology emphasize similar elements, the tug of "infantile" needs to belong and the fears of abandonment, the threat to one's valued adult identity and ego adaptation, the fear of loss of boundaries and one's sense of separate selfhood, the painful and disruptive feelings that are experienced. The patriarchal response to this threatening chaos is either to flee, denying powerful belonging needs but preserving individuality by not joining the group, or to join and try to impose order in the patriarchal model. Still another approach would be to suggest that it is precisely the chaotic and psychologically primitive aspects of group psychic life, perhaps its very assault on one's boundaried sense of self, which holds the group's most creative potential.

The patriarchal view holds that consciousness is something confined within each individual's skin, but as we explore other realities that patriarchal vision has cut off, it seems clear that the boundaries of the self are far more permeable than the heroic ego has wanted to admit. We have learned from psychoanalysis that individuals in intimate dyadic relationships share conscious and unconscious psychic life. We can describe that shared psychic life in terms of projective identification, introjection and identification, or transference and countertransference, which is a way of seeing psychic reality as somehow being transferred back and forth between two people with separate bounded psyches. Or we can say that a psychic field both in and between two people is created and experienced in the psyches of both people.

Bion saw that such an interactive field is created in group life, but only its negative destructive effects. The work of Schwartz-Salant (1989), who combines both Jungian and Kleinian perspectives, suggests a possible revisioning of Bion's work. Schwartz-Salant brings together Klein's theory of projective identification and Jung's "Psychology of the Transference," which, he asserts, is centrally about the phenomenon Klein is describing. He suggests that while Jung often saw the negative side of projective identification, such as confusion, panic, and identity loss, he was also aware of the positive side. Projective identification breaks down the ego's usual sense of boundaried separateness and moves psychic life into a wholly different realm.

Schwartz-Salant describes an imaginal and symbolic approach to the psychic field that arises in the treatment of patients with borderline personality disorders. Since from a Kleinian perspective the borderline patient is one who has failed to negotiate the paranoid/schizoid stage successfully, his work has implications for group psyche, since group members are described by the group relations theorists as being at the same developmental stage as the borderline patient. The imaginal realm Schwartz-Salant describes as the one entered into by analyst and borderline patient may also be the one entered into by individuals in groups.

Schwartz-Salant asserts that the operation of projective identification in the interaction between analyst and patient breaks down the normal sense of ego separation and involves both participants in experiences that take place in a third area, neither inside nor outside the two individuals, where notions of location and spatial consideration cease to be relevant, an area whose processes can only be perceived by the eye of the imagination. He describes this space as a transitional area between the space–time world (where processes are characterized as an interaction of objects) and the collective unconscious. This space is the subtle-body area, entered through the mechanism of projective identification, that links ego consciousness with the world of the archetypes. He suggests, citing Comfort, that the dominant quality of this realm is relatedness. Linking Schwartz-Salant's work to that of the group relations theorists, it appears that group psychic life in its very nature plunges its members into this realm, and the relational image that dominates this realm in group psychic life is that of the mother and child.

Looking from Schwartz-Salant's imaginal perspective, what Bion and the other group relations theorists regard as the regressive aspects of group life, the presence of the archetypal mother and child—the use of projective identification and other defenses, and the shared group fantasies—actually holds the promise of creative renewal from connection with the archetypal world. To see this potential in a group, again, requires a shift from the patriarchal perspective, to which we are so accustomed, to one that values chaos and disorder as harbingers of a new order. Jungian psychology tells us that for the individual to develop increasing consciousness, to integrate material which has been hitherto unconscious, it is necessary to break down old psychic structures to let in the new material arising from the unconscious. The process is never neat and linear; on the contrary, it is painful and disruptive, and the ego experiences that process as a defeat.

Schwartz-Salant's work suggests that this border realm brings renewal from contact with archetypal energies and that, in fact, other cultures have recognized that possibility and deliberately sought it out.

> The "border" has existed in myths of many cultures. It is the area in the psyche where the ego's orientation begins to fail and where powerful forces, over which one may have little control, constellate. . . . The Egyptians were conscious of the importance of the demonic qualities that raged at the "borders" and created fear and confusion. In fact, they initiated processes at the "border" for the renewal of Osiris, even though these "borderline" processes were the very ones that destroyed the principle of life and order. . . . They were able to recognize the paradoxically renewing nature of what appear to be the most destructive states of mind. (Schwartz-Salant 1989, pp. 9–11)

The work of Bion and his followers points the way to seeing the chaotic experience of group psyche as a source of renewal for individuals, as Colman describes the individual being born from the group matrix, as well as a source of renewal for the collective. What may be a departure for Jungian psychology is to suggest that we need, when acting collectively, to form a relationship with the Self-in-the-group. Jungian psychology asserts the necessity for ego and Self to be in a mutually interdependent relationship with each other in the individual psyche, with the individual ego required to act in the world in response to the enigmatic urgings of the Self. To frame a theory of the Self-in-the-group would be to suggest that in our role as group members, we need to pay attention to the relationship between what could be described as the group ego and the group Self. When Eishold says that our need to belong is as profound as our need to dream, he seems to be recognizing that belonging, like dreaming, is a doorway to the Self. Bion's work, looked at from the perspective of Jungians like Schwartz-Salant, suggests that the fertile chaos of group psychic life may bring us closer to the archetypal realm than our ordinary experience as separate selves permits and that immersion in that life can be a source of renewal and creativity.

To apply the ideas developed in this paper to group life in organizations requires a shift from the patriarchal perspective. If the creative possibilities in groups are to be realized, patriarchal assumptions about the necessity for order and for strong leadership centered in one person need to be examined. The creative potential in a group cannot be released unless group members are equally empowered in a collaborative way, until the process is recognized, even embraced, as necessarily chaotic, messy, and painful, and unless the group members each take responsibility for maintaining, to the greatest extent possible, the containing presence of the good mother. Each participant becomes a microcosm of the group, containing the archetypal mother and child within, acting out those roles, and others, in a changing and fluid manner. Each participant takes responsibility for leading and following, for sustaining the presence of the archetypal good mother who neither abandons nor intrudes. Then individual creativity and group creativity intermingle as group members attend to the group's process within themselves, with each other and the group as a whole. The child which then may emerge from the unconscious psychic life of the group carries the possibility of new life, the creative new approach to the group's task, as well as those archetypal energies that renew the individuals, the group, and the organization of which the group is a part.

References

Bion, W. R. 1959. Selections from: "Experiences in Groups." In *Group Relations Reader 1*, A. D. Colman and W. H. Bexton, eds. Washington, D.C.: A. K. Rice Institute, pp. 11–20.

Bly, R., and Thompson, K. 1985. What men really want. In *Challenge of the Heart: Love, Sex and Intimacy in Changing Times*, J. Welwood, ed. Boston: Shambhala Publications, Inc., pp. 100–116.

Campbell, J. 1949. *The Hero with a Thousand Faces*. Princeton, N.J.: Princeton University Press.

_____. 1965. *The Masks of God: Occidental Mythology*. New York: Viking/Compass.

Chodorow, N. 1978. *The Reproduction of Mothering: Psychoanalysis and the Sociology of Gender*. Berkeley, Calif.: University of California Press.

Colman, A. D. 1975. Group consciousness as a developmental phase. In *Group Relations Reader 1*, A. D. Colman and W. H. Bexton, eds. Washington, D.C.: A. K. Rice Institute, pp. 35–42.

Eishold, K. 1985. Recovering Bion's contributions to group analysis. In *Group Relations Reader 2*, A. D. Colman and M. H. Geller, eds. Washington, D.C.: A. K. Rice Institute, pp. 37–48.

Eisler, R. 1987. *The Chalice and the Blade*. San Francisco: Harper and Row.

Gilligan, C. 1982. *In a Different Voice*. Cambridge, Mass.: Harvard University Press.

Gorkin, M. 1987. *The Uses of Countertransference*. Northvale, N.J.: Jason Aronson, Inc.

Gustafson, J. P., and Cooper, L. 1985. Collaboration in small groups: theory and technique for the study of small-group processes. In *Group Relations Reader 2*, A. D. Colman and M. H. Geller, eds. Washington, D.C.: A. K. Rice Institute, pp. 139–150.

Klein, M. 1959. Our adult world and its roots in infancy. In *Group Relations Reader 2*, A. D. Colman and M. H. Geller, eds. Washington, D.C.: A. K. Rice Institute, pp. 5–19.

Keller, C. 1986. *From a Broken Web: Separation, Sexism and Self*. Boston: Beacon Press.

Jung, C. G. 1951. The psychology of the child archetype. In *CW* 9i:151–181. Princeton, N.J.: Princeton University Press, 1959.

_____. 1956. *The Collected Works of C. G. Jung*. Volume 5. Princeton, N.J.: Princeton University Press.

_____. 1959. Introduction to Toni Wolff's Studies in Jungian Psychology. In *CW* 10: 469–476. Princeton, N.J.: Princeton University Press, 1964.

Miller, J. B. 1976. *Toward a New Psychology of Women*. Boston: Beacon Press.

Rice, A. K. 1975. Selections from: "Learning for Leadership." In *Group Relations Reader 1*, A. D. Colman and W. H. Bexton, eds. Washington, D.C.: A. K. Rice Institute, pp. 71–158.

Rioch, M. J. 1975a. Group relations: rationale and technique. In *Group Relations Reader 1*, A. D. Colman and W. H. Bexton, eds. Washington, D.C.: A. K. Rice Institute, pp. 3–10.

_____. 1975b. The work of Wilfred Bion on groups. In *Group Relations Reader 1*, A. D. Colman and W. H. Bexton, eds. Washington, D.C.: A. K. Rice Institute, pp. 21–34.

Schwartz-Salant, N. 1989. *The Borderline Personality: Vision and Healing.* Wilmette, Ill.: Chiron Publications.

Stern, D. 1985. *The Interpersonal World of the Infant.* New York: Basic Books, Inc.

Surrey, J. 1984. The "self-in-relation": a theory of women's development. *Work in Progress*, no. 13. Wellesley, Mass.: Stone Center Working Papers Series.

Turquet, P. M. 1985. Leadership: the individual and the group. In *Group Relations Reader 2*, A. D. Colman and M. H. Geller, eds. Washington, D.C.: A. K. Rice Institute, pp. 71–88.

Whitmont, E. C. 1961. Individual and group. *Spring* 1961:58–79.

_____. 1984. *Return of the Goddess.* New York: Crossroads Publishing Company.

Medora S. Perlman *is currently a psychotherapist practicing in a community mental health center and a Jungian low-fee psychotherapy service, and training candidate in the Inter-Regional Society of Jungian Analysts. She has had many opportunities to observe groups as a high school English teacher, a lawyer in private practice, manager of a large banking organization, and volunteer and board member for a wide variety of organizations.*

Psychological Types, Job Change, and Personal Growth

Randall E. Ruppart
and Aryeh Maidenbaum

The field of typology is one of the more pragmatic enterprises to result from the work of Carl Jung, and type inventories have long been a staple of career counselors and educational consultants. Jung himself did not invent any personality tests. Type indicators as we know them today are largely the result of efforts in the 1940s and 1950s by Isabel Briggs Myers and her mother, Katherine Briggs, to "operationalize" Jung's theory of "personality types" (Myers 1980, preface). Their work first caught the attention not of analysts, but of personnel consultants, university professors, and assessment experts. As a result, much of their initial research was done among student populations and employment service clients, which established a solid statistical relationship between type and vocational aptitude and satisfaction.

The verifiability of these statistical data has led many researchers to regard typology as the core of a scientific Jungian approach to understanding personality. In 1968, Dr. C. A. Meier, close associate of Jung and first president of the C. G. Jung Institute in Zürich, delivered a paper at the Fourth International Congress for Analytical Psychology entitled, "Psychological Types and Individuation: A Plea for a More Scientific Approach in Jungian Psychology" (1971). "Of all the basic concepts of Jung," Meier says, "the four functions are the most basic, the most neatly defined concepts in Jungian psychology" (p. 277). He notes the contribution of both the *Gray-Wheelwright Psychological Test Questionnaire* (1946) and the *Myers-Briggs Type Indicator* (MBTI) (1962) to a better understanding of the individual psyche and goes so far as to advocate the development of additional standardized Jungian typology instruments that can be computerized for wider access. Meier reminds us that Jung understood himself as a scientist; his work on the word association test derived from his understanding of psychology as a scientific discipline.

Only as Jungian psychology meets the criteria of scientific methodology, says Meier—reliability, validity, measurability, quantification, replicability of results, predictability, and the like—will the discipline enjoy full status as a branch of knowledge, worthy of psychology department chairs in universities, research funds, recognized institutes, practitioners, and the wider dissemination of Jung's theory and ideas.

Meier threw down the gauntlet to that assemblage of Jungian analysts gathered from around the world to hear him. He suggested that membership in the International Jungian Analysts Society be limited to those analysts who test their patients at the start of and during the process of treatment to find out how (and if) typology is affected in the course of an analysis. Even if the majority of those who have taken up the challenge have not been Jungian analysts, but rather educators and career counselors, we are nevertheless documenting the effectiveness of type analysis for the process of individuation (Jung's term for individual self-realization). In particular, any form of outplacement counseling that is intentionally centered around the MBTI is surprisingly similar to a Jungian analysis highlighting psychological type.

If nothing else, type analysis is a forward-looking process, it does not rely on postmortems and reasons for failure as a technique of cure. Instead, it encourages a client to recognize present strengths and weaknesses and their relationship to choices that need to be made.

Jung's basic hypothesis was that each of us has four basic functions (sensation, intuition, thinking, feeling) and two attitudes (extraversion and introversion) with which we approach the world. Jung emphasized that all of these possibilities exist in each individual. One's "type" is determined by a preference for using certain combinations of functions more than others and, hence, becoming more developed in those areas. No single type or combination of functions is better or worse than another. Rather, from a Jungian standpoint, the task for each of us is to realize our full potential—by developing our preferred functions in a way that will bring us satisfaction and by attending to our weaker functions as sources of growth and change.

Jung himself became interested in the concept of different personality types during the final stages of his break with Freud. He felt a strong need to understand the differences in outlook that had produced Freud's, Adler's, and his own concepts of psychological development. In the first public presentation of his ideas on typology, at the Munich Psychoanalytic Congress of 1913, Jung attempted to sketch out a theory of extraversion and introversion, relating them, respectively, to William James's descriptions of "tough-minded" and "tender-minded" personality types. Over the next eight years, however, Jung expanded and developed his theory well beyond this initial effort and in 1921 published his well-known book, *Psychological Types*.

As a quick guide to understanding Jung's theory of personality types, we could do worse than to begin as he did—with the attitudes: extraversion and introversion. The popularization of these terms has made them clichés, and most people use them very casually, as though "extraverted" meant outgoing, friendly, and basically normal, and "introverted" meant shy or antisocial. Jung, however, did not use the words this way. Jung described extraverts as object-oriented; they immediately adapt to the situation at hand and require a great deal of stimulation from the outer world in order to feel comfortable. Introverts, in contrast, are oriented by their subjective reactions to the object; that is, an introvert is more aware of and requires stimulation from the inner world.

It is important to understand that extraversion and introversion are polar attitudes. If a person is highly introverted, then extraversion is very poorly developed (inferior), and vice versa. Introverts have had bad press in this country because the majority of Americans are extraverted (estimates range from 50% to 75%) and tend to interpret introversion in terms of their own weaker, less-developed attitude. In particular, the introvert's need for inner stimulation, which requires an assessment of objects and solitary engagement, is too often understood as a failure of social adequacy, even by introverts themselves.

One might speculate that Americans are traditionally extraverted because extraversion was an asset in an undeveloped country, where the ability to size up new situations quickly and to adapt accordingly assured one's survival. The downside of this kind of adaptability is the tendency to lose one's sense of self—to depend too much on the outer situation to dictate a feeling of well-being. As for the functions, sensation and intuition are essentially different ways of *perceiving* information. Sensation is fact-oriented, one-thing-at-a-time perception and focuses on the here and now (things as they are). Intuition is gestalt-oriented, whole-thing-at-once perception and focuses on the past/future (things as they might be). Thinking and feeling are different ways of *acting on* information. Thinking acts on information logically, seeking objective distance from the thing perceived. Feeling acts on information by imparting value to it, seeking subjective identification with the thing perceived.

Because the case studies to follow make use of the *Myers-Briggs Type Indicator*, it is important to point out that Myers and Briggs created a very important addition to Jung's overt model of psychological types and to the *Gray-Wheelright Psychological Test Questionnaire* by adding two further dimensions to the type scale: judgment and perception. Myers held that these two attitudes were implied in Jung's theory, and they allow a counselor to determine exactly which of the four functions is dominant in a given personality. According to Myers, "those who take a judging attitude . . . [toward life] tend to live in a planned, orderly way, wanting to regulate life and control it," while "those who prefer a perceptive process when dealing with the outer world . . . like to live in a flexible, spontaneous way" (Myers 1962, 1975, p. 6).

Although Jungian analysts are divided on their acceptance of the JP scale, in general, the identification of JP qualities means a great deal to those who seek to understand the dynamics of the broad range of behavior now associated with them through the MBTI. And counselors and analysts do agree that the concept of dominant and inferior functions is key to understanding the psychological growth patterns and potential for any one person. For users of the MBTI, the JP scale is fundamental to the determination of the order of the functions, from dominant through auxiliary and tertiary to the fourth or inferior function. (For further explanation of the JP scale, see Myers 1980.)

It should be noted that introverts are treated differently from extraverts when interpreting the JP scale. The presumption is that an introvert's preferred, or dominant function, because it is an introverted function, will operate primarily in the individual's inner world. For an introvert, relationship to the outer world is accomplished with the secondary, or auxiliary function. Therefore, a J or P attitude registered on the MBTI will indicate the orientation of the introvert's *auxiliary* function—his or her way of relating to the outer world.

It should also be noted that when MBTI profiles are displayed and discussed, the attitudes and functions always appear in the same order. E or I will always occupy the first position; S or N (for iNtuition), the second; T or F, the third; and J or P, the fourth. The first and last letters are attitudes, the middle letters are functions.

Jung's and the Myers' respective theories are referred to as "function theories," because they focus on proper and progressive development of the functions (S, N, T, F). Their implication is that people should grow and change, and that growth and change will take place according to type, with allowances for individual differences due to life circumstances. In other words, people "individualize" their types—through life experience, personal goals, relationships, and the way they live out their lives. The MBTI profiles are generally considered to reflect the functions and attitudes of the first half of life—the ego stage of development. In the second half of life, the self stage of development, the tertiary and inferior functions and attitudes begin to "surface," and the individual must come to terms with them if growth is to occur.

That being said, certain broad generalizations can be made about how each type sees the world and interacts with others. Let's take a few moments now to look at some of the highlights of the four functions modified by the attitudes. For the sake of convenience, we will describe the introverts in terms of their auxiliary functions, because we are concerned here with the function that relates to the outer world.

Extraverted thinking types (ESTJ/ENTJ) are very much attuned to the logic of a situation. Those whose sensation function is auxiliary (ESTJ) are fact-oriented, practical, and well able to set aside the emotional aspects of a confusing situation in order to make realistic decisions. Those whose intuition function is auxiliary (ENTJ) are likely to be more analytical and idea-oriented, even visionary. Whereas ESTJs are natural administrators, ENTJs are natural leaders. Extraverted thinking types in general can get so caught up in the logical requirements of a situation that feelings can strike them as merely illogical irritants. Relationships can seem less important than work.

Introverted thinking types (ISTJ/INTJ) are also attuned to logic, but more to systemic logic. Where an extraverted thinking type wants to know, an introverted thinking type wants to know *how*. Those whose sensation function is inwardly dominant (ISTJ) are likely to be quite good at organizing information, making plans, and scheduling. Those whose intuition is inwardly dominant (INTJ) are likely to be more abstract—interested in scientific systems or mathematics. Both introverted thinking types can seem arrogant in their need to demonstrate technical competence in their areas of expertise.

Extraverted feeling types (ESFJ/ENFJ) give priority to harmonious relationships; people's feelings often take precedence over other considerations. Those whose sensation function is auxiliary (ESFJ) tend to be very alert to societal mores and almost instinctively reflect the consensus as a strongly held personal opinion. Those whose intuition function is auxiliary (ENFJ) are likely to be more aware of other people's potential to contribute to the larger society. Where ESFJs preserve, ENFJs catalyze—as teachers, ministers, and counselors of all sorts. Both extraverted feeling types can be so attuned to the social norms that they become unwittingly judgmental.

Introverted feeling types (ISFJ/INFJ) are also oriented by social concerns, but are more attuned to the values behind social norms. They often divide things into "right" or "wrong," "good" and "bad." This tendency makes for great idealism and the need to find meaning in their work. Those whose sensation function is inwardly dominant (ISFJ) are very alert to people's immediate practical needs and feel a strong drive to be of service. Those whose intuition is inwardly dominant (INFJ) are more sensitive to people's unspoken needs and will generally seek an outlet—such as writing—for expressing what they intuit. Both introverted feeling types are somewhat awkward about sharing their own feelings.

Extraverted sensation types (ESFP/ESTP) are very much in the here and now. Those whose feeling function is auxiliary (ESFP) enjoy having others around, are generous, and enjoy all the sensate pleasures—good food, nice clothing, outdoor activities, friendly competition. Those whose thinking function is auxiliary (ESTP) are more interested in the sensory pleasures of skill, daring, and serious competition. Both extraverted sensation types enjoy the physical world and their immediate relation to it. Abstract ideas and philosophy generally strike them as one step removed from a life meant to be lived. They may be immediate to the point of being impulsive, and realistic sometimes to the detriment of the inner world.

Introverted sensation types (ISFP/ISTP) are also in the here and now, but their immediacy and physicality are more idiosyncratic. Those whose feeling function is inwardly dominant (ISFP) may seem to be without direction because they are so much "in the moment." Such types can make good actors and performers; they tend to lose themselves in what they do. Those whose thinking function is inwardly dominant (ISTP) are, like ESTPs, given more to the pleasures of technical competence—but in an introverted fashion. Where an ESTP may enjoy motorcycle racing, the ISTP will know how to repair and renovate the cycle machinery.

Both introverted sensation types relate well to colors, fabrics, tex-
tures, and other external sensory stimuli.

Extraverted intuitive types (ENFP/ENTP), as opposed to
extraverted sensation types, are very much attuned to the not-
here and the not-yet. They tend to see an object in terms of its
potential for change and are constantly generating new ideas.
Those whose feeling function is auxiliary (ENFP) can veer between
charismatic optimism and restless disengagement, as when the
planning stage ends and the situation begins to require tedious
detail work in order to be realized. Those whose thinking function
is auxiliary (ENTP) are more strategically inventive and ingenious,
but tend to start new projects before ending old ones and are easily
bored with routine, to the point of flouting convention. Both extraverted intuitive types tend to get in trouble with authority and are
consistently surprised by it. Both are more likely to leave a difficult
situation than to compromise.

Introverted intuitive types (INFP/INTP), like other introverts,
are geared by their subjective reactions to things. Those whose
feeling function is inwardly dominant (INFP) are like ENFPs in
their sensitivity to potential, but appear to experience it as something personally unrealized. Where an ENFP might become a minister, an INFP is more likely to have a very personal religious
drive—a need to believe in something or someone with idealistic
fervor. Those whose thinking function is inwardly dominant
(INTP) are innovative like ENTPs, but their interests are more
abstract and technical. They tend to be interested in the way
things function, how they can be made to function better, but that
interest tends to stop at the design stage. Both introverted intuitive types tend to avoid the purely physical as somewhat gross and
unworthy of their attention.

These are some of the highlights of the types, as evolved from
Jung's work. Although modern-day Jungian analysts themselves
do not utilize typology in the service of individuation nearly often
enough, many career counselors and educators who administer
and work with the *Myers-Briggs Type Indicator* have found that
counseling an individual while using the MBTI as a primary tool
helps to foster the process of individuation in their clients'
development.

Following are the MBTI profiles of two individuals who partic-
ipated in a formal outplacement program provided through a
nationally known outplacement consulting firm in the United
States. Outplacement counseling is a comprehensive career/job
transition program provided by an employer, through a third-

party counseling consultant, to an employee who is losing a job. The consultant helps the employee to cope better with the loss, prepare for new work, and find an appropriate job in a different organization. Both individuals discussed were clients in such a program. Their profiles are composites of more than one single person but were inspired by particular individuals (not their real names) for whom the critical elements were true.

Individual Study: Jocelyn Adams

When Jocelyn Adams entered the outplacement program, she had just lost her job with a multinational financial organization. Due to a large-scale reorganization and downsizing of the company, her job had been eliminated, and no alternative placement had been found for her. She was therefore offered sponsored career-transition assistance, undergirded with salary continuance and the option to convert her medical benefits after four months.

As a part of the first phase of the outplacement program, Jocelyn was asked to complete the MBTI and a career autobiography. On the MBTI she generated a profile of INTJ—introverted intuition, with a thinking function auxiliary, and a judgment attitude, meaning that she used her thinking function to relate to the outer world. In the early meetings, which were held about twice each week, Jocelyn acted and spoke in ways that could be considered consistent with this profile. However, there were aspects of her behavior and things she said that seemed to be rooted in some other profile. Further analysis of the MBTI scores brought attention to the facts that the I score was moderate, the N score was strong, the T score was low, and the J score was moderate to strong.

Jocelyn's career autobiography indicated that she was in her mid-forties, married with stability, and had two children. In college she had been good in math and earned a bachelor of science in petroleum engineering, with honors. After college, she began working in the chemicals division of an oil company, spending her time on various projects involving refineries. She traveled a great part of the time, met interesting and intelligent people, and got positive feedback from her peers and managers. After about eight years, Jocelyn began gravitating toward marketing and soon moved into work that was devoted to petrochemical marketing.

Not long after, Jocelyn was offered a position in a new company, largely in the field of petrochemicals and related products. There she conducted marketing studies, drawing on her math competence. During this period, playing to her demonstrated abilities and to many of her interests, she earned an MBA in both marketing and finance. Soon after, an executive recruiter contacted her about a possible new job. By this time, Jocelyn was fifteen years into her career, and she and her husband were managing an active family.

A few months later, Jocelyn was offered a position in a prestigious brokerage and investment organization. The company wanted her to conduct very sophisticated industry analyses and company forecasting, beginning with oil and petrochemicals. She took the position because of the industry's prestige and a belief that the work would broaden her base of experience. As it turned out, the job required long hours, was heavily oriented toward math and projective statistics, and caused her to feel that she was neglecting her family.

Within a year, Jocelyn was tired of her work and had even thought of looking for something less taxing. She was disappointed in herself. How had she let this happen? She had made "a mess" of her change of industries, but she was unable to understand clearly just what had gone wrong. Within fifteen months, Jocelyn had lost so much confidence that she couldn't believe another job at her level would be any better. These circumstances left her confused and very frustrated. This was the situation when she entered into the career-transition (outplacement) process.

The counselor sought clarification on a number of questions during the detailed review of the career autobiography. In several instances, Jocelyn's answers indicated that she was trying to be objective and decisive, along the lines of an INTJ profile, but that she was not doing so fully or with self-assurance. These responses, along with the initial uncertainty regarding the MBTI profile, prompted the counselor to present Jocelyn with and ask her about her comfort with alternate profiles among the sixteen prepared by the outplacement firm. Each profile in the series, somewhat like the descriptive highlights given earlier, contained general outlines of the characteristic attitudes, behavior patterns, values, and areas of career choice most likely for individuals with that profile. As a result, matters slowly began to become more clear.

The counselor worked through with Jocelyn why it was that she had made certain choices at particular times in her life—her college major, for instance, and the focus of her MBA studies. That process greatly helped Jocelyn through a kind of guided self-review: how did she feel about her choices, how satisfied had she been at various points? The review of the career autobiography gradually became the vehicle by which Jocelyn and her counselor were able to arrive at a point of clarity concerning the MBTI profile. This entire process led to an awareness and a mutual acceptance that the correct profile was ENFP—extraverted intuition, with a feeling function auxiliary, and a perception attitude.

With this fresh perspective, Jocelyn and her counselor were able to examine her career and her choices anew. That second review served to make the underlying pattern more conscious and went a long way toward eliminating some of the anomalies that had appeared during the earlier parts of the process. For example, it was helpful in understanding why she had done so well across the various career segments, the appeal of jobs related to marketing, her pleasure and abilities in analysis, and many of the reasons that the most recent position had had such a negative effect on her happiness and generally positive image of herself.

For a further explanation, the order of her function dominance is important to consider. The two profiles look like this:

	INTJ	ENFP
Dominant	N	N
Auxiliary	T	F
Tertiary	F	T
Fourth	S	S

Because of the dominant intuition in each profile, from a career standpoint, people with either of these profiles might prefer doing some of the same things—analysis, conceptual activities, idea generation, along with some preference for the mental patterns associated with math and languages or other symbolic processes.

However, the other functions would play different roles in the two profiles, directed by the different attitudes. Extraversion would move Jocelyn to direct her intuition outward, toward the external world, whereas introversion would lead her to "extravert" her auxiliary function, in this case, thinking. The reversal of auxiliaries is particularly important here. As an ENFP, Jocelyn would seek warm and somewhat personal relationships that brought comfort, new possibilities, and contributed to a sense of inner harmony. She would also need a good deal of stimulation from her job if she were not to feel restless, bored, and fatigued. In contrast, a person with an INTJ profile might more typically want to establish objectivity and clarity in relationships with the external world. And an INTJ would welcome the space and privacy for deep engagement with her work.

It is also important to note that a person with a judgment attitude would seek to create order in her surroundings and to be decisive, whereas a person with a perceptive attitude would much prefer to be open-ended and spontaneous. Overall, a person with an INTJ profile would likely be intense and task-oriented, in contrast to the lively sociability and restless curiosity of an ENFP individual. Both types can be interesting and enjoyable people, and both can focus on the work that is to be performed, but they would approach these events from differing standpoints and have contrasting needs to be satisfied in any situation.

What might have been at work in Jocelyn's move toward an INTJ profile? The analysis suggested that in her last position, the work tasks themselves had caused her to shift first to a TJ combination mode. Thinking function activities had been progressively required because of the extensive work with numbers and statistics. Also, with the long hours and the increasing difficulties in being with her family in a way that was satisfactory to her, Jocelyn had begun to suppress her feelings and to develop a work-focused orientation.

In many ways, it can be said that the TJ mode came to the foreground to enable Jocelyn to do what she felt she had to do. As a short-term adaptive tactic, that could be regarded as beneficial. Regarding the attitudes, Jocelyn as a perceptive type is flexible and adaptive, and as an extravert she perceives her external environment with realism and accuracy. So in summary form, she adapted; but it was an adaptation that was too extreme and beginning to last too long. Her extraverted, spontaneous, social, caring, and family-oriented self began to disappear into the background. As a consequence, she progressively lost her ability to function at her best, her self-insight diminished, her feelings got little or no real expression of a positive nature, and slowly she began to feel crushed and trapped.

For a person with an ENFP profile, such a condition brings on misery and despair. Had the restructuring in her company not caused her to find her way into a constructive counseling relationship, Jocelyn might well have begun to experience physical symptoms of her distress as a result of her unhealthy retreat into herself (constellated in the defensive adoption of an uncharacteristic introverted attitude). If she had been able to use her introverted attitude and thinking function in a positive manner—as a way to hold onto or recover her self-perspective—much of Jocelyn's unhappiness might have been avoided. She might have been able to lift herself out of her difficult situation and accomplish an appropriate and fruitful change. Her extraversion could have worked to help her see real possibilities for herself, while her less-developed introversion could have served as the quiet and personal place to evaluate pathways holding greater potential for her and her self-development.

Once Jocelyn began to incorporate the new understanding derived from the outplacement process, she responded quickly. She became almost suddenly lighter, as though a great weight had been lifted. In the working sessions, she began to laugh and to enjoy thoughts of the new possibilities that she could start to see in front of her. The social ENFP personality began to appear, and pretty soon life was fun again.

Jocelyn decided that working in a small company and being close to home were important criteria for her next job. She also wanted to move toward some form of sales, possibly in a financial area. With the aid of good research and energetic networking, Jocelyn was able to find an organization that fit her interests, skills, and many of her goals for the future. She joined a small financial services and brokerage organization where she would be trained for and eventually move into a financial consultant role, working with the firm's outside clients. When contacted by her counselor four months later, Jocelyn said that she was very happy and mindful of the insights she had gained, which had benefited her both professionally and personally.

It should be pointed out that the MBTI did not fail to perform adequately or properly in this situation. Rather, the instrument did quite well in picking up and accurately describing the actual profile from which Jocelyn was operating. Her initial scores, because of the relative strengths of the four preferences, were clues that further investigation was needed. One might question, of course, why a moderate-to-strong J score would indicate a possible preference for the opposite attitude. In its extreme, the J score can indicate a type of psychological rigidity, either temporary or long-standing in nature. That condition can be a sign that says "look deeper" to the counselor.

With Jocelyn's profile, the J score was indicative that something was being held to tenaciously. The "something" turned out to be twofold. First, she was holding her feelings in check to a very large degree. Second, she was holding to her course with a great deal of determination, because it had become her way of adapting to her situation and coping with the job and its requirements day after day. So the MBTI was extremely valuable not only in its profile display, but in its indications that the apparent reality was not at all the true reality. It is fair to say, however, that the more experience a counselor has had with the instrument, the more likely it will be that very subtle characteristics will be noted and translated into meaningful indications.

Myers addressed this type of "changeability" on the MBTI preferences when she wrote that "in work with individuals, the reported type [MBTI profile] should never be used as a fact but always as a hypothesis for verification" (Myers 1977, p. 2). Experienced interpreters of the instrument know this rule, and they employ it as part of the proper protocol in the interpretive process. In various other places, Myers and other researchers dealt with the questions of reliability. Myers commented that:

> good type development thus demands that the auxiliary supplement the dominant process in two respects. It must supply a useful degree of balance not only between perception and judgment but *also between extraversion and introversion.* (Myers 1980, p. 21)

> On the assumption that good judgment is the last of the functions to develop, Myers hypothesized that reliability values for the *TF* scale would be most sensitive to lack of full type development in the subjects. (McCaulley 1981, p. 315)

More specifically, Myers pointed out that "intuitives need the stabilizing influence of well-developed thinking or feeling" (Myers 1980, p. 110). She went on to conclude that: "Extraverted intuitives must, therefore, begin to develop judgment as early as possible" (p. 111).

From these indications and theoretical principles relating to the MBTI, the issue for the Jocelyn Adams situation was the relative strength of her type development, not the reliability of the instrument. Seen from this perspective, it is most likely that Jocelyn's inadequately developed judgment and thinking/feeling allowed her to be pulled into a work circumstance that was highly inappropriate and which progressively took its toll. Ideally, the resulting "crisis" and its resolution, aided significantly by her work with the MBTI and her counselor, served to clarify the proper function and attitude development and thereby to strengthen them in their proper roles for the future. The post-counseling follow-up suggested that indeed this had been the case.

Comments from an Analytic Perspective

One might note the similarities between Jocelyn's work in outplacement counseling and the process one often goes through in an analysis. Jocelyn reached the counselor as the result of a crisis—as is usually the case when one enters analysis. In fact, persons entering therapy for the declared purpose of "self-enlightenment" generally make no progress. One's defenses have to be down in order for any real change to take place.

Similarly, in reevaluating her career strengths and weaknesses, Jocelyn was experiencing what analysands normally go through in the course of treatment. One must look at one's life in terms of both past experience and present reality before any growth can be effected. It has been said that for a new perspective to emerge from one's psyche, the old attitude must first die.

Moreover, the counselor clearly used his own functions to find out what happened, as C. A. Meier urged Jungian analysts to do. For example, the counselor's intuitive function picked up the incongruity between Jocelyn's initial MBTI profile and her truer, more extraverted attitude. But intuition was not enough. The counselor also had to gather the facts (sensation), put them together logically (thinking), and provide empathy for Jocelyn's suffering (feeling).

Finally, as in analysis, the work was accomplished in dialogue together. Jung, in describing how a dream must be interpreted, advised analysts that the interpretation must "click" with the dreamer. The analyst alone cannot decide what is correct and what is not. The dreamer must digest and acknowledge the information imparted. This kind of mutuality is exactly what happened in Jocelyn's case.

Individual Study: George Spencer

George Spencer was fifty-three when he entered the outplacement program. Early in his career, just after high school, he had taken a job in banking, beginning in a back-office accounting function. Within nine years, he was married, had completed a bachelor of science degree in business, and was taking an officer training program at the same bank. When he first met his counselor, he had been working overall for thirty-five years. The day before this meeting, he had been terminated from his job. The termination had been a complete surprise to him.

George's career autobiography indicated that he had completed the bank's officer training program and become a commercial loan officer and a vice president. The discussions with his counselor revealed that after about twenty years in banking, when George was in his early forties, he felt restless and in need of a change. His friends became aware of his interest in doing something different, and one day a man in his fraternal lodge told him that a local community hospital needed a person with a "no-nonsense business head" in their financial office. George followed this lead and secured a new position and a change in careers at the same time.

George was proud of this accomplishment and he felt happier at the hospital. Yet his restlessness increased. He had a vague feeling that his marriage wasn't going well, and about two years later he and his wife of twenty-four years were divorced. A year after the divorce, George took another job, this time at a large metropolitan medical complex, and moved from his suburban neighborhood into a trendy urban area.

Now in the heart of the city, embarking on an excellent new job, George wanted to make a better life for himself. He thought the future looked very bright. He privately hoped that he would soon meet someone and perhaps remarry. But George took one more bold step.

A few years after the move to the medical complex, George saw a notice for a position in benefits administration. He applied for the position but was turned down because someone else had direct experience that was stronger than his own. Nevertheless, shortly thereafter, a parallel position came open, and George was offered the job. He accepted it and found himself in human resources, an area in which he had never worked before. With his financial skills and long business experience, George added a real strength to the employee benefits operation. His resourcefulness in developing a new cafeteria plan for the program earned him a bonus and a big feature story in the monthly newsletter.

Within a few years, George turned fifty, and he was promoted to the position of director, the last position he was to hold at the complex. From that point, his career went downhill, and over the next three years he became slowly but progressively, "impossible to live with." He became mired in details and focused extensively on the facts at the expense of the general idea. He was irritable and went back to smoking, having quit for twelve years. He sometimes became so buried in his work that he had no time for anyone or anything else.

Eventually, George began to complain that employees were trying to "rip off" the benefits program and that the company was too benevolent to stop them. He missed important project deadlines, and one day made a critical mistake. He failed to catch a calculation error in pension interest made by an outside agency, which resulted in a cost to the complex of $125,000. It was this error that finally cost him his job.

On the MBTI, George generated a profile of ISTJ—introverted sensation, with a thinking function auxiliary, and a judgment attitude, meaning that he used his thinking function to relate to the outside world. As he began the outplacement program, he was bitter, cynical, and generally unhappy. He didn't trust the career-transition process and would frequently challenge the counselor on any point that suggested the process might really help him find a new position.

Even though George was given a continuance of his salary and benefits for six months, he was greatly worried about finances. For the first few weeks of the program, he insisted that he would never get another job as good as the last, and that therefore the whole program would benefit him very little. On one occasion, tears came into his eyes when he began talking about what an "awful situation I'm in." He couldn't understand how he could have let it happen—especially so fast. The counselor worked with George's feelings and tried to help him through the adjustment of this early period. Logic told George that he must have played a part in his own undoing, but he didn't seem to understand the reasons for his termination, and he was troubled by that lack of comprehension.

After six months of participating in the outplacement program and searching for new work, George did get back on a good path. He found a very interesting job in the financial area of a medium-sized hospital supply company. In talking with him after he had accepted the new position, George admitted to his counselor that he was surprised to find a job of this nature in what he regarded as a reasonably short period of time. He volunteered also that the discussions on the MBTI had been more valuable to him than he had let on at the time. Those conversations had helped him to admit that when he was starting to "feel bad" a few years before, he wouldn't listen to anybody who tried to help him. He had thought that after all of the changes he had made previously he could handle just about anything. He said further that he really appreciated the help he had received and the real concern he knew his counselor had for him. In the end, George said that he hoped he could remember what he had learned and apply the lessons well in his life in the future. The MBTI had provided a framework in which growth could occur.

From that standpoint, and with a concern for type development, the main problem for George had been that he was "stuck" in the ego phase of his life development. He had not sufficiently developed his intuitive function as a balance for his dominant sensation function. Intuition makes one aware of the larger picture, that which is beyond the immediate, and of the context or set of relationships in which something exists. Secondarily, George's feeling function seemed to have gotten stuck or reverted to an earlier stage. He was overly focused on himself and showed only a small amount of consideration for and awareness of the needs of others.

When his own, more self-centered needs could not be met, his feelings turned sour, and he appeared to others as a misanthrope. One might even go so far as to hypothesize that his inward turning diverted his outward attention to such an extent that he failed in one of his typical areas of greatest strength: spotting errors of fact (use of the sensation function). Had he allowed his intuitive function to come more to the foreground in a consciously differentiated way, George might have been able to attain some perspective on his work and the associated problems. He might have managed his numerous tasks, deadlines, and interactions instead of getting mired in them. The minimal use of intuition also accounts for the fact that George didn't realize how deeply in trouble he was (loss of perspective) and how close he was to making a critical mistake that would lead to termination of his job.

Therefore, when it came, George was shocked. He was even dismayed, because in his mind at the time, *he* was the hard worker, *he* was the loyal one looking out for the organization's money, and *he* was the one who would implant a real business orientation in that place if it was the last thing he did. Pictorially, George was the runaway train that sped onward without relief. His termination was akin to slamming into the brick wall that came up out of nowhere. So much of this condition was rooted in his failure to develop intuition's ability to see what's coming and to foresee the possible consequences of one's actions. As a result of the outplacement, serving as a constructive intervention, George understood much better what he had to do and on what he would have to work in the future. That awareness, in and of itself, gave cause for hope that he could and would change.

Comments from an Analytic Perspective

Jung has pointed out that major shifts in our psyches take place at key transition points: puberty, adolescence, career change, marriage, divorce, mid-life, and so forth. Important archetypal dreams generally occur at these times, as well as outer, dramatic shifts in our lifestyles. George, who might well have been categorized as having a mid-life crisis, was in the midst of just such a transition point when his world came crashing down. One might say that intuition and feeling, his inferior functions, compensated his one-sided approach to life by raising up the possibility of new situations and greater satisfaction. But these functions were not under George's conscious control. He didn't "use" them; they took him over, and he reacted defensively by holding more tenaciously to the functions that had always served him. As he became more of a stereotype of his former self, his inferior functions became all the more insistent.

Another way to look at this is to say that George began to identify the archetype of change called up by his inferior function, intuition. To use a Jungian term, he became inflated and lost touch with reality. In the process of analysis, a new analysand often reacts in similar fashion. In fact, analysts often warn new patients not to make any significant changes in their lives during the first few months of therapy. This is because there is a strong tendency toward inflation, which sets in almost invariably at the first contact one has with the self—or even, as in George's situation, when one first confronts previously undeveloped aspects of the unconscious.

Luckily for George, his particular counselor, intentionally or not, followed a path similar to the one that a good analyst would take. Beginning with the anamnesis (gathering background, case history, and material) and proceeding on toward confrontation with the shadow, that is, in this case, George's inflation engendered by overidentification with his inferior function, George's outplacement counselor was able to help his client toward individuation. The use of Jung's psychological types model proved an excellent vehicle in this process.

Jungian analysts have something to learn from the consulting business in its use of Jung's types model. Cases such as the two we have just discussed make clear the fact that the types are not cubbyholes or rationalizations for behavior. They are dynamic, reflecting not only preference, but circumstance, and the will to adapt and to survive. A good counselor/analyst will recognize the confluence of elements contributing to a client's test results and use that knowledge to explore the client's approach to life. Such work, in the true spirit of Jungian psychology, necessarily goes beyond vocational guidance, ultimately touching on the development of the whole person to further the process of individuation.

References

Carlyn, M. 1977. An assessment of the Myers-Briggs Type Indicator. *Journal of Personality Assessment* 41 (5):461–473.

Carskadon, T. G. 1979. Clinical and counseling aspects of the Myers-Briggs Type Indicator: a research review. *Research in Psychological Type* 2:2–31.

Jung, C. G. 1921. *Psychological types. CW*, vol. 6, H. G. Baynes, trans. R. F. C. Hull, ed. Princeton, N.J.: Princeton University Press, 1971.

_____. 1961. *Memories, Dreams, Reflections.* New York: Random House.

Kleinberg, J. 1988. Utilizing career crises to prepare patients for intensive psychotherapy. *Journal of Contemporary Psychotherapy* 18(3):240–248.

Kroeger, O., and Mitheusen, J. 1988. *Type Talk.* New York: Dell Publishing.

McCaulley, M. H. 1981. Jung's theory of psychological types and the *Myers-Briggs Type Indicator.* In *Advances in Personality Theory,* 5, Paul McReynolds, ed. New York: Jossey-Bass, pp. 295–352.

Meier, C. A. 1971. Psychological types and individuation: a plea for a more scientific approach in Jungian psychology. In *The Analytic Process: Aims, Analysis, Training,* I. Joseph Wheelright, ed. The Proceedings of the Fourth International Congress for Analytical Psychology. New York: G. P. Putnam Sons, for the C. G. Jung Foundation for Analytical Psychology, pp. 276–289.

Murray, W. O. G., and Rosalie, R. 1987. *When ENFP and INFJ Interact.* Gladwyne, Penn.: Type & Temperament, Inc.

Myers, I. B. 1962, 1975. *The Myers-Briggs Type Indicator.* Palo Alto, Calif.: Consulting Psychologists Press.

_____. 1977. *Supplementary Manual: The Myers-Briggs Type Indicator.* Palo Alto, Calif.: Consulting Psychologists Press.

_____. 1980. *Gifts Differing*. Palo Alto, Calif.: Consulting Psychologists Press.

Myers, I. B., and McCaulley, M. H. 1985. *Manual: A Guide to the Development and Use of the Myers-Briggs Type Indicator*. Palo Alto, Calif.: Consulting Psychologists Press.

Newman, L. E. 1979. Personality types of therapist and client and their use in counseling. In *Research in Psychological Type* 2:46–55.

Quenk, A. T. 1984. *Psychological Types and Psychotherapy*. Gainesville, Fla.: Center for Applications of Psychological Type, Inc.

Sharp, D. 1987. *Personality Types*. Toronto: Inner City Books.

Spoto, A. 1989. *Jung's Typology in Perspective*. Boston: Sigo Press.

Stein, M. 1983. *In Mid Life: A Jungian Perspective*. Dallas: Spring Publications.

Randall E. Ruppart, Ph.D., is president of Ruppart and Associates, Inc., an international human resources consulting firm in Forest Hills, N.Y., which focuses on organization and career development. He is an experienced interpreter of the Myers-Briggs Type Indicator and a charter member of the Association for Psychological Type. He regularly writes and lectures on applications of type and is currently a member of the Board of Trustees of the C. G. Jung Foundation for Analytical Psychology of New York.

Aryeh Maidenbaum, Ph.D., is executive director of the C. G. Jung Foundation for Analytical Psychology of New York. He is a graduate of the C. G. Jung Institute of Zürich, maintains a private practice in New York City, and teaches courses in Jungian psychology at New York University and Herbert H. Leman College.

Jung's Typology in
the Workplace

June Singer

Individual differences in personality, or "psychological types," play an important part in determining how organizations function. According to K. Owen Ash:

> As uncomfortable as it may be, our perception needs to be continually challenged by those whose experience is dissimilar to our own. Differing perceptions need to be understood, not rebuffed. Truth and reality generally lie beyond the mere collection and analysis of unprejudiced facts. Even within our own discipline, viewpoints from colleagues in different countries and work environments help to mature and broaden our perspectives. Only when our minds expand to understand the perceptions of others will our own biases be put into appropriate perspective. (Ash 1990)

Background: Jung's Seminal Work in Psychological Types

Modern psychology was born in 1900. With the arrival of the new century came two dramatic and diametrically opposed events: in that year John B. Watson, who would become "the father of behaviorism," earned the first doctorate in psychology given by the University of Chicago, with a dissertation on maze learning in rats; and Sigmund Freud published *The Interpretation of Dreams*. Psychology inherited traits of its two prime progenitors, one devoted to the method of purely objective measurement and the other committed to the process of introspection and subjectivity as a means of gathering and analyzing data. No wonder this young discipline developed with an internal basis for conflict! It is not surprising that the controversy between objective and subjective approaches is still raging as modern psychology approaches the century-mark of its existence.

In 1900, C. G. Jung was beginning his career in psychiatry in Zürich. In him, the two strands of psychology were embodied. He was engaged in experimental research in psychology using objective measures in a clinical setting (Jung 1957), and he was soon to join Freud and his Vienna group where cases were discussed from the subjective viewpoints of the early psychoanalysts.

Jung's pioneering work, *Psychological Types* (1921), was written during the period immediately following his break from Freud and his disaffection from the Vienna psychoanalytic circle in 1913. His book reflected his analysis of the differences in personality styles, both in his own experience and in classical literature. Looking back in his autobiographical *Memories, Dreams, Reflections*, Jung wrote:

> This work sprang originally from my need to define the ways in which my outlook differed from Freud's and Adler's. In attempting to answer this question, I came across the problem of types; for it is one's psychological type which from the outset determines and limits a person's judgment. My book, therefore, was an effort to deal with the relationship of the individual to the world, to people and things. It discussed the various attitudes the conscious mind might take toward the world, and thus constitutes a psychology of consciousness regarded from what might be called a clinical angle. (1961, p. 207)

Jung's theory of psychological types created a bridge between the two opposing forces in psychology. His typology has been successfully used in the context of individual therapy as well as for the basis of several objective inventories which profess to measure personality factors.[1]

Jung's work on psychological types yielded several insights, the first being that perfectly normal, healthy individuals view themselves, their world, and their interactions from very different points of view, and they often come to very different conclusions. He first identified two opposing attitudes: *introversion*, where individuals direct their energy inward primarily and are concerned with the effects of the environment upon themselves, and

---

[1]Throughout this article, the terms *therapy* or *individual therapy* will be employed to include psychoanalysis and Jungian analysis (analytical psychology), these latter being forms of depth psychotherapy in which unconscious material is evoked and analyzed.

extraversion, where the energy is primarily directed outward and persons are more concerned with their effect on the world. He also distinguished four functions of consciousness: thinking, feeling, sensation, and intuition, and asserted that these represented four primary ways of perceiving and processing information. In *Psychological Types*, Jung also showed how one could observe many relationships and interpersonal struggles throughout history from the perspective of typology. He asserted that while no person sees things in their entirety, opposing points of view may be complementary to one another, and therefore that people of very different typologies may engage in productive relationships with each other.

In his early work, Jung classified personality factors into eight distinct types, namely, introverted thinking, extraverted thinking, introverted feeling, extraverted feeling, introverted intuition, extraverted intuition, introverted sensation, and extraverted sensation. He further postulated that thinking and feeling were opposites, as were sensation and intuition, and introversion and extraversion. Thus introverted thinking was opposed to extraverted feeling, and so on. He assumed that these opposing types were mutually exclusive, so that if one were highly developed in introverted thinking, for example, that person must be weakest in extraverted feeling. We must bear in mind that this crucial assumption was only that, an assumption. Jung never did any objective research on this and as far as this writer has ascertained, neither, for many years, did anyone else test the bipolar assumption using the standard methods of research in psychology.

During the first half of the twentieth century, Jung's theory of psychological types was utilized exclusively by Jungian therapists in their work with individual clients. It was not until the advent of psychological testing during World War II that the possibility of adapting Jung's theory to an objective measure was considered. As instruments based on Jung's typology began to be developed, they had to confront the controversy that arose over the relative merits of clinical (or interviewer) judgment versus objective measures. That controversy continues and is now more important than ever in light of the extensive use of personality inventories based on Jung's typology.

The Controversy over the Relative Value of Clinical (or Interviewer) Judgment versus Objective Measures

Let us consider these two viewpoints as they are currently being expressed by those who deal with the assessment of personality factors, both in the consulting room and in business and industry.

The Case for Clinical (or Interviewer) Judgment

A personal interview provides, first of all, an opportunity for direct observation by the interviewer of the person being interviewed (the client). The case can be made that what one observes in a personal interview is far more important to consider in evaluating the client than anything that may be demonstrated in a paper-and-pencil test or similar performance measure. Therapists know (even if they rarely admit it) that often one can make a fairly accurate diagnosis in the time it takes for the client to walk in the door and seat himself or herself opposite the therapist. Anxiety, depression, carelessness, agitation, lack of self-confidence, all look very different from calmness, optimism, attention to details, secure repose, and self-assurance. These visible factors, which can be extracted only minimally in a personality inventory and then without a great deal of certainty, may be extremely important in coming to a judgment about how well the client will do in a particular situation.

A second value provided by the personal interview is in the flexibility of the interviewer to adapt to the attitude of the client. For example, suppose the client is responsive to the interviewer most of the time but periodically appears to be somewhat distracted. The interviewer wonders what this is all about and can ask, "Is something bothering you?" The client is then able to say, "My child was up all night with a high fever, and I guess I'm not quite with it today." Or, the client may try to cover up with the pretense that nothing is wrong. Either way, the interviewer finds out something about the client that an objective measure could scarcely divulge.

A third factor has to do with the potential for the interviewer to create an emotional climate that would be useful for evoking the special abilities, or weaknesses, of the client—both of which may need to be evaluated in relation to the requirements of the work-place. Is the interviewer interested in whether the client is capable of learning new skills in a facilitating environment? If so, the inter-view can be structured to provide an atmosphere of empathy and encouragement that allow the client to take risks in the interview itself, thereby indicating a potential to do so in other aspects of life and work. Is the interviewer eager to find out how the client will function under stress? By observing the client's responses to cer-tain questions, the skilled interviewer can sense which areas seem to be more emotionally charged than others and can elicit responses that might well serve to highlight sensitive areas such as complexes, phobias, or defenses.

The effect of the interviewer is thus clearly a factor when subjective measures are used. The attitude and approach of an interviewer can influence the evaluation of a client. In addition, whenever there is a significant interaction between two people, there are always unconscious factors on both sides that feed into the equation of the interview. In psychotherapy these uncon-scious factors are referred to as transference and countertransfer-ence, the first being related to the unconscious factors brought into the setting by the client, and the second being the uncon-scious response of the therapist or interviewer to the client. It is important for the interviewer to understand something about these two interrelated mechanisms, since they play such an important role in assessment. It has already been suggested that much that is unconscious in the client is fairly well demonstrated in such nonverbal communication as manner, dress, posture, voice, etc. These nonverbal messages can be more informative than words.

Interviewers need to be aware of their responses to clients on a more than superficial level. They must ask themselves such questions as: What is my initial reaction to this person, and why? Does this person remind me of someone I know, and am I attribut-ing that person's qualities to the individual before me? Am I preju-diced against something about this person: race, religion, sex, poli-tics, social class, educational level, appearance? Am I hesitant to employ or work with this person because he or she doesn't see things the way I do, or because I would not choose this person as a friend? The interviewer should know that it is a natural tendency for people to feel more favorably disposed toward someone like themselves, but that this is not necessarily the person who is needed to fill a particular role in a job or in any other interpersonal setting.

With this in mind, an interviewer who understands typology in sufficient depth will not find it too difficult to assess the typology of an individual in interviews and to conduct the investigations that industries and organizations require for dealing with personnel and with interpersonal situations. The interviewer ought to have a sense not only of the client's psychological type, but also of the typological requirements of the position in which the client is likely to be placed. For example, a highly intuitive interviewer interviews two prospective applicants for a position which requires careful record keeping in a company. One applicant appeals personally to the interviewer because she presents many ideas for effecting improvements in the company, an interest the interviewer shares; the second, carefully groomed and dressed in a conservative and well-coordinated fashion, asks exactly what she will be expected to do, what are the working hours, and what are the fringe benefits of the position thus showing a detail-mindedness suitable for the position. The interviewer who is cognizant of the value of typology in helping to select candidates for suitability rather than charisma will have no difficulty making the wiser choice. Others may be seduced by the allure of a reflection of their own self-image.

Another feature of the more subjective approach to personality assessment in industrial and organizational management relates to the specific interactions that can take place between interviewer and client. After having talked with a client for some time, an interviewer begins to imagine situations in which the client might find himself in a particular work situation. The interviewer might then verbally create a situation to which the client would be asked to respond directly. The spontaneity and appropriateness of the response would give the interviewer information rarely obtainable through the use of objective measures.

It would be possible to cite innumerable instances in which the nonobjective circumstance of the one-to-one interview might prove to be the most valuable way of assessing the factors that relate to performance or potential performance of a client. There is no substitute for the personal relationship, the empathy, and the feedback that can only occur in a face-to-face meeting. However, proponents of objective measures have another point of view, one which must be considered when we look at how best to utilize Jung's insights on personality typology in the industrial or organizational setting.

The Case for Objective Measures

Since the end of World War II, when psychological testing was introduced on a large scale by the United States military, objective measures of intelligence, performance, mental status, and personality have been in vogue. These tests and measures have proved useful in evaluating sizable numbers of people when individual interviewing has not been practicable. They have been used for testing intelligence, assessing aptitudes, and predicting performance in a wide variety of areas. In evaluating the efficacy of these objective measures, some test users have found *undesirable* the very characteristics that the proponents of the more personal approach have cited as *desirable.*

Objective tests eliminate such descriptive factors as a subject's personal appearance, race, sex, physical ability or disability, or socioeconomic background as evidenced by dress or manners. Reliance is placed upon the test results only, and these, it is claimed, are unaffected by personal prejudice, conscious or unconscious. (Of course, this does not take into account the possibility that psychological tests may be culturally biased, but, in all fairness, test constructors who follow approved scientific research methods are aware of this potential and make reasonable attempts to avoid it.)

In the administration of objective tests, attempts are made to create an identical atmosphere for all testees, on the basis that objective assessment requires impartiality. In contrast, in interview situations, the interviewer usually tries to devise an atmosphere for the assessment of the person that will facilitate the individual subject's optimal functioning.

Proponents of the use of objective measures say that the effect of the test administrator on the testing process is, or should be, minimized through the use of testing. The person administering the test is usually not the person who does the scoring or interpretation. This practice serves to distance the subject from the person who will make the necessary judgments. From the Jungian point of view, this should eliminate the factors of transference and countertransference, which could be deemed prejudicial to the subject.

Another contention of those who prefer objective measures is that, in general, self-assessment as demonstrated by a test in which the testees supply information about what they would or would not do, or would or would not prefer, tends to be more accurate than a subjective clinical assessment by another person.

Even a highly trained psychotherapist would be wary of predicting an individual's future behavior, recognizing that the therapeutic or interview situation is particular unto itself and does not necessarily reflect the whole range of behaviors in which an individual might engage. The clinician only sees the client in the consulting room, not on the job, or at home, or at parties, or in various kinds of social relationships. A well-constructed objective test can provide models for a variety of situations and conditions.

The last but surely not the least important point that is brought out by the proponents of objective testing is that the test really is "objective." This means that when test results are obtained from the testee and are scored impartially, they can be viewed by the testee and the counselor together as a statement of the testee that reflects his or her own self-image.[2] It is not a question of what the tester thinks about the individual over and against the individual's own self-presentation. It is there in black and white, and the question is not whether it is true or not, but rather, what does it mean? The counselor and the person who has been tested can together evaluate the results in terms of what they show about the individual in relation to the task at hand, be it employment screening, promotion, relations with other workers, aptitude, or potential areas of difficulty. What this method offers, say the proponents of testing, is an opportunity for self reflection, an impartial evaluation of the results of this self-reflection, and an assessment by a qualified person based on the data at hand.

Are Objective Measures Prejudicial to the Individual?

Again, the answer to this question must be a qualified "yes" and "no." *The presentation and interpretation of test results may have devastating effects if they result in decisions on the part of management based solely on test performance.*

---

[2]"Counselor" here means the person in industry or in the organization who is designated to communicate test results either to individuals who have been tested or to management. The counselor may be a staff person or a trained consultant specially employed for this purpose.

Potential Dangers in Using Tests and Measures

Let us consider a few of the potential dangers to the individual who is given various tests to determine suitability for a particular task, position, or ability to interact with others. Some people suffer from test anxiety and cannot perform well in a testing situation, but may be extremely effective on the job. Others enjoy the anonymity of the testing setting just because they do not easily relate to people. Testing procedures do not allow for individual differences; everyone is measured by the same yardstick. They do not take into account the particular state of mind of the person taking the test. No matter how objectively test results are presented, there is the possibility of untoward effects on the person who has taken the test. Self-esteem may fall when the results are not according to the testee's expectations. A person who has little self-confidence may be emotionally shattered when test results suggest that the individual will be unable to function successfully in certain areas. On the other side, the person whose test results indicate potential high performance in a certain area may go forward with greater confidence than is warranted and may fail because of factors that are not measurable by an objective test. For these reasons, extreme care should be taken to ensure that the results of personality testing are communicated accurately and in as positive a manner as possible. The point should also be made that tests have their limitations and that there are many valuable aspects of personality that cannot be adequately measured in an objective test.

Potential Advantages in Using Tests and Measures

Objectivity, freedom from prejudice, and fairness to all are the factors most frequently cited by those who favor objective tests. Efficiency is another important factor. It is possible to examine a large number of people simultaneously with an objective test and to select the few best suited for the particular tasks and responsibilities that are projected.

The Use of Jung's Typology in Psychological Testing

It was not surprising that Jung's theory of psychological types would be seized upon by people who were interested in determining the effects of different personality factors on individuals' functioning in every arena of their lives. The Jungian therapists who first used his theory as a framework for clinical evaluation in the course of psychotherapy and analytic work found it useful to evaluate individuals in the typological groups Jung described (1921, pars. 556–671). They soon discovered that the typology of the therapist was as important as that of the client, for in the intimate interaction of psychotherapy the personalities of both therapist and client go into the same crucible, and what comes out is an amalgam of the workings of the two. Jungian analysts and therapists recognized the importance of knowing the factors that predominated in their own personalities as well as those in their clients'. For many years the method by which these therapists evaluated their own typology and that of others was purely intuitive. After all, this was the way Jung himself came to the idea of typology.

Trial and error played an important part in refining Jung's theory and still does today as clinicians continually modify their intuitive impressions of a client's typology. There must be many clients who have suffered from being mistyped as a result either of some confusion in the transference/countertransference process or simply because of the limitations imposed by the therapeutic setting. The use of typology by Jungian therapists in their practices is far from universal. Many have come to distrust it, simply because they have seen mistakes made to the detriment of the client. They hesitate to categorize people, and the conventional way of looking at Jung's typology does open itself to that possibility.

Over the course of time, however, Jung moved far from his tendency to categorize people and from his bipolar stance of the 1920s. In his later work, he indicates that one of his major objectives in achieving the integration of the person is the "bringing together of the opposites." The individuation process, as he describes it, involves the integration of the unconscious factors into the more conscious realm. This requires raising to consciousness the "shadow" element, which he thought was linked to the inferior, or least-developed, function. Toward the end of his life, forty years after his statement about the mutual exclusivity of the types, Jung's main thrust was in the direction of harmonizing the opposites. He made this clear in his last major work, *Mysterium Coniunctionis*, where he wrote:

> [J]ust as there is no energy without the tension of opposites, so there can be no consciousness without the perception of differences. But any stronger emphasis on differences leads to polarity and finally to a conflict which maintains the necessary tension of opposites. This tension is needed on the one hand for increased energy production and on the other for the further differentiation of differences, both of which are indispensable requisites for development of consciousness. But although this conflict is unquestionably useful it also has very evident disadvantages, which sometimes prove injurious. Then a counter-movement sets in, in the attempt to reconcile the conflicting parties. (1955, par. 603)

One of the most valuable aspects of Jung's work on typology has been to identify opposite forces in the psyche so that they can be brought into a more conscious relationship with one another.

Personality Inventories Based on Jung's Typology

It was inevitable that personality inventories would be devised to measure typology using Jung's concepts. The first such inventory, published in the 1940s, was the Jungian Type Survey (JTS), also known as the Gray Wheelwrights Test (Wheelwright, Wheelwright, and Buehler 1964). Joseph and Jane Wheelwright are two Jungian analysts whose extensive analytical work with clients led them to see the importance of understanding typology and of creating a useful inventory to measure typology in Jung's terms. Gray, and later Buehler, worked with the Wheelwrights on the construction of the inventory. The Jungian Type Survey was widely used by Jungian therapists and continues to be employed by them and by others today. It is available through the C. G. Jung Institute of San Francisco.

After a great deal of research, the Myers-Briggs Type Indicator (MBTI) (Myers 1962) was published by Consulting Psychologists Press. A more sophisticated instrument than the JTS, it addressed itself not only to therapists and individuals, but also to educators, vocational counselors, industrial and organizational management, and to a variety of other persons. As the MBTI became more and more widely used, a large database was developed. Extensive research based on these data effectively demonstrated many and varied applications of Jung's typology.

To the dimensions of introversion/extraversion, thinking/feeling, and intuition/sensation, the MBTI added another bipolar pair, judging/perceiving. This resulted in a matrix of sixteen categories. Each category was composed of four factors, each representing one-half of each bipolar pair. A category, for example, would be identified as "ESTJ," which would stand for the extraverted-sensation-thinking-judging type. Research was carried out to correlate aptitudes for certain kinds of activities or vocations with the sixteen categories, or types. Over a long period of time, useful descriptions of the sixteen categories and the characteristics and aptitudes associated with each of them were developed. Using this test, which is easy to administer and score, it is possible to place an individual within one of these categories and to make certain assumptions about that person based on the performance of others whose test results had placed them in the same category. The MBTI "is not trying to *measure* people, but to sort them into groups to which, in theory, they already belong" (Myers and McCaulley 1962, p. 140). Consequently it became widely used, and continuing research has increased the scope of its appeal and popularity. The MBTI deserves credit for bringing Jung's seminal concept of personality types to the attention of an ever-increasing public. Among its most significant contributions has been the furthering of a healthy respect for individual differences in our pluralistic society.

Other inventories based on Jung's theories have since been developed, but until 1984 the JTS and the MBTI were the two most widely used. While these instruments have proven to be very useful in making gross distinctions among individuals, certain problems arose related to their bipolar construction. In the 1970s, articles began to appear questioning the bipolar assumption. Cook (1970) asked, "Is Jungian typology true?" Jarrett (1979) raised the question, "How opposite is opposite?" C. A. Meier, a Jungian analyst and close associate of Jung, made a plea for "a more scientific approach in Jungian psychology" (1971, pp. 276–289). Rothenberg (1971) suggested that the process of "Janusian think-

Table 1. *Profile Changes When Scaled Items Replaced Forced-Choice Items*

	GW	MBTI	Total
Number of subjects in the study	120	79	199
Changes in superior function	86 (72%)	36 (46)%	122 (61%)
Inferior not opposed to superior function	66 (55%)	29 (36%)	95 (48%)

ing," the ability to look in opposite directions at the same time, played an important role in creativity.

In 1975, Mary E. Loomis and I (Singer and Loomis 1984) tested the bipolar assumption utilized by both the JTS and the MBTI. We reconstructed both of the existing instruments so that each half of the bipolar question would be answered and scored independently of the other. For example, a forced-choice question which was supposed to be answered by "a" or "b" was split into two questions. Each could be answered by selecting a number on a scale, indicating the degree of agreement or disagreement with the statement. Experimental subjects took both versions of a single test, the forced-choice version and the scaled-item (independent rating) version. The reasoning behind this was that if the bipolar assumption was correct, the subjects' scores would place them in the same category no matter what version of the test was used. The results of this experiment indicated that, with both the JTS and the MBTI, there was a significant difference between the results when different versions of the tests were used. The superior function often differed on the reconstructed test from what it had been on the original version of the test, and the inferior function was not necessarily the opposite of the superior function—as would be anticipated in a forced-choice–based inventory. The results are shown in Table 1.

On the basis of these findings and subsequent research, Loomis and I, both Jungian analysts, devised a new instrument for personality assessment, the Singer-Loomis Inventory of Personality (SLIP). The SLIP abandoned the bipolar assumption in favor of measuring each personality factor independently using scaled scores. This led to a score for each of the eight cognitive modes: introverted thinking, extraverted thinking, introverted feeling, extraverted feeling, introverted sensation, extraverted sensation, introverted intuition, and extraverted intuition. Each score yielded a number showing its strength relative to the other scores. No matter what is the leading cognitive mode, it is possible for any one of the other seven cognitive modes to be second, third, fourth, etc., when the SLIP is used. Thus, instead of defining individuals in terms of a limited number of categories, the SLIP provides a wide variety of individualized profiles. It also shows the relative strengths and weaknesses of every cognitive mode in a given individual. Because the numerical score indicates the strength of each cognitive mode, it becomes possible to chart the development of the different cognitive modes through subsequent administration of the inventory.

After nearly ten years of research and preparation, during which the SLIP was revised twice, a third version of the inventory was published in an experimental model by Consulting Psychologists Press in 1984, and has since come into wide use. A validity study was performed on this version in order to ascertain whether the personality profile obtained with the use of the SLIP corresponded with the self-image of the individuals who took the inventory. The method used gave six groups of subjects an opportunity to read a brief description of introversion, extraversion, judging, perceiving, and each of the four functions taken from the *SLIP Interpretive Guide* (1984), rating themselves on each one. Then the inventory was given and the results of the self-rating based on the *Guide* were compared with those obtained from the inventory profile. The overall validity of the *SLIP Interpretive Guide* was 74%, which means that the statements drawn from the *Guide* were congruent with the SLIP scores three out of four times. Agreement ranged from a high of 88% for the intuition statement to a low of 59% for the perceiving statement. Variations between groups were not as great. The highest group's agreement was 79%, while the lowest group's was 72%. It is interesting to note that the group with the lowest agreement was composed of candidates training to be analysts at the Jung Institute in Zürich, Switzerland. This group had been studying Jung's theory of typology in a setting where the bipolarity aspect of Jung's typology was being emphasized. On the other hand, the group with the highest agreement was composed of people in Grosse Pointe, Michigan, who had little or no previous knowledge of typology. This suggests the possibility that in making self-assessments, people who might prejudge their typology on the basis of their knowledge about the bipolarity assumption tend to be correct less often than those who rely upon their self-assessment and the descriptions in the *SLIP Interpretive Guide*. Details on the validity experiment are shown in Table 2.

Table 2. Validity of the SLIP Interpretive Guide

As shown by a comparison of subjects' self-descriptions with their SLIP profiles. The numbers below indicate the number (N) of subjects whose self-descriptions agreed with SLIP profile.

SITE	Number	Introversion	Extraversion	Judging	Perceiving	Thinking	Feeling	Sensation	Intuition	Agreement	
PA	13	11	11	10	6	10	11	8	9	76	73%
GP	19	16	17	15	12	15	16	13	16	120	79%
CH	11	10	8	6	7	9	10	7	10	67	76%
RO	23	19	16	14	13	15	17	20	19	133	72%
NY	57	44	41	41	36	38	43	37	53	333	73%
ZU	17	15	10	11	8	12	15	11	16	98	72%
Total	140 / 140	115 / 139	103 / 140	97 / 140	82 / 140	99 / 140	112 / 140	96 / 140	123 / 140	827 / 1119	74%

Sites: PA = Palo Alto, Calif.
GP = Grosse Pointe, Mich.
CH = Chicago
RO = Royal Oak, Mich.
NY = New York
ZU = Zurich

The SLIP was originally hand-scored, but computer scoring along with a narrative profile has also been available since 1989. This makes a detailed written analysis of each individual's personality profile easily accessible. With the addition of computerization, a database is being created for the SLIP, which will facilitate further research.

How Can Tests and Measures of Personality Best Serve Industry and Organizations?

Tests and measures should never be used alone as the sole determinants of management decisions. Put simply and directly, tests and measures of an objective nature can best serve industry and organization when they are used in conjunction with personal contact, interviews, and reports on the past and present performance of individuals. For reasons stated above, there must be a variety of approaches to assessing human personality and its vagaries.

Understanding typology and using tests and measurements of personality in organization management helps to ensure that individuals are able to work in areas compatible with their individual personality structures. When people are aware of their less well developed areas, they can focus on these as their "growing edges," the places where new ways of functioning can be encouraged.

When personnel practices are designed to use either personal interviews or objective tests or a combination of the two, a flexibility of approach is possible which helps to discern individuals' cognitive styles. This approach can be useful in designing methods of training people for particular kinds of work. Different individuals respond to different approaches: those who are strong in thinking will appreciate a step-by-step logical process of training, while for those whose leading cognitive mode is extraverted feeling, a personal and empathic approach will work best. Sensation-function people will want all the details and will pay careful attention to them, while intuitive people will grasp the whole picture quickly and begin from the general, moving toward the particular. People do their best work when they are understood and when their work is compatible with their natural tendencies. What is true for training is also applicable to personnel development and to making decisions about advancement within an organization.

The same concepts that led Jung to an understanding of why Freud and Adler so often disagreed are useful today in furthering the resolution of conflict. Jung's first notions about typology arose out of his analysis of how different psychiatrists would interpret the same case material in their own idiosyncratic ways, but with a consistency which led each individual to formulate his own psychological theories that he believed to be universally applicable (Jung 1917)! This same tendency, to believe that one's own views are the correct ones and that the other person's views are wrong, continues to be evident in people who do not understand the extent of individual personality differences; and this attitude leads not only to conflicts among employees, but also to conflict between labor and management and to the failure of businesses to thrive. In dealing with interpersonal problems among personnel, the use of typology is invaluable. When people are given basic information about how typology works, they are better able to understand why conflicts arise and how a knowledge of typology helps to resolve them.

A grasp of the various personality structures and their needs makes it possible to create a facilitating environment that can provide for the needs of different types of individuals. The workplace environment is both physical and interpersonal. The physical environment must be such as to encourage a variety of work spaces and a range of activities within them. The interpersonal environment should be one in which individual styles are recognized and each one is valued for the contribution it makes to the whole.

Issues Around the Training of Persons Administering, Scoring, and Interpreting Personality Inventories

Personality inventories should be administered by people who are specially trained for this task. Since this is an "objective measure," care should be taken to keep the testing conditions as uniform as possible for all those who are to be tested. A good inventory supplies explicit directions for administering it, and these must be closely followed. It is important to minimize "test anxiety." Since a personality inventory is a self-assessment, testees should be informed by the test administrator when the test instructions are given that while the inventory is designed to indicate individual personality characteristics, no one personality type is more desirable than any other. They should be told also that these inventories do not measure intelligence or emotional stability and that individuals are not going to be compared with each other; the primary purpose is to identify the individual's strengths. While most tests of this nature have no time limit, the individual should be encouraged not to mull over each item but to move quickly from one to another. This should lead to a more genuine response, rather than a contrived one.

The interpretation of the personality profile that results from an objective test often can be done with the use of the manuals and guides supplied with the inventory, or it can be provided by a computerized scoring and interpretation procedure. How detailed an interpretation is given to the testee depends upon the purpose for which the individual was asked to take the test. Evaluating the interpretation in terms of the purpose for which the test was given and communicating this evaluation to the organization who has ordered the test or to the person who was tested requires more training, skill, and experience. Training workshops may be given for people in management and personnel to enable them to utilize the instruments and their interpretations within their organizations. Test publishers often determine who is qualified to use specific tests and measures, based on training and experience. Personnel officers who lack such qualifications should call upon outside consultants with experience in testing and with a working knowledge of Jung's theory of psychological types.

Conclusions

The use of objective measures based on Jung's theory of typology in industry and organizations is widespread today. There is no question but that this usage leads to an appreciation of individual differences and helps to make it possible for people to work together with optimal respect for individuals' temperament and singularity.

The ongoing controversy over the relative merits of the clinician's or interviewer's judgment versus the information provided by objective testing continues. But, as Jung was fond of saying, it is not a case of either/or, but of both/and. Each approach has its advantages and its limitations. When we can bypass our prejudices in favor of one or the other, we will recognize that the two approaches are complementary. As we have learned from the research on psychological types, one approach need not exclude the other. With both the interview and the inventory as part of their assessment resources, organizations can increase the possibility of obtaining the accurate information that will allow them to make informed and fair choices that are in the best interests of people at all levels.

References

Ash, K. O. 1990. The editor's column. *Journal of the International Federation of Clinical Chemists* 2, 2. Slough, England: ISC House, Progress Business Centre.

Cook, D. 1970. Is Jung's typology true? A theoretical and experimental study of some assumptions implicit in a theory of personality types. Ph.D. dissertation, Duke University.

Jarrett, J. L. 1979. The logic of psychological opposition: or how opposite is opposite? *Journal of Analytical Psychology* 24:4.

Jung, C. G. 1957. *Experimental Researches. CW* 2. Princeton, N.J.: Princeton University Press, 1973.

_____. 1917. The psychology of the unconscious. In *CW* 7:8–117. Princeton, N.J.: Princeton University Press, 1966.

_____. 1921. *Psychological Types. CW*, vol. 6. Princeton, N.J.: Princeton University Press, 1971.

_____. 1955. *Mysterium Coniunctionis. CW*, vol. 14. Princeton, N.J.: Princeton University Press, 1970.

_____. 1961. *Memories, Dreams, Reflections.* New York: Pantheon Books.

Meier, C. A. 1971. Psychological type and individuation: a plea for a more scientific approach in Jungian psychology. In *The Analytic Process*, J. B. Wheelwright, ed. New York: G. P. Putnam's Sons, pp. 276–289.

Myers, I., and McCaulley, M. 1962. *The Myers-Briggs Type Indicator.* Palo Alto, Calif.: Consulting Psychologists Press.

Rothenberg, A. 1971. The process of Janusian thinking in creativity. *Archives of General Psychiatry* 24:195–295.

Singer, J., and Loomis, M. 1984. *Manual for the Singer-Loomis Inventory of Personality*. Palo Alto, Calif.: Consulting Psychologists Press.

_____. 1984. *Interpretive Guide for the Singer-Loomis Inventory of Personality*. Palo Alto, Calif.: Consulting Psychologists Press.

Wheelwright, J. B., Wheelwright, J. H., and Buehler, J. A. 1964. *The Jungian Type Survey*. San Francisco: Society of Jungian Analysts of Northern California.

June Singer, *Ph.D., is a Jungian analyst and member of the C. G. Jung Institute of San Francisco. She is also a founding member of the C. G. Jung Institute of Chicago and of the Inter-Regional Society of Jungian Analysts. Her books include* The Unholy Bible: Blake, Jung and the Collective Unconscious, Boundaries of the Soul: The Practice of Jung's Psychology, Androgyny: The Opposites Within, Love's Energies, Seeing Through the Visible World: Jung, Gnosis and Chaos, *and the forthcoming* A Gnostic Book of Hours.